Cabinets in Eastern Europe

Cabinets in Eastern Europe

Jean Blondel
Robert Schuman Centre
European University Institute
Florence, and
University of Siena

and

Ferdinand Müller-Rommel
University of Düsseldorf

Editorial matter and selection © Jean Blondel
and Ferdinand Müller-Rommel 2001
Chapters 1–16 © Palgrave Publishers Ltd 2001

First published 2001 by
PALGRAVE
Houndmills, Basingstoke, Hampshire RG21 6XS and
175 Fifth Avenue, New York, N.Y. 10010
Companies and representatives throughout the world

PALGRAVE is the new global academic imprint of
St. Martin's Press LLC Scholarly and Reference Division and
Palgrave Publishers Ltd (formerly Macmillan Press Ltd).

ISBN 0–333–74879–4

This book is printed on paper suitable for recycling and
made from fully managed and sustained forest sources.

A catalogue record for this book is available
from the British Library.

Library of Congress Cataloging-in-Publication Data
Blondel, Jean, 1929–
     Cabinets in Eastern Europe / Jean Blondel and Ferdinand
     Müller-Rommel.
       p. cm.
     Includes bibliographical references and index.
     ISBN 0–333–74879–4 (cloth)
      1. Cabinet system—Europe, Eastern. 2. Europe, Eastern–
     –Politics and government—1989– I. Müller-Rommel, Ferdinand.
     II. Title.
     JN96.A58 B57 2001
     321.8'043'0947—dc21
                                                          2001032127

10   9   8   7   6   5   4   3   2   1
10   09 08 07 06 05 04 03 02 01

Printed and bound in Great Britain by
Antony Rowe Ltd, Chippenham, Wiltshire

Contents

List of Tables

Notes on Contributors

Svetzosar Andreev is a researcher at the European University Institute, Florence.

Jean Blondel was full-time Professor of Political Science and is currently member of the Robert Schuman Centre at the European University Institute in Florence and Visiting Professor at the University of Siena.

Luisa Chiodi is a researcher at the European University Institute, Florence.

Slavko Gaber was former Minister for Education in Slovenia and is currently member of the Faculty of Education, University of Ljubljana.

Ole Hersted Hansen is a researcher at the Department of Political Science, University of Aarhus.

Gabriella Ilonszki is a member of the Department of Political Science, University of Economics, Budapest.

Darina Malova is a member of the Department of Political Science, Comenius University Bratislava.

Zedenka Mansfeldová is a member of the Czech Academy of Science, Prague.

Silvia Matteucci is a researcher at the Centro per l'Europea centro-orientale e balcanica in Bologna.

Ferdinand Müller-Rommel is Professor of Comparative Politics at the Department of Social Sciences, University of Düsseldorf.

Ole Nørgaard is Professor at the Department of Political Science, University of Aarhus.

Ioanna Penescu is a researcher at the European University Institute, Florence.

Francesco Privitera is Professor at the University of Bologna and Researcher at the Centro per l'Europea centro-orientale e balcanica in Bologna.

Senada Selo Sabic is a researcher at the European University Institute, Florence.

Georg Sootla is Professor in the Department of Government, Tallinn University of Educational Sciences.

Preface

This volume on *Cabinets in Eastern Europe* is a parallel work to the volume on *Cabinets in Western Europe* which first appeared in 1988 and had a second edition in 1997. The evolution of Eastern Europe in the course of the 1990s seemed to entail that an inquiry be made into the way post-communist countries were being governed, intrinsically because of the extraordinary changes which had taken place after 1989 in the way the national executive was being organised in these polities and practically because of the high probability that some, if not all, the countries of the area would sooner or later join the European Union. As a matter of fact, what was striking was the extent to which the new regimes of Eastern Europe were modelled on those of Western Europe – much more so, for instance, than those of the countries belonging to the Commonwealth of Independent States (CIS).

It is particularly interesting to study the way the national executive has been restructured in Eastern Europe because what the cabinet system of government has been adopted everywhere in an area in which one might have expected a form of presidentialism to prevail, as indeed it has tended to be the case further East, whether in Russia or in other republics, even if in a manner different from the presidentialism of America and Latin America.

The cabinet system has been praised for generations for having enabled Britain and several other countries to move smoothly towards a responsible system of executive rule: but the cabinet system has been successful in a minority of countries only, principally Western European or in parts of the Commonwealth. Examples of failure have been numerous, not just in Africa after 1960 but in Western Europe itself. Post-First World War Italy, Weimar Germany, Republican Spain, Third and Fourth Republic France or 1967 Greece are only some of the examples of the pathology of cabinet government. Meanwhile, other countries ruled by cabinet government are sometimes regarded as providing examples of difficulties and perhaps ineffectiveness, an accusation which was even levelled at Britain in the 1970s.

These difficulties stem in large part from the fact that cabinet government, which takes place in the context of the parliamentary system, is rather like a complex instrument which can work very well when all the parts are in order but can easily be disrupted if one or more parts are deficient. The cabinet system requires among other things a working party system, a spirit of collaboration among the parties and in particular among their leaders and a high level of trust between politicians in government and the civil servants who are working alongside them. Not all these character-istics prevail widely and in particular in countries which have been under authoritarian rule for generations. To have adopted the cabinet system constitutes for Eastern Europe therefore a kind of act of faith in the ability of the new regimes to achieve, almost instantaneously, what many countries had taken years, decades or even centuries to reach. It is there-fore most interesting to see how far Eastern Europe has been able to meet the challenge in the course of the first decade of liberal democratic rule.

Cabinet government has come to take a variety of shapes in Western Europe where it was born. There is no longer one model only of 'good' cabinet structure and cabinet decision-making, a model largely based on the Westminster pattern. As was pointed out in *Cabinets in Western Europe*, 'the cabinet system now functions – and functions well – with coalitions as well as single-party governments, with strong prime ministers as well as with politicians who are only "chairmen", with ministers who are basically "amateurs" as well as with specialists. This diversity has naturally led to very different "types"; and it is increasingly suggested that there might be alternative ways in which cabinet government can be stable and efficient' (Jean Blondel/Ferdinand Müller-Rommel (eds), *Cabinets in Western Europe*, (1997) p. x). In analysing the national executives in Eastern Europe, it is naturally essential to discover how diverse the new cabinets of these countries were and what models they were consciously or accidentally fol-lowing.

The study has benefited from the help of a number of institutions. The European University in Florence as well as the universities of Sienna, and Düsseldorf (Ministerium für Schule Wissensraft and Forschung, NRW) provided generous financial support. Ferdinand Müller-Rommel also wishes to express his gratitude to the German *Volkswagen Stiftung* for a scholarship which enabled him to finish the project on a full time basis during his six months visits at the European University in Florence and the Centre of Democracy at the University of California, Irvine. Both institutions provided invaluable assistance and an academic home throughout the visits.

This volume has also been made possible because of the help provided by many scholars from the countries of Eastern Europe. In addition to those colleagues who contributed as co-authors in this book, a substantial number of researchers from the European University Institute in Florence and the University of Düsseldorf have generously devoted their time to this study. Furthermore, leaders and researchers from the Centro per l'Europea centro-orientale e balcanica in Bologna have enthusiastically been willing to parti-cipate in the project. Without their help, this volume would not have been possible: we only hope that, as a result and whatever its imperfections, this work reflects accurately the state of development of cabinets in an area in which the establishment of an efficient structure for the national executive is a condition sine qua non of the success of the liberal democratic order.

Sticciano, Tuscany   June 2001

Jean Blondel

Ferdinand Müller-Rommel

Cabinets in post-communist East-Central Europe and in the Balkans: Introduction

Jean Blondel

Cabinet government as the common pattern

No one, or almost no one, expected in the mid-1980s that the Eastern European countries, which had been under authoritarian communist rule for half a century, would be, a decade later, working democracies with a cabinet form of government. That there should be many problems is no surprise but that the polities of the area should have transformed their political life so profoundly and, by and large, so smoothly, is one of those happy accidents which rarely occur in world politics.

This accident is particularly happy since the region scarcely had a tradition of liberal democratic government, not only before 1989, but also before 1939. At the end of the nineteenth century, only three of the sixteen countries of East-Central Europe and the Balkans were independent, all three indeed in the Balkans, Romania, Bulgaria and Serbia, while Hungary was substantially autonomous but in the context of a much larger 'half' of the Austro-Hungarian empire which incorporated many 'nations'. The rest of Eastern Europe belonged then to one of four empires – German, Russian, Austro-Hungarian and Turkish. As a result of the peace treaties which ended the First World War, the Baltic States (Estonia, Latvia, Lithuania), Poland, Czechoslovakia, Hungary and Albania did become independent, Yugoslavia incorporated, alongside Serbia, parts of the Austro-Hungarian and Turkish empires, and Bessarabia (much of which was to become Moldova) became part of Romania. But, if Czechoslovakia succeeded in maintaining a working parliamentary system for the next twenty years, all the other polities sooner or later were to be run in an authoritarian manner before being forcefully absorbed by Nazi Germany, Fascist Italy or the Soviet Union.[1]

What occurred in the area in the last decade of the twentieth century was thus a complete transformation, where authoritarianism, imported or indigenous, had prevailed in the past, a working liberal democracy has emerged almost everywhere. A civil society was in the process of being constituted where there had been none. A pluralistic party system had taken root in all the sixteen countries, even if, in a few cases and in effect essentially in Serbia, significant restrictions to the free operation of parties did exist and even if, in many countries, the new parties were often, not surprisingly, without strong roots in the society. A representative cabinet system of a parliamentary or 'semi-presidential' kind functioned nearly everywhere broadly satisfactorily.[2]

One can therefore take stock, not only as has been the case in the abundant literature on the subject in relation to public opinion and to the party system, but also in relation to the national executive, which has so far remained almost wholly uncovered.[3] It is particularly interesting to see how far these national executives have come to resemble those of Western Europe in the sixteen countries of what was known as 'Eastern Europe' and what is now more often referred to as 'East-Central Europe and the Balkans'. Included in this group are the Baltic States and Moldova, as these four countries have acquired political characteristics and in particular governmental arrangements more akin to those of the rest of 'Eastern Europe' than to those of what was most of the Soviet Union. In these sixteen countries, the cabinet form of government has become generally adopted, while this is far from being a widespread feature of the Commonwealth of Independent States (CIS).

The national executive in East-Central Europe and in the Balkans has come to resemble, at least in its general configuration, what it is in Western Europe, where, as was pointed out in the volume on *Cabinets in Western Europe* on which the present work in modelled, the government 'is linked to the legislature, in contrast to the presidential system which prevails in the United States and Latin America. A government cannot remain in office if it ceases to have the confidence of Parliament but it can, in fact, remain in being as long as it enjoys this confidence as there is no fixed term to its life. The arrangement is also based, somewhat more technically but none the less quite importantly, on the notion that the government constitutes a collective body: the ministers form a cabinet which is more than the sum of its members as it is ultimately responsible as a body to Parliament and through Parliament to the nation for the conduct of the affairs of the country'.[4] In this, East-Central Europe and the Balkans are no different from Western Europe.

The extension of the cabinet system of government to Eastern Europe constitutes a major development for that form of government. It was pointed out in the *Cabinets in Western Europe* that '[p]arliamentary or cabinet government is.... one of the fundamental characteristics of Western European governments... [I]t is one of the important ways in which Western Europe has political unity, as it follows from the adoption of this system by all Western European countries, except Switzerland, that a large number of rules and of modes of behaviour – of political understanding – are common to Western European countries while these rules, modes of behaviour, and understanding do not apply to most other countries of the world . . . Western Europe is both internally similar and distinct as a group from the rest of the world where, except for some Commonwealth countries, Israel, Japan, and, since the early 1990s, a number of Eastern European countries, systems of government are based not only on different broad principles but on different specific arrangements'.[5] The adoption of the cabinet system in Eastern Europe thus constitutes a significant increase in the scope of that form of government across the world.

General problems posed by cabinet government

Towards the end of the twentieth century, it had become rather fashionable to assert that the cabinet system of government was not only successful, but indeed inherently more successful than the presidential system, which is the other widespread formula of liberal rule in the contemporary world, with Switzerland – and perhaps the European Union – being the only examples of a third system.[6] Such a conclusion is rather hasty, however. Cabinet systems have often been unsuccessful, both in the Third World since the Second World War and in Western Europe at various points in the twentieth century, the last example of the collapse of such a regime in that area being in Greece in 1967.

To be successful, cabinet government has to overcome two hurdles, that of party system fractionalisation and that of weak leadership. If these two hurdles are not overcome, governments are likely to be very unstable and the regime may collapse, the French Fourth Republic being a well-known example of such a scenario. To prevent these developments, arrangements are sometimes introduced in constitutions to stabilise governments, somewhat artificially, by rendering the use or the operation of the censure motion more difficult. These arrangements may have some effect, but only if they are accompanied by the streamlining of the party system and a concomitant strengthening of the leadership. Thus the provisions of the French Constitution of 1958, which instored the Fifth Republic, would not have been as effective, had De Gaulle not imposed his style on the new regime and indeed had he not set up his own party. Similarly, the arrangements of the 'constructive motion of confidence' introduced in the German Basic Law of 1949 would probably have had little effect had they not been accompanied by a marked simplification of the party system under Adenauer's leadership.

On the whole, Eastern European countries appear to have benefited from the experience which Western Europe acquired over the previous decades. Thus, in most countries thresholds were introduced barring very small parties from obtaining seats in the legislature. The party system was *ipso facto* streamlined and the effect was truly dramatic in both Hungary and Poland, for example, although similar hurdles have not prevented cabinets from falling frequently in the Baltic States. Meanwhile, perhaps somewhat surprisingly, strong democratic leadership emerged in several Eastern European countries. On the one hand, only in few cases, Serbia and Croatia being the major examples, were the polities of Eastern Europe dominated by authoritarian leaders. On the other hand, only in a minority of countries have heads of government been so weak that they had little grip on the politics and society. Given the economic and social upheavals problems which the countries of the region have been facing, such an overall positive picture is remarkable.

Despite this overall positive picture, three types of problems of varying degrees of seriousness have emerged in the area. First, there are the tragic cases of Bosnia-Hercegovina and of Yugoslavia, although both Croatia and Serbia appear to have moved towards 'normal' politics in 2000. Second, while a democratic type of leadership has emerged in most countries of the region, there are significant exceptions to this trend, while in many of these cases substantial governmental instability is also occurring. Third, there are misgivings about the efficiency of the governmental machinery almost everywhere, although deficiencies appear more pronounced in some countries than in others.

The major problems posed by Bosnia-Hercegovina and the new Yugoslavia are so well-known that little needs to be said about them on this broad matter. What needs merely to be pointed out in relation to Bosnia-Hercegovina is that the government of the overall country seems to function only under major pressure from the representatives of the international community and that the government of the component Serb Republic, since 1999 at least, appears not to be operating at all. Moreover, although the September 2000 election has shown that Serbia was on the way towards democracy, the problem posed by the status of Kosovo is far from being solved or even tackled.

The question of the strength of the governmental leadership has arisen particularly, on the one hand, in the Baltic States and in Poland, and, on the other, in several of the countries of the Balkans. These problems are in part associated with the question of the relative role of president and prime minister and of the spread of forms of 'semi-presidentialism' somewhat patterned on the French model under de Gaulle and Mitterrand. In the Baltic States and in Bulgaria, prime ministerial leadership has often been weak and governmental instability substantial. In these countries, the role of the president has consisted in attempting, as in Italy, to build governments able to muster a majority and to rule the country efficiently. These efforts have been more or less successful over the period. The difficulties seem to have been largely overcome in Bulgaria by the late 1990s.

In Moldova, in Romania, and to an extent in Albania throughout the period as well as, in the first half of the 1990s, in Poland, the problem of weak governmental leadership has been associated with the part played by the president in the conduct of governmental affairs. Whether 'semi-presidentialism' in the strong sense of the word applies (or, in the case of Poland, has applied) to all four countries is debatable as much depends on the character and authority of particular presidents. Iliescu in Romania, Snegur in Moldova and Berisha in Albania played a major part in government when they were in office; Walesa tried to do the same but was less successful. When these heads of state were replaced, the scope of semi-presidentialism was markedly reduced. In Poland, the leadership of the prime minister was established. In Albania, Berisha's successor, Mejdani, was not able – or willing – to intervene markedly. In Romania, the president of the centre-right, Constantinescu, elected in 1995, played a key part in political life only reluctantly, but the return of Iliescu in 2000 may mean the return to a semi-presidential form of government in the country. In Moldova, Snegur's successor, Lucinschi, did endeavour to affirm his power but had only limited success. Finally, in one of the two countries where authoritarian presidents dominated the polity, Croatia, semi-presidentialism seems abandoned, while in the other, Serbia, it is not easy to predict the effective role of Kostunica. It is thus difficult to state whether any form of 'semi-presidentialism' is taking roots in Eastern Europe.

It is also difficult to ascertain whether, where semi-presidentialism occurred, this development has been due to or been the cause of the absence of prime ministerial leadership: the case of Poland under Walesa is highly ambiguous in this respect. What can be stated with assurance is only that some presidents, especially in the Balkans, have played a major part in political life: this was indeed also the case in Macedonia up to the change of government which occurred in 1999, but in a context in which there was also strong and durable prime ministerial leadership. In the majority of the countries of East-Central Europe, prime ministerial leadership has therefore been remarkably well established and only in the Balkans does the question of semi-presidential rule constitute a possible impediment to the development of that prime ministerial leadership.

Meanwhile, across the region, there are problems about the administrative working of the government. This field is more difficult to investigate, although the Sigma group associated to the Organization for Economic Co-operation and Development (OECD) has analysed both aspects in detail for most of the countries.[7] Cabinet committees, for instance, do not always meet regularly; nor do they often wield as much power as do their counterparts in the West. As a result, the cabinet is often overloaded, a situation which is in itself not surprising given the extent of change which governments had to undertake. The effect is to prevent reforms from taking place as rapidly as they should. Nor is support provided by the secretariat always adequate. This, may not be surprising either, given the fact that structures of this kind did not exist in the past and had therefore to be created from scratch. Yet rapid turnover, overload of cabinet meetings and the relative inefficiency of the secretariat combine to create problems in the life of governments in many, perhaps in most, of the countries, and probably more in the Balkan states than in East-Central Europe.

Framework helping to compare Eastern European cabinets

It would ideally be most valuable to be able to undertake a truly comparative analysis of cabinets in Eastern Europe and thus to be able to assess fully the achievements of each of the countries in relation to the whole of the region. This is manifestly impossible at this stage. Our limited knowledge of many aspects of the operation of cabinets, as was pointed out in the previous paragraph, makes it unrealistic to aim for a fully comparative exposition of the characteristics and life of cabinets in post-communist Eastern Europe. As a matter of fact, it is also essential, in particular in a first presentation of the characteristics of these cabinets, to examine the specific context, cultural and historical, in which constitutional arrangements, parties and party systems and leadership have emerged in each country of the region since the fall of communism. This is why, as in the case of *Cabinets in Western Europe*, the analysis is conducted on a country-by-country basis according to a common framework which is being used for the presentation of each country.

As was pointed out in that volume, 'what needs to be grasped is not just the bare bones of the structure – the relationship between government and parliament, the nature of collective responsibility – but also the delicate manner in which the different elements of the cabinet system combine. We need for instance to appreciate better how cabinets are formed – whether this is a slow or rapid process ... We need to assess what prime ministers can effectively do with respect to their colleagues ... We need to understand the ways in which the meetings of the cabinet are being used, whether these are occasions for debate or merely for formal ratification, whether they are organs of initiative or merely responsive. We need to see to what extent other bodies develop around the cabinet and prepare the decisions'.[8]

The country contributions which are presented here have therefore been deliberately modelled on the structure adopted for *Cabinets in Western Europe*. That structure makes it possible to analyse systematically the characteristics of cabinets in each country; comparisons become also possible both among the Eastern European countries and between those countries and Western Europe. We are therefore following the same distinctions in each chapter as in the earlier 'companion' volume, namely the successive examination 'of the general political setting within which [cabinets] operate, of their current structure, of the main aspects of their life and of the shape which decision-making takes among their members'.[9] While adapting the description of the contents of each of these four chapter sections to the Eastern European cases, the remaining developments of this Introduction follow closely the pattern adopted in the earlier volume.

Cabinet setting

Cabinet government, as any form of government, is shaped by the setting within which it develops. As in Western Europe, the constitutional setting is broadly similar among the Eastern European countries, but the socio-political conditions on which constitutional rules apply are diverse. One of the reasons why the institutional setting is not very different with respect to the cabinet as such is that, by and large, constitutions do not devote much space to the structure and operation of the executive. More is sometimes, although not always, said about the conditions under which governments may be formed or fall, largely because in Eastern Europe and in some Western European countries, the fear of governmental instability has led to restrictive conditions being applied to the use of motions of confidence and censure. This is the case, for instance, in Hungary and in Romania, where the model which is followed is that of Germany in the first instance and that of Fifth Republic France in the second.

Generally, constitutions give little guidance, on the other hand, about the organisation of cabinets. It is sometimes stated that decisions are to be taken collectively or a particular role is assigned to the prime minister. For the most part, however, the solution of cabinet decision-making problems is left to practices rather than to rules, as is indeed also the case in Western Europe. It seems that, in some Eastern European countries, more indeed perhaps than in Western Europe, major decisions come to the cabinet to be decided even if this means a degree of overload. As in Western Europe, too, the need to give individual ministers an area of responsibility within their particular sector of government constitutes a further problem.

Constitutions are typically more concerned with matters of appointment and dismissal of government members and in particular with the role of the head of state in this respect. Texts usually give presidents the power to participate in cabinet formation, but are often unclear about powers of dismissal. Difficulties occurred in Romania in 1999 on this very matter when the president wished to dismiss a prime minister who insisted that the head of state had no power to do so.

Where there is a two-party system or where there are two clearly defined coalitions, the question of the power of the head of state may not be of great practical relevance. In the majority of Eastern European countries, however, where parties are sometimes numerous and tend not to be, naturally enough, well established, the head of state, as in France, but also as in the Netherlands and Belgium, may be very influential in the process of government formation. The role of the president in this respect may be either in effect to find an acceptable prime minister in a situation in which there is no clear majority – as occurs often in the Baltic States or has occurred in Bulgaria – or the president has real influence, as in the French case outside situations of 'cohabitation', and can in effect select at will one of the prominent politicians of the majority parties. This has occurred in Romania, in Albania and, under Walesa up to 1993, in Poland.

Thus the general setting within which cabinets operate is provided in broad terms by the constitution (or the constitutional conventions), but detailed contours depend to a large extent on the practice. In the case of Western Europe, this practice has developed over decades and sometimes over one or two centuries. An important discriminating element is typically constituted by the extent to which the representative principle, embodied in the parties in the government, is accompanied and somewhat modified by a bureaucratic tradition, as has for instance been the case in Austria, France or Finland. Moreover, the effect of this representative principle may also be different depending on the extent to which the cabinet system is principally based on a the majoritarian principle or on 'consociationalism', the contrast between Britain and Belgium or the Netherlands being sharp in this respect in Western Europe. As Eastern Europe only had one decade of liberal democracy at the beginning of the twenty-first century, practices have not had time to gel. Contrasts between countries are therefore not as marked as they are in Western Europe, although, by and large, majoritarianism, even though it is based usually on coalitions, has tended to prevail over consociationalism. This may in part be because of the unwillingness of many of the political parties which did not have links with the communist past to be associated with parties that did.

Cabinet structure

The structure of cabinets, East or West, is scarcely defined, as we saw, by constitutional documents. Yet an interesting development has had to take place in Eastern Europe because the structure of governments was more complex and indeed idiosyncratic under communist rule. As economic activities were wholly controlled by the state, the number of ministries tended to be larger than in the West and pyramidal arrangements in the government (with a 'presidium' on which sat the prime minister and a number of deputy prime ministers, for instance) were more marked. Thus the end of communism led to a decrease in the size of the national executive in many Eastern European countries, although the move towards 'slimmer' governments had sometimes already begun in the 1980s, in Bulgaria for example.

As a result of these changes, cabinets in Eastern Europe tend to have, as in Western Europe, around 15 to 20 members. Yet these smaller cabinets, smaller than in communist governments, are nonetheless too large, in Eastern Europe as in Western Europe, to be fully involved in all aspects of the decisions which have to be taken. This is particularly so in Eastern Europe, given the needs for economic restructuring which forced cabinets to be involved in more fundamental decisions than most Western European cabinets. Cabinet meetings cannot therefore have an informal character but need on the contrary to be well-structured and well-prepared.

A number of developments designed to achieve these goals have been introduced in Eastern Europe, typically as a result of the direct influence exercised by representatives of Western countries or of international organisations. As a result, Eastern European cabinets have not had the slow and sometimes diverse evolution of Western European cabinets. This gave rise, as in Western Europe, to what can be described as a cabinet *system* in which the prime minister (or occasionally the president) plays a major part, in which 'second-class' government members, that is to say 'junior ministers', are appointed in many countries and, perhaps above all, in which a variety of 'preparatory' bodies often have come to be very influential. One must not exaggerate the extent to which these developments are truly effective in East-Central Europe and in the Balkans, however, given the speed with which they were introduced.

The authority and effective power of the prime minister varies among Eastern European countries. Not all prime ministers can in effect appoint or dismiss ministers more or less at will, for instance. Not all of them have a large staff at their disposal. Not all of them even have real control over the agenda of cabinet meetings. Indeed, in contrast to what seems to be the case in the other countries of the region, prime ministers in the Baltic States seem often to be 'first among equals', although some have been described as having had an 'authoritarian' style and as attempting to impose their views.

It would be interesting to know to what extent, around the prime minister, an oligarchy of ministers emerges at the top. A decade of cabinet government is manifestly not sufficient for practices of this kind to be well established. There seems to be a move towards such an oligarchy, occasionally at least, in the Baltic States for example, when ex-prime ministers are given a ministerial portfolio in subsequent cabinets. However, in many countries of the region at least, ministers of finance do not seem to be as influential as in Western Europe; ministers of justice play a greater part, perhaps because of the large amount of new legislation which these countries have had to adopt.

As in the West, while ministers are at any rate formally equal to prime ministers, there exists a second tier of ministers, often usually known in the region as 'state secretaries' who, being junior ministers, do not have the same rights as full ministers and in particular do not normally attend meetings of the cabinet except to replace 'their' minister if he or she happens to be absent. To this extent at least, as in the West, governments are not even formally fully collective.

Meanwhile, several cabinet committees with wide powers have been formally set up in many Eastern European countries, their role being to speed up the process of decision making. They obviously reduce the real importance of cabinet meetings, although they help to maintain a degree of collegiality. The practice of setting up these committees is not universal, however, although Western European and other international advisers have been pressing the governments of the region to introduce them. Even when they are formally established, proposals may either bypass them or come to the cabinet meeting without having been fully debated and approved in a cabinet committee. On this, there seem to be substantial differences among countries.

The other set of structures which are part of the cabinet 'system' are the cabinet secretariats and the prime ministers' offices. In this respect, too, Eastern European governments have been markedly influenced by practices in Western Europe, although wide variations appear to exist in the extent to which these secretariats and offices are able to control the flow of proposals coming to and emanating from cabinet meetings. But their role is recognised everywhere as being essential to ensure efficiency in cabinet decision-making.

Eastern European cabinets are thus in a state of 'development'. Western European structures have been 'imported' by and large eagerly, ostensibly at least. This is either because they were genuinely felt to be of value or because it seemed highly 'politic' to Eastern European governments not to oppose suggestions made by Western European advisers or international organisations. It will take more than a decade to ensure that these new structures fully take roots and therefore truly shape the reality of the life of Eastern European cabinets.

Cabinet life

There is both an external and an internal aspect to the life of cabinets. Externally, cabinet life is affected by the way the government relates to the main actors with which it has to deal – groups, parties, parliament and the bureaucracy. The strength of the relationships and the forms which these relationships take are affected by the extent to which an 'administrative' tradition exists and by the configuration of the socio-political forces. As a result, groups or parliament may or may not play a large part in the pre-occupations of ministers. In Western Europe, at least in general, groups tend to play a larger part than parliament; in Eastern Europe, the situation seems to be the converse, also in general. Groups – the 'civil society' – have usually not had time to form a powerful network; parliament, on the other hand, is regarded as having substantial power, in part because legislatures had very little influence, if any at all, under communism – and they are regarded as key institutions in a democratic regime – and in part because the parties are still often relatively weak and liable to splits or rebellions.

The role of parliaments does vary, admittedly, but these often intervene in a substantial manner in the governmental legislative process. In several countries, the boundary between government and opposition is not entirely clear, to begin with: coalitions are liable to shift and it is in parliament that these shifts occur. This appears to be particularly true in the samller countries – the Baltic States and Slovenia – these being also the countries where the distinction between Left and Right or between 'socialists', on the one hand, that is to say typically, except in the Czech Republic, between the ex-communists and their allies, and, on the other hand, the 'anti-communist' parties, that is to say parties set up after the collapse of the old regime which often experienced ups and downs, collapses and mergers.

Thus governments often find themselves unable to maintain discipline among the members of parliament belonging to the parties nominally supporting the coalition and even among the ministers representing these parties in the coalition. There are major variations and these stem in part from the very character of the coalitions. The coalitions can include two or three clearly defined parties, as generally in Hungary or the Czech Republic; they may on the contrary be composed of 'confederations' resulting from alliances in which the component bodies still claim a marked degree of autonomy, often due to their representing different social or geographical constituencies, as has been the case in Romania and, but less so, in Poland with the governments of the centre-right in particular.

Meanwhile, the bureaucracy's relation with cabinets is less well defined in Eastern Europe than in Western Europe. Under communism, the distinction between politics and administration was obscure – politics was alleged to infiltrate the whole of public life. The very idea of the 'neutrality' of the civil service was unknown. What the bureaucracy could and could not do in the context of a democratic system had therefore to be learnt, not only by the politicians, but also by the civil servants. Yet by far the majority of these civil servants was trained under the old regime and find it difficult to understand exactly what it is expected to do and not to do. 'Advice', 'preparation', 'following up' are all processes which imply subtle distinctions between what is expected to be done to speed up decision making and what must not be done it is the preserve of politicians. Moreover, the roles of the truly political advisers who belong to prime ministers' offices and the 'mere' administrative counsellors in cabinet secretariats can be difficult to identify, especially when, as occurs in some cases, the prime minister's office forms part of the cabinet secretariat.

Thus both the external and the internal aspects of the life of Eastern European cabinets create many tensions which are seemingly rather different from those which exist in Western Europe. Difficulties arise in particular because the change of political system was rapid, even brutal, and that the functions which governments have to fulfil since the change are profoundly different from those which governments exercised in the calmer climate of the communist regimes where little which was unpredictable was ever taking place. Thus, not surprisingly, there is so much within Eastern European governments seems inefficient to Western observers. These governments may have an air of 'normality' which is in part illusory and hides a sense of impotence or of confusion about what is to be done. Cabinets do exist, however, and, on the whole, operate on the lines of the arrangements which they were made to adopt and as a result of the advice which they received. This at least is an indication that the machinery of government is moving in the right direction in most of Eastern Europe.

Cabinet decision-making

Decision making in Eastern European cabinets has therefore to be seen as taking place in the context of a conflict among contradictory patterns of relationships. The cabinet system is a network composed of the prime minister, of perhaps some important ministers such as the minister of finance or the minister of justice, of some party leaders who may be outside the government, of the ministers, individually and in groups, for example in ministerial committees, and of several ministerial advisers, probably closer to the prime minister than to other members of the cabinet. To these men and women must be added, in some cases at least, the president of the republic who may intervene, perhaps in an unpredictable manner, in aspects of decision making.

There are thus likely to be variations in the arrangements. There will be differences in the extent to which the cabinet meeting is genuinely involved in decisions and is not just ratifying proposals made by other bodies. There will be variations in the extent to which committees speed up the decision process. On the whole, Eastern European cabinet meetings seem to last longer than those of Western Europe an governments. Processes of streamlining, committee preparation and informal discussions, at both the political and the administrative levels, are not as higly 'routinised' in the East as in the West. Conflicts among ministers and among coalition partners may frequently surface and have to be resolved in cabinet meetings.

The result will be either a compromise or the collapse of the government. Conflicts leading to cabinet collapse have been rare in Eastern Europe, however. This suggests that cabinet members seem able to agree on many issues whether in the few single-party governments which have existed in the region or in the coalitions, although detailed coalition agreements have been relatively rare.

On the whole, the cabinet meeting has maintained greater importance in Eastern Europe than in the West. This may be because parties are less well structured and, in the background, because parliament often modifies what the cabinet decided. Thus the cabinet meeting would seem to be in Eastern Europe, not just, as in Western Europe, 'an arena in which final appeals can be and are made, as well as (at least in some countries) a place where ideas are discussed',[10] but a place where the various interests represented by the various ministers come to be ironed out.

This conclusion may be regarded as indicative of the fact that decisions of the cabinet are not prepared well enough, whether in the committees or in the cabinet secretariat, perhaps because the members of these bodies have not had sufficient training required to enable them to undertake their tasks.

Western European cabinet decision-making processes include long 'preparations', often supervised or directed by the prime minister or the minister of finance; in Eastern Europe the 'gate keepers' to the cabinet are less 'firm' or less systematic in their control of access. This state of affairs may be temporary. The same forces which have reduced the role of the cabinet in the West may well operate in Eastern Europe in the course of successive decades, but, at the beginning of the twenty-first century at least, the cabinet meeting continues to be an occasion of some importance in many countries of the area.

The role of the Eastern European prime minister is also still 'in the making'. It varies appreciably from country to country – as in Western Europe, but not perhaps entirely for the same reasons. First, the president of the republic may be influential both with respect to the choice of the prime minister, as, at one extreme, in the Baltic States, because of the fragmentation of the party system and, at the other, in Serbia and, up to 2000, in Croatia because, on the contrary, the party of the president dominates political life. The role of the prime minister depends also on the nature of the party system. Where the parties in power are rather rudimentary or are loose 'confederations', as in Romania with the centre-right government, the authority of the prime minister may be seriously undermined. Yet there are also many cases where the prime minister is the real leader, as in the Czech Republic, Hungary or Slovenia, as well as occasionally elsewhere, in large part because of the personality of the incumbent. Unlike in the West, however, and probably because party systems are less structured, there is seemingly little difference in the role of prime ministers as a result of the 'consociational' or 'majoritarian' character of the political system. Whether prime ministers are 'chiefs' rather than 'chairmen' depends therefore more on the extent to which the parties have 'solidified' and on the personality of the prime minister than on the extent to which politics is 'adversarial' or not.[11]

The comparative study of cabinets in post-communist Eastern Europe thus provides both a means of discovering similarities and differences and of examining the process of building the institution of the executive in a context as subtle and as flexible as the cabinet. Imitation plays a large part: to an extent, the cabinets of the countries of East-Central Europe and the Balkans resemble each other in terms of the trappings – in particular of the administrative trappings – of a modern national government. There are major variations in the extent to which the formal arrangements are implemented, however. The informal arrangements must therefore be monitored as they may be more important than the formal design. Thus Eastern European cabinets are more complex to analyse and categorise than Western European cabinets. They are a series of buildings, as yet unfinished, and their overall shape and colour can be expected to alter appreciably in the course of the first decades of the twenty-first century.

Notes

1   Authoritarianism came in the Eastern European states as early as 1919 in Hungary and 1920 in Romania. It developed from 1926 in Latvia, Lithuania and Poland and from 1928 in Yugoslavia; it arrived in 1934 in Estonia and Bulgaria. See S. Berglund, T. Hellén and F. H. Aarebrot, *Handbook of Political Change in Eastern Europe* (Cheltenham: Edward Elgar, 1998) pp. 14–16, 25–6.

2   According to the 1997 freedom ratings quoted in S. Berglund *et al.* (note 1) p. 3, the following nine countries were regarded as being 'free': Estonia, Latvia, Lithuania, Poland, Hungary, the Czech Republic, Slovenia, Romania, Bulgaria; a further six countries were regarded as being 'partly free': Slovakia, Croatia, Bosnia-Hercegovina, Macedonia, Albania and Moldova, while (the new) Yugoslavia was held to be 'not free'. By 2001, it would seem that at least Slovakia, Croatia and Macedonia and even Serbia had moved into the category of 'free' countries.

3   One exception is A. Agh, *Emerging Democracies in East Central Europe and the Balkans* (Northampton, MA: Elgar, 1998), in which there is a chapter on executives, but the developments do not examine specifically the characteristics of cabinets. The study of Hungary by A. Korosenyi, *Government and Parliament in Hungary* (Central European University Press, 1998) does examine in detail the 'cabinet system' of that country.

4   J. Blondel and F. Müller-Rommel (eds) *Cabinets in Western Europe* (2nd edn, Basingstoke: Macmillan, 1997) pp. 1–2.

5   Ibid., p. 2.

6   The Swiss system is based on the idea of a 'council' whose members are appointed by parliament, formally at least on an individual basis, for a fixed period. The characteristics of the appointment and composition of the European Commission of the European Union are similar in many ways to this model.

7   Sigma, an organisation financed by the European Union but closely associated with the OECD, has analysed in considerable detail the administrative characteristics of most of the countries of East-Central Europe and of some of the Balkan countries. Much of the description of these characteristics in this volume are based on the information provided by Sigma.

8   J. Blondel and F. Müller-Rommel (note 4) p. 5.

9   Ibid., p. 6.

10   Ibid., pp. 14–15.

11   The expressions are from B. Farrell, *Chairman or Chief, The Role of Taoiseach in Irish Government* (Dublin: Gill & Macmillan 1971).

Part 1
East-Central Europe

1
Estonia

Ferdinand Müller-Rommel and Georg Sootla

Cabinet setting

Estonian developments since 1987

Estonia's move towards independence was similar to that of the other two Baltic States. In Estonia, two different movements developed in the late 1980s – the reform communists and the nationalists. The reform oriented communist opposition grew in strength after the Popular Front of Estonia (PFE) was founded in April 1988. This new group, which consisted of many members of the Estonian Communist Party, advocated the transformation of the USSR into a confederacy, thus expecting a greater political and economic autonomy for Estonia. The nationalist movements, however, formed the Estonian National Independence Party (ERSP), which claimed independence for Estonia, demanded the adoption of Estonian as the language of the state and opposed a compromise with Russian minorities over voting rights.

In March 1990, the Estonian Supreme Soviet conducted a referendum on the issue of independence. The result was clear: 83 per cent of the registered electorate participated in the elections and 78 per cent voted in favour of Estonian independence.

One month later, the Estonian Supreme Soviet elected Edgar Savisaar, the leader of the PFE, as prime minister. One of the first acts of the new government was to restore the first five articles of the 1938 Estonian Constitution. The old Republic of Estonia was independent again, complete with the state emblems and flags. The Soviet Union immediately declared that proclamation void and sent troops to Estonia.

A few days after the Soviet Union military troops occupied Tallinn, the members of the Estonian Supreme Soviet declared full and immediate independence of the Estonian Republic on 20 August 1991. The Soviet *coup d'état* failed and Estonia was recognised as an independent state by more than thirty countries. Two weeks later, on 6 September 1991, the Soviet Union recognised the independence of all three Baltic States.

The new constitution established a parliamentary system with a president who would be elected in the first instance by the people and thereafter by the members of parliament. Combined presidential and parliamentary elections were held in September 1992. It was the first fully free election held in Estonia since 1934. The franchise was limited to about 690,000 Estonian citizens while 602,000 non-Estonians, mostly ethnic-Russian were not eligible to vote. The turnout was only 68 per cent.

The electoral law, which was based on a modified D'Hondt system of proportional representation with a 5 per cent threshold, forced numerous small parties to form electoral alliances. Thus, a total of 633 candidates representing some 40 parties and movements were grouped into nine alliances, with the following results:

- The Pro Patria Alliance Isamaa (NFP), a group of five Christian democratic, republican, liberal democratic and conservative parties which obtained the largest number of seats (29 out of a total of 101).
- The Estonian National Independence Party (ERSP), which had been in existence as a nationalist, anti-communist movement since 1988 obtained 10 seats.
- The Moderates (MOD), which was a coalition of the Tallinn- and Tartu-based Social Democrats and Centre–Rural parties won 12 seats.
- The electoral union Popular Front (PFE), formerly a left-wing reform orientated movement, which had become moderate won 15 seats.
- The Safe Home group, essentially a group of former Soviet industry managers obtained 17 seats.
- The Estonian Citizens Alliance, an extremely nationalist populist alliance led by a former US colonel, won 8 seats.
- The Monarchist Party, obtained 8 seats mostly as a protest vote.
- The Greens failed to pass the 5 per cent threshold but gained one direct seat in the university city of Tartu
- The Entrepreneurs' Party, a small group of centre-oriented politicians also missed the 5 per cent hurdle but gained one constituency seat.

The first President of Estonia was to be directly elected by the people, but none of the four candidates won on overall majority of the votes at the first ballot. The outgoing President Rüütel, who was leader of the former Estonian Communist Party, came top with 42 per cent of the total vote, followed by former Foreign Minister Lennart Meri, candidate of the Fatherland Alliance, with 30 per cent. The third place was taken by Rein Taagepera, an American-Estonian political scientist supported by the Popular Front who received 24 per cent of the total vote. The fourth, Mrs Parek, who was a candidate of the ENIP party, obtained only 4 per cent of the vote.

According to the Estonian Constitution, the final choice for the nomination of the president was to be made by parliament. Dominated by the

Pro Patria Alliance, parliament (*Riigikogu*) elected Lennart Meri to be Estonia's first president after independence.

Cabinets since 1992

Between 1992 and 1999, Estonia had four prime ministers and seven cabinets. These cabinets were the following:

- Laar (1) (NFP), majority coalition government, October 1992 to October 1994
- Tarand (MOD/IND), majority coalition government, October 1994 to April 1995
- Vähi (1) (KMÜ), majority government, April 1995 to October 1995
- Vähi (2) (KMÜ), majority government, November 1995 to November 1996
- Vähi (3) (KMÜ), minority government, December 1996 to February 1997
- Siimann (KMÜ), minority government, March 1997 to March 1999
- Laar (2) (NFP), majority coalition government, since March 1999.

Cabinets lasted twelve months on average; they lasted less immediately after independence. In less than three years there were two prime ministers.

In the first centre-right government, which was in office during 1992–94, the Pro Patria Alliance together had 38 per cent of the cabinet posts, while the Nationalist Independent Party had about 25 per cent and the Moderates 25 per cent. Together, these three parties commanded a 54 per cent majority of the seats in parliament. This first cabinet ended after two years because of the resignation of the prime minister.

Immediately thereafter, President Meri appointed the President of the Bank of Estonia, Siim Kallas, as the new Prime Minister. However, the members of the Estonian parliament refused to follow this nomination. Consequently, the president had to appoint a second candidate who has been former minister of environment, a supporter of the Greens but non-party affiliated. The new Prime Minister, Tarand, formed the second Estonian coalition government consisting of the Pro Patria Alliance (NFP), the Moderates, the Nationalists (ERSP) as well as smaller centre-right groups. In this second cabinet, the NFP lost ministerial posts. The winners have been independent, non-party affiliated professionals, who held a total of 26 per cent of the ministerial positions. This cabinet was not expected to last more than five months in office, since the second national parliamentary elections were scheduled for April 1995.

By then several political parties had changed their name and their organisation. Thus, the former centre-left wing Popular Front (PFE) became the Centre Party, while the former Safe Home Alliance emerged as the Coalition Party and Rural People's Union (KMÜ) comprising various agrarian parties and the Pensioners' and Families' League. The KMÜ focused on pro-market reforms, increasing protectionism and social benefits for citizens.

Voter turnout at the 1995 election was again low at 69 per cent. Four party alliances and three parties won seats in national parliament. The KMÜ, which comprises centre-right and centre-left parties, became the largest parliamentary party with 41 out of 101 seats. It was followed by the newly founded Estonian Reform Party (ER), which obtained 19 and the Centre Party which obtained 16. Both the Pro Patria Alliance, in electoral union with ERS and the Moderates, lost support and obtained only 8 and 6 seats respectively.

Immediately after the election the president nominated , Tiit Vähi, leader of the KMÜ, to form the government. He entered into negotiations with the centre-left party with which he signed a coalition agreement, in which both parties agreed to press for the integration of Estonia in Western and European institutions, to improve relations with Russia, to balance the budget, to exempt smallholders from income tax payments and to reduce credits for agriculture. Thus, Vähi established the smallest possible 'minimum winning' coalition based on two parties only.

From 1995 to 1999, the dominant Coalition Party, which formed an alliance with the Rural Union, the Pensioners' and Families' League and the Rural People's Party, held 53 per cent of the cabinet posts in the first coalition and only 40 per cent in the second coalition. In the fourth cabinet, the Reform Party (ER) received a significantly high number of seats in cabinet given to their relatively low representation in parliament. In the fifth cabinet, the strength of the KMÜ in cabinet increased again. They now held 53 per cent of the ministerial posts, while 34 per cent had been distributed among independent politicians. The end of the Vähi era was determined by the resignation of the prime minister in February 1992.

President Meri then appointed the former leader of the KMÜ parliamentary party, Mart Siimann, as new prime minister. He too formed a single party near-majority government with the 41 seats of the KMÜ parties in parliament, appointing also four independent ministers. The composition of the Siiman cabinet was half technical and half political. In the sixth Estonian cabinet, the KMÜ could increase its cabinet strength to 60 per cent. As the KMÜ held only 40 per cent of the seats in parliament, one portfolio was given to the small Progressive Party, the successor of the Centre Party, thereby increasing the parliamentary strength of the coalition government to 56 per cent. Although some changes in its composition took place, the government remained in office up to the third general election of 7 March 1999.

This election shifted Estonian politics back to the centre-right of the political spectrum. Former Prime Minister Laar formed a coalition with the Reform Party and the Moderates and the parliament constituted the seventh Estonian cabinet. In this new cabinet the posts were equally divided among the governing parties. Thus, the Pro Patria Alliance (NFP), the Radical Party (ER) and the Moderates each received 33 per cent of the ministerial posts. This distribution also reflected the parliamentary representation of the governing parties – while the NSF and the ER each held 18 seats in parliament, the Moderates had 17 members in parliament.

Compared to most other East-Central European cabinets, the Estonian governments consist of a fairly high number of non-party affiliated ministers. On average, independents held 19 per cent of the cabinet posts during the period from 1992 to 1999.

Cabinet structure

Constitutional framework

According to the new Constitution of 1992, which is based on that of 1938, Estonia is a parliamentary system in which the government holds the executive power and the legislative power rests with a parliament of 101 members. Elections take place every four years on a proportional representation basis. Parliament passes laws and resolutions, adopts the budget and decides on the holding of referendums. It also authorises the prime minister to form the cabinet.

The head of state is the president, elected by secret ballot in parliament for five years. The power of the president is rather limited. As in other parliamentary democracies the president of Estonia has mainly the ceremonial role of representing the state; yet the president of Estonia has used his position to influence public policy and political processes. On about thirty occasions since 1992, the president has used his right of suspensive veto on bills passed by parliament. The president has also the authority to appoint several categories of civil servants as well as ambassadors.

In contrast to Latvia, the term 'cabinet' does not appear in the Estonian Constitution. The main responsibilities of 'The Government of the Republic' are described in articles 86–101. The Constitution stipulates the maximum time which the formation of governments may take. The president has to nominate a candidate for the post of prime minister within 14 days after the previous government has resigned. The nominated candidate has to present to parliament the basic lines of the programme of the new government within a further 14 days, after which parliament decides by a vote on the quesiton of giving the candidate for prime minister the authority to form a government. Having received that authority, the prime minister must present the names of the members of the government to the president within seven days. The president then has to appoint the ministers within three days. The formation of a government cannot take more than six weeks.

The constitution also mentions the State Chancellery and in particular the state secretary, who serves as head of the chancellery and is appointed and dismissed by the prime minister. He or she has the constitutional right to attend cabinet meetings with the right to participate in the discussions. He or she has the same rights as the head of the State Chancellery as those of a minister at the head of a department, except the right to issue regulations. The main functions of the State Chancellery are to manage the operations of and provide support services for the government and the prime minister, to manage the relations of the government with the parliament and other constitutional institutions and to coordinate the work of the State Information System and the co-ordination of the training of state officials and local government officials. All administrative support structures of the prime minister belong formally to the State Chancellery.

The Constitution also specifies some characteristics of cabinet meetings. Article 96 says that government sessions should be closed, unless the government decides otherwise. Government decisions are taken on the basis of proposals made by the prime minister or by ministers. To be valid, government decrees require the signatures of the prime minister, of the respective minister and of the secretary of the chancellery. This gives the latter more political responsibility than is usually the case.

Article 97 regulates the vote of no-confidence. At least one-fifth of the members of parliament have to submit a written motion during a session of parliament. If a no-confidence motion is passed against the prime minister or the government, the president may, on the proposal by the government and within three days, dissolve parliament. A no-confidence motion on the same issue may not be presented unless three months have elapsed since the previous no-confidence vote.

To avoid corruption or conflicts of interest, the Constitution stipulates that cabinet members may not hold any other public office or belong to the leadership or of the board of a commercial undertaking.

Cabinet life

Political characteristics

The first Estonian centre-right majority cabinet was formed one month after the election in 1992. The first half of this government lasted for only 15 months, as the Prime Minister Laar announced that he wished to undertake a simultaneous reshuffle of the defence, foreign, economy, and finance posts. At first, President Meri did not accept the proposal, arguing that a discontinuity in key ministries would seriously hurt Estonia's relations with Russia and NATO. This unconstitutional move caused a serious contest of politicians and key lawyers. President Meri was forced to sign the new ministerial appointments but publicly made clear that he would have rather seen Prime Minister Laar resign. However, the prime minister stayed in office but promised to give more information on cabinet work to parliament and to the president.

The second half of the Laar government lasted only nine months, the parties being internally divided, largely because the prime minister became too dependent on interest group lobby. Several ministers resigned and the Pro Patria Alliance split as a new Republican and Conservative Popular Party was being created.

In addition, it was announced that Laar has approved the secret plan to sell Russian roubles during the monetary reform. This led to a vote on a no-confidence motion, which was passed by 60 members of parliament. Laar resigned in October 1994.

His successor, Prime Minister Tarand was only in office for six months because of the national parliamentary elections in 1995, which was won by the left-wing parties. New Prime Minister Vähi survived only seven months in his first cabinet. It collapsed because the Minister for the Interior from the Centre Party, Edgar Savisaar, had been involved in a phone-tapping scandal. Prime Minister Vähi dismissed Savisaar, but the Centre Party refused to accept this decision. As a result, the prime minister and all ministers from the KMÜ tendered their resignations, thus leaving a minority group of Centre Party ministers in cabinet. President Meri did not accept this rather peculiar arrangement and reappointed Vähi, asking him to form a new government.

The second Vähi cabinet remained in office for one year only, the KMÜ having signed a 'party-to-party memorandum' with the former junior coalition partner, the Centre Party. The Reform Party considered this behaviour as a prelude for including the Centre Party into cabinet and asked the KMÜ to respect the memorandum. This was refused by KMÜ party officials and all Reform Party ministers formally resigned. Vähi then continued in office at the head of a single party near majority government commanding 40 per cent of the seats in parliament.

Early in 1997, the opposition parties accused the prime minister of corruption following allegations of his involvement in suspect real estate deals while speaker of Tallinn City council. Although a legislative vote of no-confidence in the prime minister was defeated by a narrow margin, Vähi resigned as prime minister while denying the allegations made against him. Mart Siimann (1997–99) became the new Prime Minister.

Duration ministers

Between 1992 and 1999, 61 different persons were in office; the average duration of service of these ministers was eighteen months, six months higher than the average cabinet duration. Major ministerial changes took place under Prime Minister Laar, as we noted, in 1994. Another major reshuffle took place under Vähi: he recruited a total of 33 ministers for the 14 governmental posts. Cabinet stability increased significantly after 1997 and under Siimann, only three ministers were replaced, in part because of the large number of independents among the ministers, as these are experts and professional managers and not party officials.

Administrative characteristics

As in most other countries, the administrative features of cabinet decision making are co-ordinated and monitored by the State Chancellery, which in Estonia consists of 140 persons who hold permanent positions, except the advisers to the prime minister. They are expected to co-ordinate the technical and procedural work of the government and advise it on legal matters.

The staff of the Prime Minister's Office (PMO) is rather small (nine positions). When Prime Minister Laar came into office first in 1992, he abolished the section which mirrored the structure of the departments. Since then, the main role of the prime minister's staff has been, first, to harmonise policy proposals with the general line of the coalition agreement, second, to provide background information on proposals coming out of the departments, and third, with the assistance of specially selected civil servants, to elaborate alternative proposals for the prime minister, for instance on budgetary matters.

The State Chancellery headed by the state secretary manages the operations of and provides support services to the cabinet. It also manages the relations between cabinet and parliament. In this context, the state secretary is formally responsible for the preparation of cabinet meetings and the examination of proposed bills from the viewpoint of their legal correctness before these are presented to the cabinet for approval. This technical role may be politically important in Estonia, as the quality of the legal advice given to ministers is often rather low. The diminishing role of the Ministry of Justice has increased the involvement of the department of legislation of the State Chancellery as the final filter before decisions are taken in cabinet.

The Bureau of Public Administration (PAB) and the European Integration Office (EIO) are sub-units of the State Chancellery. The main function of these units is to collect and analyse relevant information. The EIO was established when the co-ordination of EU matters was with the Minister of Foreign Affairs. This was one of reasons why matters concerning EU accession were for a long time poorly co-ordinated. One of the main tasks of the EIO is to prepare and conduct meetings of the Council of Higher Civil Servants (CHCS). It co-ordinates and monitors European integration issues. The office is thus a filter between cabinet and prime minister, since it informs ministers about political problems and channels politically sensitive issues which need to be decided on to the prime minister.

The role of the Bureau of Public Administration is to define the objectives of public administration reform in Estonia, a task which is difficult to fulfil as the office cannot count on the support of the departments. Most ministers consider such a reform as leading to probable political failure and as an unlikely to bring about 'fast political profit'.

The Estonian cabinet meets at least once a week, normally on Tuesdays. The prime minister chairs the sessions. In principle, only the prime minister, the ministers and the secretary of state have the right to speak. However, the legal chancellor and the auditor general may participate in cabinet meetings in matters within their competence. The prime minister may also invite others to attend a cabinet meeting, but this rarely occurs. Among the political officials invited by ministers who may also attend, but only to hear the discussion of issues presented by these ministers, is one representative of county governors, representatives of local government associations, secretaries general of ministries and representatives of the president of the republic.

Additional unofficial meetings of cabinet members occur regularly once a week on a Tuesday evening after the official cabinet meetings. These meetings aim at 'pre-cooking' policy proposals before the final decision is taken in cabinet. The prime minister invites the all ministers and sometimes party leaders to these meetings. The political implications of proposals are discussed and reviewed before being formally submitted to the cabinet. Occasionally, informal decisions taken at these meetings have had a most decisive impact on final decision making in cabinet.

For ironing out politically and technically complex policy proposals, the prime minister may set up one of three different types of committees – a *ministerial committee* composed of the secretary of state and of those ministers who would have to implement the proposal under discussion, an *interministerial committee* consisting of officials from various governmental agencies, including local and county governments, or an *expert committee* comprising public officials and persons from the private sector. According to the Constitution, these committees may not have executive power.

Several prime ministers established committees with a very broad remit. This resulted in a segmentation of government decision-making, which rendered discussions and decisions more time-consuming and less effective. Ministers thus started to delegate the attendance at these committees to civil servants, who took decisions on behalf of politicians. When issues were broadly defined, ministers usually did not devote enough time to details. Ministerial committees became therefore in effect inter-ministerial committees. In addition, the committees have appointed small ad hoc expert committees for the resolution of specific conflicts among cabinet members. These were established rather informally. As these expert committees consisted of persons occupied outside the government, the result was an increase in the impact and access of interest groups to cabinet decision-making.

The agenda of cabinet meetings is publicly available. It is distributed, with all relevant attachments for cabinet discussion, seven days before the Tuesday meeting, to ministers, the auditor general, the legal chancellor, representatives of county governors, local government associations, the Office of the President of the Republic, the advisory staff of the prime minister, officials in the State Chancellery and journalists. This gives political representatives and civil servants enough time to consult ministers and public officials on the items proposed for cabinet decision.

Only the prime minister and the ministers may propose drafts for cabinet decision, which must be submitted to the State Chancellery seven days before the cabinet agenda is approved. All formal and legal aspects of every single policy proposal are discussed finally at the regular meetings of the state secretaries of ministries, which usually take place on Friday mornings. Thus, only well-prepared proposals are dealt with in cabinet.

Cabinet decisions are minuted and the discussion is recorded on tapes. The minutes are sent to all governmental bodies affected by the decisions. The State Chancellery monitors the implementation of cabinet decisions. It keeps records of the decisions taken in cabinet and presents regularly an overview of the implementation process, but it does not have the power to intervene in these processes.

Cabinet decision-making

The decision-making process in Estonian cabinets has varied over time, according to the leadership style of the prime minister. Yet, irrespective of this style, prime ministers have all made intensive use of the informal meetings which take place before matters are decided on at the regular meetings of the cabinet. Informal decisions have also been taken in coalition council meetings, where no written records are taken. In addition, consultations with the parliamentary parties are frequent as well as seminars with members of the coalition parties on issues which have to be decided in cabinet.

The impact of individual leadership style on cabinet decision-making can be assessed by examining the very different mode of behaviour of two prime ministers, Siimann (1997–99) and Laar (1992–94, and from 1999).

After the March 1995 election, the Coalition Party (KMÜ) under Prime Minister Vähi formed a coalition with parties from the centre-left and the right. Because of different scandals in which the prime minister was alleged to be involved, as noted earlier, the government fell and a minority cabinet led by Siiman (KMÜ) was formed in 1997. The new prime minister promised to open the policy process and to consult even opposition parties on policy proposal. As we also noted, he recruited seven of his fifteen ministers among experts without party affiliation.

The new 'consultative policy style' opened the decision-making process first to civil servants, many of whom attended informal cabinet meetings as advisers to politicians or as observers. Siimann allowed general discussions and hard bargains to take place on policy issues.

As the number of participants increased, the duration of the decision-making process also increased at these informal meetings became much longer and the probability that proposals would be ready for the cabinet declined. This led to more 'unprepared' policy proposals coming to the cabinet. Unable to deal simultaneously with the extended number of these proposals, the prime minister started to delegate decisions on these matters to other institutions and to political actors, for example, to ministerial committees, to individual ministers and to expert groups. In the ministerial committees, civil servants soon began to play a major part, as much of the discussion dealt with technical issues which were more within the competence of the civil servants than of the ministers. Indeed, the more technical issues became, the less ministers were competent to discuss proposals at ministerial committee meetings. Thus a greater number of proposals came from the departmental civil servants, who at their own discretion started to elaborate draft policy programmes and ministers often approved these proposals *ex post facto*.

The political power of ministers individually grew markedly during the Siimann cabinet. As only half of the cabinet members belonged to a party, the impact of interest groups on political decision-making became large, while ministers belonging to a party tended to follow the guidelines of their organisations. Indeed, ministers belonging to a party tend to inform their respective parliamentary party about their ministerial activities once a week when parliament is sitting.

However, the consensual-consultative style introduced by Siimann thus gave considerable responsibility to individual ministers and resulted in a markedly more open form of governmental decision-making than that which had characterised previous Estonian cabinets.

Mart Laar, on returning to office after the March 1999 election, reduced ministerial autonomy and relocated political decision-making in the centre of government. His leadership style is based on the dominant role of the prime minister. Parties became more important; co-ordination of decision making was given to politicians and not to civil servants and the decision-making process became more formal. Civil servants were barred from attending informal cabinet meetings.

The main purpose of these informal meetings is to have the discussion of these matters in an informal environment, as this helps to increase collegiality among the decision makers. These meetings lasted much longer than regular cabinet meetings – on average four hours even during the cabinet of Laar – with each issue being allocated about twenty minutes. Ministers, parliamentary party leaders, the prime minister and his personal advisers, the government advisers and state secretaries participated. The staff from the Bureau of Public Administration Reform and from the Bureau of European Integration attended only once a month. The time devoted to the discussion of particular items at these meetings came to be limited in time and there was concentration on political rather than on technical issues. If a serious controversy occurred among members at informal cabinet meetings, the matter was sent to an ad hoc working group led by ministers. Votes were taken on proposals.

The consensual leadership style was replaced by a more rigid bargaining style. The role of the prime minister in cabinet decision-making became markedly more pronounced. This new leadership style substantially increased the decision-making capacity in a cabinet which had a rather heterogeneous party composition.

In sum, cabinet decision-making in Estonia, up to 1999 at least, has been more consensual and more open than in most countries of East-Central Europe. Critical issues have been discussed in advance either informally or in cabinet committees and they either have been solved by means of discussions or have not appeared on the cabinet agenda at all. Voting in cabinet has been rare. The fact that cabinet agendas have been sent to journalists and cabinet decisions taped underlines the transparency of cabinet decision-making in the country.

2
Latvia

Ferdinand Müller-Rommel and Ole Nørgaard

Cabinet setting

Latvian developments since 1989

The road to independence was less smooth in Latvia than in the other two Baltic States because about one third of the population are ethnic Russians. Thus, political conflicts between pro- and anti-Soviet Union positions were foremost in the public debate in the first years after independence.

Organised Latvian opposition against the Soviet Union began in the mid-1980s. One of the strongest opposition movements was a group of anti-Soviet intellectuals known as the Latvian Writers' Union. It was established in 1987 and put forward a resolution proposing that Latvia became an internationally recognised sovereign state. Moreover, the movement demanded complete autonomy in financial matters and in education, and an end to censorship and human rights violations in Latvia. In October 1988, the group formed the Popular Front of Latvia (PFL).

The founding congress of the PFL adopted a charter advocating greater economic and political autonomy for the republic: an immigration policy that would keep non-Latvians from entering the country; free democratic elections; an independent constitutional court; territorial armed forces; separate diplomatic representation abroad; and religious instruction in schools. By the end of 1988 the PFL had become the largest and most influential political force in Latvia. In March 1989 candidates supported by the PFL won 26 of the 34 contested Latvian seats in the USSR's Congress of People's Deputies.

Under these new political circumstances the governing Latvian Communist Party (CP) changed its position. The majority of CP members in the Latvian Supreme Soviet decided to abolish the clause in Article 6 of the Latvian Constitution guaranteeing the 'leading role' of the Communist Party. In addition, the Latvian Supreme Soviet passed a law restoring the official use of the original flag, state emblems and national anthem of independent Latvia in place of those used by Soviet Latvia.

In March 1991 all permanent residents of Latvia aged 18 and over (excluding members of the armed forces stationed in the republic) were asked to vote in a referendum on independence for the Latvian Republic. The result was striking. The turnout was 87 per cent, and 74 per cent of those who voted voted in favor of independence for Latvia. Support for independence was greater than expected among ethnic Russian and other minorities. Although the result fell short of a two-thirds majority of registered voters, which would have been a primary condition under the 1990 USSR legislation for the secession of a republic, the Soviet Union formally recognised Latvian independence in September 1991.

After independence was declared, the Council took several important steps designed to establish a democratic system. First, by a majority, members decided to grant citizenship to anyone who had held Latvian citizenship before the Soviet occupation (1940) as well as to their descendants, even if they were not currently Latvian residents. However, the Council did not allow dual citizenship: Latvians had to renounce Soviet or any other citizenship. The Council also decided that anyone else who wished to obtain Latvian citizenship had to have lived in Latvia for at least 16 years. Citizens had to be fluent in the Latvian language, conversant with the Latvian Constitution and swear allegiance to the Latvian Republic. Second, the Council approved proposals for amendments to the language law. These acknowledged the right of minorities to use their mother tongue, but guaranteed education only in the Latvian language. Russian-speaking members voted against this proposal. Third, the Council passed a resolution nationalising all Soviet Army bases on Latvian territory and banning former officers of the Latvian State Security Committee (KGB) from working in defence, internal affairs and security bodies. Fourth, major organisational changes were introduced in the government. The new prime minister of the Council, Ivars Godmanis, who was appointed in November 1991, proposed that a cabinet be set up in which the number of posts would be reduced from 23 to 16 and each minister would be responsible for determining how the privatisation process would take place in the field in which he or she was concerned.

The first free election to the 100-seat new Latvian parliament, which took place in June 1993, attracted a very high turnout: nearly 90 per cent voted. Twenty-four parties competed in the election, but, because of the 4 per cent threshold, only nine of these came to be represented. Both moderate and nationalist parties won: Latvian Way, a political movement established in February 1993 and covering a wide range of political views, obtained 32 per cent of the vote and 36 seats in the Saeima. The National Independence Party and the National Movement of Latvia obtained 25 per cent of the vote and 28 seats. On the other hand, the Latvian Popular Front, which had been the largest party in the outgoing Council, failed to pass the 4 per cent threshold.

The large support for both nationalist and moderate parties was in part the result of the electoral law which gave the vote only to citizens of pre-1940 Latvia and to their descendants. The 27 per cent of the population which was ethnic Russian was excluded from the election and these citizens were represented by six deputies only.

During the first plenary session of the Saeima, Guntis Ulmanis was elected president of the republic. He appointed Valdis Birkavs, a leading member of Latvian Way as prime minister. Birkavs formed a minority coalition government composed of members of Latvian Way and of the Latvian Peasants' Party, but the latter was given only the Agriculture and Welfare portfolios. That party announced in July 1994 its withdrawal from the government. It was a strongly nationalistic party which disagreed with the protectionist import tariffs introduced by Latvian Way and with the general agricultural policy of the government. Attempts by the president to form a new coalition government comprising Latvian Way and the Latvian National Conservative Party (LNNK) failed. Latvian Way then formed a two party coalition with the a new 'Political Union of Economists'.

That new minority government was approved by 49 votes to 33 in the Saeima and on the basis of this vote, President Ulmanis appointed Maris Gailis of Latvian Way as prime minister and Valdis Birkavs became Minister for Foreign Affairs. The new prime minister appointed nine ministers from Latvian Way and three independent non-party 'experts' who were not members of the Saeima.

That second cabinet resigned after the 1995 general election, which resulted in a very fragmented parliament. Nine parties were represented, and none of these obtained more than 16 per cent of the vote. In particular, Latvian Way, formerly the strongest party, lost considerable support. The newly established Democratic Party Saimnieks (DPS) obtained the largest number of seats (18). It was ideologically left of centre with some populist undertones. The second largest group in parliament was the extreme right wing People's Movement for Latvia (LVP), which gained 16 seats. That party had campaigned on a nationalistic and anti-Russian platform. Other populist parties that did well were the Union for Fatherland and Freedom (TB) on the right, and the Unity Party (SP) led by orthodox communists on the left. It seemed that Latvian Way and the Latvian Conservative Party (LNNK) had lost to populist parties because of widespread dissatisfaction with the economic and social reform policies which had been pursued.

In what was to be the third government of the new republic, parliament passed a vote of confidence in a cabinet led by Andris Skele, a businessman and compromise candidate belonging to the DPS. That cabinet was to be the broadest coalition in Latvia so far, as it included six parties and excluded only the right wing People's Movement for Latvia and the National Harmony Party.

That majority coalition held office for 14 months only, however, during which the prime minister reshuffled the cabinet twice in order to have a more cohesive team. Rather surprisingly, the prime minister resigned in January 1997. He had been widely criticised for his authoritarian leadership style and for his choice of a new finance minister. He was nonetheless re-appointed after the president stated publicly that he regarded Skele as the prime minister best able to continue to implement economic reforms. The new Skele majority government consisted of member of the three major parties and of two smaller groups. That government remained in office for six months only, however, during which several ministers were dismissed or resigned after having been accused of corruption. The cabinet began to disintegrate and Skele announced his resignation.

President Ulmanis appointed Guntars Krasts, the outgoing minister of economy, to form the government. Krasts was a member of the former Union for Fatherland and Freedom which had merged with the Latvian National Conservative Party (LNNK). The new prime minister formed a five-party centre-left coalition. Yet Krasts' first cabinet ended in April 1998 after the DPS announced its withdrawal from the ruling coalition. The prime minister remained in office as the head of a second cabinet consisting of four parties only, which jointly held a majority in parliament. That cabinet lasted for only a few months and ended with the national election of 3 October 1998.

Prior to that election, three developments had had an impact on Latvian politics. First, in May 1998, former Prime Minister Skele founded the People's Party, of which he was elected chairman. That party attracted significant support because Skele was considered an expert in economic reforms, while also attracting support from members of parliament who had been disillusioned by the Krasts governments. Second, the threshold to secure parliamentary representation was raised to 5 per cent for parties competing singly and to 7 per cent for party alliances. Third, amendments to the citizenship law were passed which gave automatic citizenship to anyone born in Latvia after 21 August 1991. The amendments also simplified the language requirements for older residents wishing to obtain citizenship. These changes were designed to make it easier for non-citizens (particularly ethnic Russians) currently living in Latvia to obtain Latvian citizenship. While these new rules were welcomed by the international community, a group consisting of 38 members of parliament asked the president to call for a referendum on this issue. The referendum was held simultaneously with the general election on 3 October. The electorate voted by 53 per cent in favour of the reform. Meanwhile, at the general election, the People's Party became the largest party, gaining 21 per cent of the vote and 24 seats, while the largest party of the former government, Latvian Way, won 21 seats and the Conservative Union for Fatherland and Freedom/LNNK 17 seats. Only six of the twenty-one parties that contested the election passed the new 5 per cent threshold.

Yet the fragmented nature of the Saeima implied that at least three parties needed to co-operate to form a majority. After extensive talks involving all the parties in parliament a three-party minority coalition was constituted, consisting of Latvian Way, the Conservative Union for Fatherland and Freedom/LNNK and the New Party. The three parties signed an accord of co-operation with the opposition Latvian Social Democrats, who agreed to support the government and in return received the agriculture portfolio. Prime Minister Vilis Kristopans of Latvian Way headed the new cabinet.

The government lasted to June 1999. On 30 June Kristopans announced on radio his resignation because the coalition partners did not support his policies.

After two weeks of negotiations a new coalition government was formed, once again headed by Andris Skele; it included three parties, Latvian Way, the Union for Fatherland and Freedom (LNNK) and the People's Party. It was unstable from the start, however, being affected by the autocratic leadership of Skele and by intensifying conflicts over privatization strategies. Not surprisingly, the government fell in April 2000. This resulted in the setting up of the third government of the legislature and with the prime ministership returning to Latvian Way. The new government, headed by Andris Berzins, included three parties in addition to Latvian Way, the Union for Fatherland and Freedom, the People's Party and the New Party.

Cabinets since 1993

Latvia had five prime ministers and eight cabinets between 1993 and 2000. Cabinet instability has therefore been substantial. These cabinets were:

- Birkavs (LC), minority government, August 1993 to September 1994
- Gailes (LC), minority government, September 1994 to December 1995
- Skele (1) (DPS), majority government, December 1995 to February 1997
- Skele (2) (DPS), majority government, February 1997 to August 1997
- Karsts (1) (LNNK), majority government, August 1997 to April 1998
- Karsts (2) (LNNK), majority government, April 1998 to November 1998
- Kristopans (LC), minority government, November 1998 to June 1999
- Skele (3) (DPS), majority government, July 1999 to April 2000

The first two cabinets as well as the Kristopans government consisted of minority coalitions supported by small opposition parties. The five cabinets under the leadership of prime ministers Skele and Krasts were consensus-orientated majority coalitions.

Latvian cabinets have been comparatively small. The number of posts of ministers has varied between 12 and 17, but there have also been between two and nine ministers of state, each of whom is attached to a department.

They are entitled to vote at cabinet meetings only on subjects regarding their department.

All governments in independent Latvia have been coalitions. These coalitions have started and ended in different ways. Two were formed after national elections, four after a coalition crisis and another three ended because of the resignation of Prime Minister Andris Skele.

Interestingly, the Latvian Way (LC) has been represented in all eight cabinets. It is the 'oldest' party in the Latvian post-independence system. The party was formed in 1993 and represents a wide range of political views. From 1993 to 1999, four out of the five prime ministers and 23 of a total of 57 ministers came from this party. Its greatest influence was in the first two cabinets as it was then the largest party. Its political impact decreased during 1995–97 when Skele was prime minister for the first time. It became once again dominant in cabinet from 1998 onwards, except during the short interlude of the second Skele government. The second most influential party in cabinet is the conservative LNNK, which merged in 1997 with the Union for Fatherland and Freedom. It has been in government since 1995 and held between 44 per cent (seventh cabinet) and 31 per cent (fifth cabinet) of governmental posts. It had 11 ministers of the 57 ministers and one of its members, Krasts was twice prime minister. The left-wing Democratic Party Saimnieks, which merged with the Latvian Union Party in 1996 to form the Latvian Social Democratic Union, was strongly represented in the two Skele and the first Krasts cabinet, where they held between 21 and 31 per cent of governmental posts. The other parties in cabinet have had a minor role. There were independents in the second minority cabinet of Prime Minister Maris Gailis only.

Ministerial posts in Latvia have been similar to those of Western countries. There has been a position of deputy prime minister since the Skele cabinet in 1995. Ministers without portfolio only existed in the Birkavs cabinet and the first Skele cabinet. The ministerial posts in the recent cabinet were Deputy Prime Minister and Minister of European Integration; Environmental Protection and Regional Development; Defence; Foreign Affairs; Finance; Economy; Interior; Culture; Education and Science; Agriculture; Welfare; Transport; Justice; Special Tasks for Co-operation with International Financial Institutions.

Cabinet structures

Constitutional framework

The Latvian constitution establishes a parliamentary system with a cabinet responsible to parliament (Saeima). According to the 1922 constitution, restored in 1993, the president is head of state and head of the armed forces. The president is elected by secret ballot by parliament for a three-year term, extended in December 1997 to four years, and may not serve for more than two consecutive terms. The president does not participate in national decision-making as such, but has the right to convene and to preside over extraordinary cabinet meetings and to determine the agenda of these meetings. The president is also entitled to dissolve the Saeima, has the right, within seven days, to send bills back to parliament for an additional reading and with suggestions for amendments. If the parliament decides not to change the bill, the president must promulgate it.

The cabinet, which is appointed by the president, hold the executive power. All administrative institutions of the state are under its authority, but it needs the continued support of parliament, which is composed of 100 members elected on a proportional representation basis. Only in cases of urgent necessity does the constitution entitle the cabinet to issue decrees which the force of law between sessions of the Saeima, but these decrees become void if they are not presented to parliament within three days after the opening of the new session.

Cabinet life

Political characteristics

The many cleavages penetrating Latvian political life, together with proportional representation have resulted in a high degree of fractionalisation: this in turn renders coalitions inevitable, whether of a minority or of a majority character. Moreover, personalities have tended to count more than parties. In contrast to those of most countries in Western Europe, political parties in Latvia are not mass organisations with a broad membership. They tend to be clubs more akin to parties in the early phase of their development in Western Europe.

They are mostly financed by private businesses which also influence the nomination of candidates for government. The most prominent example is Latvian Way, which originated in the early 1990s from the so-called 'Club 21'. The party was and is an elite coalition which brings together previous communist nomenclature politicians, intellectuals, professionals of the Soviet-type middle class and representatives of the Latvian diaspora. Although it has occupied a central position in all governments, the party never had more than between 100 and 200 members. The same applies to other parties, where very few persons at the apex of the party organisation control party decisions. Hence, parties play only a minor role in cabinet. Governmental politics in Latvia is dominated by a rather narrow group of politicians located in the capital, Riga. The high 'survival rate' of individuals in successive governments is another expression of this elitism.

However, parliament is a much more heterogeneous (and uncontrollable) body, reflecting a confusing mixture of regional, political and ideological interests. The professional standard (and ethics of behaviour) of many parliamentary members is also relatively low, adding further to the unpredictability of parliamentary behaviour.

The elite nature of Latvian politics in conjunction with the immaturity of parliament has therefore made coalitions the logical solution to government formation. By setting up coalitions rather than single party minority governments, the political elites have been able to keep central decision making behind closed doors. A single party minority government would to a much larger extent be at the mercy of the unpredictable parliament.

Coalition negotiations in Latvia are always lengthy affairs, a characteristic which can be explained in two different ways. On the one hand, the limited number of persons involved in Latvian elite politics has to be contrasted with the intensity of the conflicts to be resolved. On the other hand, Latvia does not have a consensual political culture in which the interests of opponents are accepted as legitimate parts of the political process and compromises are a necessary part of a democratic policy. A compromise would thus be perceived as a loss by both sides. Hence, both (or all) sides in coalition agreements are unwilling to give in on what they regard as their most important issues. One result is that coalition agreements bear more resemblance to long shopping lists than to plans for strategic action. In Western Europe coalition agreements usually consist of an agreed platform of action and a work plan but in Latvia, all coalition partners seem to list their priority issues in more or less random order. Coalition agreements have therefore never constituted an adequate basis for government action. The full texts of the coalition agreements have never been published, moreover, but kept as confidential documents among the coalition partners.

The president has never played an active role in the process of cabinet formation. Elected by parliament, he, and more recently, she, lacks an independent political base, and is furthermore constrained by very limited economic and organisational resources. The bulk of presidential influence is acquired through public agenda setting. First, this agenda setting power is manifest when the president sends bills back to parliament for reconsideration. President Guntis Ulmanis (1993–95) returned 17 bills, while Vaira Vike-Freiberga (elected 1999) had returned three bills by mid-2000. The laws which the president returned to parliament cover a wide range of issues, but in particular those where parliament has been at odds with international standards and advice. This was for instance the case with laws relating to the citizenship issue. Second, when addressing the press in relation to certain issues, the president is able to attract the attention of the public and of politicians about some topics. President Vaira Vike-Freiberga, elected in 1999, and who is of Canadian origin, consciously uses this medium. Direct contact with the cabinet is limited to ceremonial events and to weekly dinners with the prime minister.

Turnover of ministers

The average duration of cabinets in Latvia has been under 12 months. Although this gives an impression of instability, there is in reality substantial stability among the major political parties and elite in cabinet. The stability of Latvian Way (LC) in cabinet, for instance, is best demonstrated by the longevity of former Prime Minister, Foreign Affairs Minister and Minister of Justice Valdis Birkavs, who was in office from June 1994 to May 2000. Another example is that of Kristopans, former Minister of Transport, who held office from 1995 until 1998, when he became prime minister.

Overall, the duration of ministers in office has been 19 months and is thus appreciably higher than the duration of cabinets. Ministers have tended to retain the same posts while in cabinet. Only three former prime ministers received ministerial positions after their resignation as head of government – Birkavs who became Foreign Affairs Minister and later Minister of Justice, Gailis who became Minister of the Environment, but remained in office only for seven months, and Krasts who became deputy prime minister.

In the first two Latvian cabinets there were reshuffles affecting only two ministers, but the number of new ministers increased significantly in the fragmented majority coalitions under Skele. In his third cabinet, Skele replaced six ministers out of fourteen, nearly half the total. In his fourth cabinet, which lasted only six months, three ministers resigned. The resignation of all four ministers of the left-wing Democratic Party (DPS) resulted in the end of the fifth Latvian government.

Administrative characteristics

The cabinet meets once a week on Tuesdays and is chaired by the prime minister. Extraordinary cabinet meetings are convened only on the initiative of the prime minister and of the president. Only the prime minister, the ministers and persons given special assignments have the right to vote. Decisions in cabinet are taken by majority vote, there being a quorum if more than half of the ministers are present. In case of a tie, the prime minister's vote prevails.

Decision-making in cabinet is formally co-ordinated by the chancellery of the cabinet, which includes both a legal and an administrative section and consists of five departments, Public Administration Reform, Civil Service Management, Secretariat of the Cabinet, Policy Planning, and Review and European Integration.

All cabinet proposals must be submitted to the chancellery and supplemented by a letter outlining the need for the proposal in light of anticipated political, social and financial consequences. In addition, the consistency of the draft with EU legislation must be demonstrated.

The Latvian cabinet has adopted a consensual mode of processing decisions. This mode was originally based on a complex committee structure that has been simplified. Since 1998 only one cabinet committee, instead of several, is charged with the preparation of all proposals going to cabinet meetings. This committee, which comprises all ministers, top civil servants and invited experts, meets every Monday before the Tuesday meeting of the cabinet. This new arrangement avoids the need to send proposals to state secretaries and to the Association of Latvian Local Governments, which were previously asked for opinions.

Having received the approval of the chancellery, cabinet proposals are transferred to the regular meetings of the state secretaries, the formal title of the administrative leaders of the ministries. If there is a disagreement about a proposal between two departments, the draft bill is re-submitted to the cabinet committee for decision. If the issue is still not resolved the prime minister may declare the proposal a cabinet matter, in which case it will be decided in cabinet. All decisions are signed by the prime minister and countersigned by the minister responsible for the implementation of the policy.

Debates and decisions at cabinet meetings are recorded. Minutes are distributed the day after the meeting to ministers and other officials who are responsible for monitoring policy implementation. The director of the state chancellery supervises implementation and regularly reports to the prime minister about the matter.

Cabinet decision-making

Latvia is a new democracy with a low level of institutionalisation and a high degree of individual influence by the political elite. Most recently, the centre of decision making in government is not the cabinet but the newly founded coalition which comprises the leaders of the coalition parties. The council has replaced a so-called inner cabinet, with which the prime ministers of earlier governments surrounded themselves with a close groups of like-minded ministers. In 2000, several government decisions were taken in the coalition council by a simple majority vote. However, all salient issues, such as those related to citizenship and privatisation can only be taken on a consensus basis.

The Prime Minister's Office (PMO) is a second, although weak, locus of decision making. The PMO and the chancellery of the cabinet co-ordinate the activities of other ministers. As in most Western European countries, the role of the PMO depends to a certain extent upon the leadership style of the prime minister. Andrijs Skele, for example, was a strong prime minister with a clear agenda and an ambition to control and direct the initiatives of other ministers. A contrasting example was Vilis Kristopans (November 1998 to July 1999), who practised a much more consensual leadership style.

The third major actors in the decision-making process are the civil servants. One important (and unfortunate) legacy of the Soviet era is the tendency of civil servants to pursue their own narrow departmental interests. In many cases the ministers have virtually become the captives of the departments that they are supposed to lead. Communication and co-ordination with other ministries is also limited and there is a general tendency for all ministries to try first to put forward their own departmental (or sector) interests. Only afterwards do they consider how their actions may infringe upon the activities of others or whether their behaviour is in accordance with the interests of the broader society.

In sum, the role of the Latvian government in the overall decision making has increased over the past decade. Correspondingly, the importance of parliamentary committees have declined. In the first half of the 1990s, when political mobilisation remained relatively high and the citizenship issue was still central on the political agenda, governmental efficiency was low because competing party elites in the successive coalition governments blocked decision making in cabinet. Yet it was a time when inefficiency was matched by a relatively high level of transparency and popular participation, as reflected in the greater parliamentary involvement in decision-making. Since the mid-1990s the role of cabinet in the decision-making process has increased. After the citizenship issue was solved, privatisation of state enterprises became the most prominent issue on the political agenda. During this time, several former politicians exchanged their position for business careers, using their political or administrative skills to benefit from the spoils of privatisation. In order to avoid outside government political decision-making by the new economic elite, the government attempted to limit the number of ministries and concentrate decision making in smaller and more manageable bodies. The cabinet thus became the major institution in which political decisions were taken.

3
Lithuania

Ferdinand Müller-Rommel and Ole Hersted Hansen

Cabinet setting

Lithuanian developments since 1989

The transition from dependence within the Soviet system to independence of a Lithuanian State was markedly influenced by two key political developments, the activities of the Lithuanian Reconstruction Movement (Sajudis) and the change of the Lithuanian Communist Party programme.

Sajudis emerged in the spring of 1988, after the security forces had prevented an unofficial demonstration to celebrate the 70th anniversary of the Lithuanian declaration of independence from Russia. In the following months, the movement was responsible for the organisation of several mass demonstrations, for instance, against the 'russification' of the national culture and against environmental pollution in the country. It also openly demanded the setting-up of an independent Lithuanian state and the use of the Lithuanian language. At its national congress in October 1989, the Sajudis movement passed a resolution, demanding political, economic and cultural autonomy for Lithuania. It also asked for a separate Lithuanian currency and for citizenship.

The Communist Party of Lithuania reacted to the challenge of the Sajudis movement by changing its political leadership to render the party more attractive to the majority of Lithuanians. Communist Party first secretary Songaila resigned and was replaced by Algirdas Brauzaskas. Under this new secretary the Communist Party adopted a programme which was much closer to that of Sajudis. Moreover, in 1989, the Communist Party stated that it would sever its links with the CPSU, arguing to the authorities in Moscow that this was the only way for the party to avoid being massively defeated by Sajudis at the 1990 election for the Lithuanian Supreme Soviet.

The most serious challenge to the Soviet Union occurred in December 1989 when the Lithuanian Communist Party declared itself independent from the Soviet CPSU, a declaration of party independence which was approved by 855 votes to 160 at the party convention. The first secretary of the party stated in his keynote address that party independence was needed to break with the Stalinist past. He also emphasised the need to create new conditions of political pluralism and an independent free market economy. In addition, he argued that the main goal of the new Communist Party would be to create a democratic, sovereign Lithuanian state. A few months later, the party adopted a new programme, which supported multi-party democracy. In addition, with the support of Sajudis, the party approved a declaration of Lithuanian sovereignty in the Supreme Soviet.

Despite the measures initiated by the Communist Party, the Lithuania Supreme Soviet election of 1990 was won by Sajudis, which obtained an absolute majority of seats. The movement leader, Vytauta Landsbergis, became the chairman of the new Supreme Soviet, which was soon to be renamed parliament and to be given once more the traditional Lithuanian name of Seimas. The application of the Constitution of the USSR was suspended in the country and, in March 1990, Lithuania became the first Soviet republic to declare independence.

Soviet military forces stationed on Lithuanian territory reacted immediately to that declaration by occupying several buildings in the capital Vilnius and by taking control of the printing presses. The Soviet Union declared a fuel embargo against Lithuania. This lasted for two months until Lithuania accepted a six-month moratorium to discuss the declaration of independence. But the negotiation ended without having found a solution to the problem acceptable to both sides.

A few months later, in January 1991, Soviet troops exercised pressure once more by occupying the Vilnius broadcasting station, an operation which resulted in several people being killed or wounded. Popular support for independence was strengthened by this attack and, in a referendum organised in February 1991 to demand the re-establishment of Lithuanian independence and the withdrawal of Soviet troops from the country, 90 per cent of the electors voted in favour. By then, German unification had taken place and all of Eastern Europe had abandoned communism. The Soviet Union had no realistic alternative but to give up its military intervention policy in Lithuania. A few months later, in September 1991, it recognised the independence of Lithuania together with that of the other Baltic States. Independence having been achieved, the Lithuanian government ordered the withdrawal of Soviet military forces and banned the Lithuanian Communist Party. This last measure had little practical effect, however, as, having been outlawed, the party was reconstituted under another name. Most of its members and leaders joined the newly created Lithuanian Democratic Labour Party (LDLP).

Cabinets since 1992

Between 1992 and 2000, Lithuania had six cabinets and six prime ministers. The average duration of Lithuanian cabinets (19 months) was about the

same as that of most Eastern European cabinets. However, there were substantial variations in the duration of these cabinets. The shortest cabinets
were the first, that of the caretaker administration of Lubys, which lasted
four months and the fifth, that of Pakas, which lasted seven months; the
longest was the single party majority cabinet of prime minister Slezevicius,
which lasted almost three years (35 months). Overall, the cabinets were

- Lupy (LDLP), single party majority, December 1992 to March 1993
- Slezevicius (LDLP), single party majority, March 1993 to Februrary 1996
- Stankevicius (LDLP), single party majority, February 1996 to December
  1996
- Vagnorius (CPL), coalition majority, December 1996 to April 1999
- Pakas (CPL), coalition majority, April 1999 to October 1999
- Kubilius (CPL), coalition majority, since October 1999.

Lithuania's first post-Soviet parliamentary election was held in November
1992 on the basis of a newly adopted electoral system based on a combination of majority voting and of proportional representation with party lists.
To the distress of Sajudis, on a 75 per cent poll, the newly founded LDLP
won: it obtained 43 per cent of the votes and took 73 of the 141 seats in the
Seimas, while Sajudis had only 21 per cent of the votes and 28 seats. Brazauskas, the reformist leader of the Communist Party in 1989, became
speaker of parliament and acting head of state pending the presidential
election. He proposed to Sajudis the formation of a broad coalition. Sajudis
refused and went into opposition. Brazauskas then appointed as prime
minister in early December 1992 Bronislovas Lubys, who had been deputy
prime minister in the previous Sajudis-based government, with the task to
form a transitional single party cabinet which was to last only up to the
presidential election, due to take place three months later in February 1993.

The principle of a direct election of the president, with two ballots if no
candidate obtained 50 per cent of the votes at the first ballot, as well as the
date of that election were part of the new Constitution of the country which
had been adopted by the Seimas and subsequently approved by popular
referendum in October 1992. The election duly took place in February
1993. There were two candidates only, one of whom was Algirdas Brazauskas
for the LDLP. He obtained 60 per cent of the votes in a 79 per cent poll, while
the candidate supported by Sajudis obtained 38 per cent. Brazauskas was
therefore elected outright. As agreed before the presidential election, the
new president nominated a different prime minister, Adolfas Slezevicius, of
the LDLP, former deputy Minister of Agriculture, in March 1993.

The Slezevicius single-party government was to encounter major difficulties in the course of its four-year existence, especially from 1995. It had a
majority in parliament, which enabled it to ride attacks from the opposition,
win votes of confidence and survive a marked decline in popular support;

but the economy was in serious trouble, so serious that a number of banks collapsed. Meanwhile, the privatisation programme moved very slowly. Political scandals also came to the fore, one of which involved the prime minister himself, when it became known that he had withdrawn his personal savings from a bank shortly before it collapsed.

Asked to resign by the president and the leaders of his own Labour Party, the prime minister refused. A crisis within the cabinet ensued, as the ministers of defence and of foreign affairs tendered their resignation, but these were not accepted by the president. The president then asked parliament to replace Slezevicius with Laurynas Stankevicius, hitherto Minister of Government Reform, as prime minister. The Seimas agreed and dismissed Slezevicius in February 1996. The Stankevicius cabinet, the third since independence, lasted only ten months, until the general election scheduled for November.

That election demonstrated the massive decline of the LDLP. Its support in the country dropped from 43 to 10 per cent and it lost 61 of the 73 seats it had won in 1992. Meanwhile, Sajudis, which had changed its name in 1993 to become the Conservative Party of Lithuania (CPL), obtained 30 per cent of the votes and, with 70 seats, came one seat short of an absolute majority in parliament. A coalition agreement was negociated and signed by the Conservative Party and the Christian Democratic Party of Lithuania (CDP), which had obtained 10 per cent of the votes and 16 seats in parliament. The CPL and the CDP formed, in December 1996, under the prime ministership of Gediminas Vagnorius, a new centre-right majority government in which the smaller Lithuania Centre Union (LCS) also participated.

In early 1999, the newly elected President Valdas Adamkus openly criticised the government and in particular attacked Prime Minister Vagnorius for being unable to deal adequately with corruption in the public sector. Vagnorius felt obliged to resign in April. The President appointed the former mayor of Vilnius, Rolandas Paksas, and asked him to form a new cabinet, which only lasted until October 1999.

Ministerial posts in Lithuania have been similiar to those in Western countries. The posts in the Pakas cabinet have been the following: National Economy; Finance; National Defence; Culture; Social Security and Labour; Justice; Transport and Communication; Health Care; Foreign Affairs; Internal Affairs; Agriculture; Education and Science; Environment; Public Administration Reforms and Local Authorities.

Cabinet structure

The constitutional framework

The formal powers of the Lithuanian government are listed in the Constitution of 1992. That document constituted a compromise between the various political forces in the country, which had markedly different views on the nature of what the nature should be of the new regime. The former communists, reorganised in the Labour Party (LDLP), wanted a parliamentary system; the Sajudis movement, about to become the Conservative Party (CPL), was in favour of a strong president who should have the power to form and dismiss governments without parliamentary support as well as to veto legislation.

The only solution was to adopt a mixed arrangement analogous to that which had prevailed in France as a result of the practice more than because of the text of the 1958 Constitution itself and, admittedly, as a result of De Gaulle's prestige and authority. In Lithuania, president, government and indeed the judiciary were to share power, while citizens were to be given the right to decide by referendum on important public issues.

The system is thus semi-presidential. The president is elected by universal suffrage for a five-year term and can only serve for two consecutive terms. There is no vice-president, as in Bulgaria, France or Finland; if the president dies, is incapacitated or is removed from office, the powers of the presidency are exercised temporarily by the speaker of parliament.

Although the president holds a prominent political position, the effective powers of the president are limited in comparison to other semi-presidential systems. He does suggest the basic lines of foreign policy and signs international treaties, but this can be done only after consultation with the government since the foreign minister is also involved in determining foreign policy. The president also has a right of 'suspensive veto' on decisions taken by parliament, but the president's veto can be overridden by a simple majority of the members of parliament.

The president selects the prime minister, but parliament must confirm the choice made by the head of state and indeed approve the governmental programme. There are also no limitations in the right of parliament to pass no-confidence motions against either individual ministers or the government as a whole. The president may veto legislation but this veto can be overturned by a simple majority of the members of parliament. Decrees signed by the president must be countersigned by the prime minister and by the relevant minister.

The position of the president became even weaker after a constitutional reform that took place in 1998. This change was initiated by the right wing Conservative Party of Lithuania (CPL) which held the majority in parliament. The Conservative Party was fearing at the time possible interventions by the new head of state from the junior partner in the centre-right coalition, the Lithuanian Centre Union since its leader, Landsbergis, had been defeated at the presidential election. The constitutional court stated that the right of the president to initiate policies stemmed from the governmental programme which had to be approved by parliament.

The president has some important powers in other respects. He proposes, for instance, the Supreme Court candidates and the three Constitutional

Court judges to the Seimas. He appoints and dismisses state officers as well as judges and chairpersons of district and local district courts. The president also proposes to the national parliament candidates for state controller and the chairperson of the board of the Bank of Lithuania. Furthermore, the president appoints and dismisses, on the approval of the parliament, the commander-in-chief of the armed forces and the head of the security service.

The Lithuanian Constitution also regulates the process of cabinet formation. The prime minister has to present the members of the cabinet as well as the governmental programme to parliament within 15 days after having been appointed. If more than half the ministers are replaced in the course of a legislature, the government must receive a new investiture or resign. This nearly occurred with the second Lithuanian cabinet, when Prime Minister Selzevicius replaced eight of the sixteen ministers. The Constitution also specifies that the government must resign if the Seimas refuses twice in succession to approve the government's legislative programme.

The responsibilities of the Lithuanian prime minister are similar to those of prime ministers in parliamentary systems. The prime minister appoints the ministers and chairs the cabinet meeting. In essence, the role of the Lithuanian prime minister is to be a 'chairman' rather than a 'chief'. All ministers have full and equal rights; they also have final responsibility for proposals related to their departments. To avoid corruption within the government, prime minister and ministers may not be employed in business, commercial or other private institutions or companies. They may not receive any remuneration other than their salary as members of the government.

Cabinet life

Political characteristics

Compared to some Western European countries, notably the Netherlands and Italy before 1992, cabinet formation in Lithuania is rapid. As was pointed out earlier, the prime minister is formally compelled by the Constitution to determine the composition of the cabinet within two weeks after his/her nomination. The composition of the cabinet and the distribution of portfolios in the three majority LDLP governments were thus 'pre-cooked' within the party well before a new cabinet was formed.

Since 1996, Lithuania has been governed by party coalitions, a development which has substantially altered cabinet life. For the first time, the centre-right governing parties have signed written coalition agreements. Moreover, the fourth cabinet led by Vagnorius included one non-partisan minister and the minor coalition partner, the Christian Democratic Party, held strategically important ministries, such as the ministries of Foreign Affairs and of Defence.

Political parties have always been played a large part in the cabinet itself. During the majority governments of 1992–96, the leaders of the parliamentary party had direct access to the prime minister and the cabinet. After 1996, the heads of the political parties have always been cabinet members. Algirdas Saudargas, who chaired the Christian Democratic Party, has been Minister of Foreign Affairs since November 1996. The current prime minister, Kubilius, also chairs the executive committee of the Conservative Party. Yet it is difficult to assess the true impact of the parties, as policy making in Lithuania (as in most other Central European countries) is centred on political personalities who also happen to hold prominent party positions.

Turnover of ministers

The rate of duration of ministers in Lithuania was higher than that of cabinets. On average, Lithuanian ministers stayed in office 23 months; some ministers did last appreciably longer, moreover, for instance Minister of Foreign Affairs Gylys, Minister of Justice Prapiesties and Minister of Transport Birziskis, all of whom were at the head of their department in three successive cabinets and thus were in office for four years. This may have contributed to the relative overall stability of foreign and domestic policy in Lithuania.

Between 1992 and December 1996, the Lithuanian cabinets were composed only of ministers drawn from the Labour Party, most of whom had belonged to the Communist Party before independence. Overall, 35 of the ministers who held office in Lithuania from 1992 to 1999 belonged to the Labour Party. Twenty ministers from the Conservative Party held office in the centre-right coalitions which followed the Labour governments between December 1996 and April 1999. The duration of those ministers in office was scarcely different from that of the Labour ministers who had preceded them – 22 months against 24.

The end of Lithuanian cabinets

Two Lithuanian cabinets of the 1990s ended 'normally', so to speak, the first because of the election of the first president and the second because it was defeated at a general election. Three other cabinets ended as the prime minister was in effect forced to resign by the president, Slezevicius because of a personal scandal, Vagnorius because he was under attack from the president and Paksas because he disagreed with a privatisation programme which the rest of the majority wanted.

Administrative characteristics

A highly idiosyncratic characteristic of the Lithuanian government is constituted by the nature and composition of its meetings. These are in effect semi-public, with 60 to 70 persons in attendance. They take place weekly, usually on Wednesdays, and include an inner and an outer circle. Prime minister and ministers belong to the inner circle and they are the only participants who have the right to speak. Members of the outer circle physically sit in a second row and may only intervene if they are invited to do so by the prime minister. Among those who form the outer circle and regularly attend cabinet meetings are the secretary and the deputy secretary of the government, the government chancellor, the press officers of the prime minister and of the government and the heads of divisions of the government office. The chairman of the Bank of Lithuania, the state controllers, the prosecutor general, representatives of parliament and of the president's office, secretaries of state and senior officers of the regions are also entitled to attend cabinet meetings, but they do not do so regularly. Heads of governmental agencies, mayors, chief executives of the regions and other key state officials may also attend cabinet meetings if the issues under discussion concern them.

The cabinet is served administratively and politically served by the cabinet office which includes a staff of about 150. The members of the office belong to one of two categories, that of A-level political appointments, who are referred to as counsellors, and that of B-level administrative appointments, who are referred to as advisers. This second group is composed of permanent officials and includes approximately 130 persons, while the prime minister can appoint and dismiss at will the 'advisers' of whom there are approximately 20.

The two key persons in the cabinet office are the secretary of the government and the chancellor. The secretary of the government co-ordinates cabinet proposals, advises the prime minister on non-political issues and prepares the agenda of cabinet meetings. The secretary of the government is responsible for the B-level officials. The chancellor heads the division of the government office known as the 'chancery' and is responsible for the implementation of the government programme with the political and administrative help of about 20 A-level officials, about a third of whom come from business. They collect and control information relating to legislative proposals. The chancellor is helped by a deputy chancellor who is responsible for the relationship between the cabinet office and parliament.

One of the main tasks of the cabinet office is to supervise the implementation of the government programme. This programme has two parts, an action programme and an implementation plan. The action programme is a political document, containing all the bills to be submitted to parliament during a legislature. The implementation plan is based on the responses of departments to the action programme. When a new cabinet is formed, the prime minister asks ministers for detailed descriptions of the policy initiatives which they plan to implement during the legislature. The cabinet office collects this information and on this basis drafts the implementation plan, which outlines all the policy initiatives to be taken by each department as well as the date by which these initiatives are to be completed. The cabinet office is thus a key institution. It not only links the prime minister to the ministers and their departments but also constitutes a clearing house for the bills which are submitted and an institutional watchdog over the activities of the ministries.

The 'advisers' in the cabinet office, who are civil servants, closely supervise the implementation of cabinet decisions. They report to the prime minister cases of non-implementation of cabinet decisions and heads of divisions in the cabinet office are required to ask departments for explanations. Indeed, ministers who fail to implement cabinet decisions receive a few days before the cabinet meeting a list of the decisions which have not been taken and may be asked in cabinet to account for this situation.

Cabinet decision-making

To maximise the effectiveness of cabinet decision-making, four cabinet committees have been set up and these prepare most of the proposals which come to cabinet. These are the committees on law enforcement, foreign policy, finance and the economy. They are chaired by the relevant minister and include the ministers concerned with the subject matter of the committee. They usually meet once a month to prepare the draft proposals which are sent to the cabinet meetings for final decision.

In addition to the committees, the cabinet secretary has major administrative responsibilities in cabinet decision-making. In preparing the draft of agenda of cabinet meetings, he or she has also to provide cabinet member with the background information they need to take the relevant decisions. He or she has to co-ordinate the requests of those who attend cabinet meetings as all those who are allowed to attend cabinet meetings may propose items for discussion in cabinet. In addition, 'advisers' who are part of the cabinet office may propose items to be placed on the cabinet agenda, though they rarely use this opportunity in practice. Draft suggestions have to be submitted to the cabinet secretary who passes them to the prime minister who then decides on these matters before finally approving the cabinet agenda.

Around four-fifths of the draft bills come from departments. Before finalising these drafts, the ministers concerned are required to consult the Ministry of Justice and any interest group which might be affected by the proposed legislation. When sent to the cabinet secretary, the draft of a bill must be accompanied by a covering memorandum outlining the aim of the project and explaining why it should be adopted. There must also be estimates of costs and a statement from the finance department.

In principle, the cabinet agenda includes first the most important items, such as new bills or changes to existing laws. Then come the drafts which have been discussed in committees or inter-ministerial meetings prior to cabinet meetings. The full cabinet agenda file, including all relevant materials, is distributed to members of the inner and the outer circle of the cabinet as well as to parliament three working days before the cabinet meeting. To increase the effectiveness of decision making the secretaries of state of the ministries meet a day before the cabinet to discuss the issues on the agenda.

The cabinet votes if different opinions are expressed by the ministers present about a proposal. In contrast to some Western European countries, neither the prime minister, nor the finance minister nor any other minister may veto a cabinet decision. Decisions are then recorded in the minutes of the meeting which are finalised by the cabinet secretary and signed by the prime minister. They are then filed by the document editorial division of the cabinet office. After each cabinet meeting, the press officer publicly announces the decisions taken by the cabinet.

As in most political systems, the role and the function of the prime minister in the process of cabinet decision-making depends upon individual personalities. Formally, the prime minister holds most power; the leadership style of Lithuania's prime ministers has varied significantly, however. Gediminas Vagnorious, who headed the cabinet for more than two years, relied primarily on the permanent officials, whereas Rolandas Paksas asked his personal staff and individual ministers for advice. Thus in the Paksas cabinet some ministers enjoyed considerably more influence than others. Decisions were taken under a collegial basis rather than on a collective basis.

Prime Minister Andrius Kubilius followed a more open and co-ordinating style. He discussed policy proposals with his personal staff, with individual ministers, with the permanent officials and with members of parliamentary committees. The prime minister also created a 'committee for strategic policy-making' to initiate cabinet proposals: in practice, this committee resembled an 'inner cabinet'. It consisted of the prime minister and of the ministers of Finance, Economy, Administrative Reform and Local Government. The prime minister chaired the meetings. In some cases, other ministers as well as state secretaries and the chancellor were invited to participate in the meetings.

In conclusion, cabinet decision making in Lithuania went through two different phases: during 1992–96 the cabinet was a rather closed decision-making body. Power was essentially concentrated on the prime minister, these having led a single party majority government. They gave political directives and the role of cabinet was limited to providing a final check on the general lines of the prime minister's policy. Thus, decisions were approved rather than made by the cabinet. From 1996 until 1999, the cabinet system became more open. Apart from the ministers and the prime minister, high-ranking civil servants enjoyed considerable autonomy in the formulation and preparation of policy proposals. The cabinet became a kind of political committee, as this was once felt to be the case in the textbook model of the parliamentary system.

4
Poland

J. Blondel and F. Müller-Rommel

Cabinet setting

Polish developments since 1988

One of the characteristics of Polish politics had indeed been considerable political and ministerial instability. After 1980, Poland followed a unique 'impetuous' and 'restive' course, the most important event being probably the creation of the illegal trade union Solidarity (Solidarność) which, under the leadership of Lech Walesa, then a worker at the Gdansk shipyards, which attracted millions of supporters and which the government could not effectively repress. As a result of the unrest which Solidarity directed, the regime felt obliged to soften the opposition by a variety of measures, ranging from the release of detainees to the creation of a Council of State which was to be independent from the Polish United Workers' Party (PZPR), the name which the Polish Communist Party had adopted. From 1988 onwards, the situation came to be out of control: the government by then had effectively abandoned the hope to govern alone. In a climate of demonstrations and strikes, the government appeared to have no alternative but to recognise fully and to negotiate with Solidarity in the early months of 1989 in what came to be known as the 'Round Table' talks. A compromise was struck which was essentially designed to preserve as much as possible of the old order. A new upper chamber, called the Senat, was set up, to which Solidarity was allowed to compete freely; but, in the existing chamber, the *Sejm*, only 35 per cent of the seats were to be freely contested while the majority was to be retained for the Communist Party and its allies. The election took place in July 1989.

On what was to be a record turnout for a parliamentary election (62 per cent) and to its great surprise, Solidarity won this 'semi-free' election on a massive scale. It took all but one of the 100 seats in the Senat and all the 161 seats in the *Sejm* for which it was allowed to compete. For a short while the Workers' Party (the PZPR) tried to remain in control, together with the United Peasant Party and the Democratic Party, which had been satellite organisations of the Workers' Party throughout the period of communist rule. The Workers' Party succeeded in ensuring the re-election of Jaruzelski as president of the country – a post which he had held since 1985 – but its candidate for the post of prime minister, General Kiszcsak, could not form a government. The PZPR then effectively gave up and communist rule ended as Tadeusz Mazowiecki, a journalist who was a member of Solidarity, became prime minister on 24 August 1989. A few months later, in January 1990, the PZPR recognised its final defeat by dissolving itself. A Social-Democratic Party was established in its place. It was soon to be form part of a Left Democratic Alliance (SLD). Symbolically, January 1990 was to be also the month in which the *Sejm* decided that the country would no longer be a 'people's republic' but return to its old name of Republic of Poland.

The Maroziewcki government proposed a programme of far-reaching economic reforms ranging from price liberalisation to an attempt at introducing a limited convertibility of the currency, the zloty. Yet, after a few months, the prime minister found himself in conflict with the more 'radical' elements of Solidarity, among whom was Walesa, who wanted quicker reforms and more privatisations. Mazowiecki came to be increasingly isolated and indeed unpopular. On a 61 per cent turnout, he was roundly defeated at the first ballot of the presidential election which took place in November 1990, obtaining 18 per cent of the votes as against Walesa's 40 per cent. He had to withdraw from the contest while Walesa went on to win at the second ballot in December with 74 per cent of the votes. Mazowiecki resigned immediately.

The fall of Mazowiecki was only the beginning of what seemed to be the same pattern of instability as the one which had beset communist governments in Poland, in particular from the 1980s. To replace Mazowiecki, Walesa had to select successively two different persons, Olszewski and Bielecki, before a new government could be formed in January 1991. This pattern was repeated less than a year later, towards the end of 1991, when, following Bielecki's resignation, Walesa first selected Geremek and then Olszewski to form the government and, in June 1992, when, with the fall of Olszewski, Pawlak was first chosen but had to give way to Mrs Suchoka before a government could be formed.

There were thus both governmental instability and major obstacles in forming new governments. Yet these problems were compounded by conflict within the governments. Thus the Minister of Finance of the Olszewski cabinet resigned early in 1992 just before the economic programme of that cabinet was being presented. These problems were in part due to Walesa's proclaimed intention to play a major part in governmental formation and activities. He did benefit to an extent from the highly fractionalised character of the *Sejm*. After the 'semi-free' parliament elected in 1989, the first wholly free election took place in October 1991, the 1989 *Sejm* having decided to dissolve itself in order to render such a truly free election possible.

The election of 1991 resulted in no less than 29 parties being represented in the *Sejm* and the largest of these, Mazowiecki's Democratic Union (UD), having only 12 per cent of the votes and 62 of the 460 seats, while a further six parties had gained at least 7 per cent of the votes. Coalition combinations were therefore extremely numerous and instability highly likely.

It was particularly difficult to avoid instability since, as under communist rule, major social unrest occurred at various points in 1991 and 1992, with strikes and demonstrations taking place at a time when the economy was, as elsewhere in Eastern Europe, in severe decline. Not surprisingly, perhaps, discontent with the 'achievements' of the new regime manifested itself in a very low turnout at most contests. Thus, while 62 per cent of the electors voted at the 'semi-free' 1989 parliamentary election and 61 per cent at the 1990 presidential election – not a very high turnout in either case anyway – only 43 per cent of the electorate voted at the 1991 parliamentary election, the first which was fully free. Not surprisingly, too, this major popular discontent manifested itself in an increase of the votes of the Left Democratic Alliance (SLD) at the September 1993 election. This took place when Walesa refused to accept the resignation of Mrs Suchocka's government after a vote of censure and dissolved parliament. This time turnout was a little higher, at 52 per cent.

Yet the coming to power of a new majority made out of the SLD and of the Polish Peasant Party (PSL) was possible only because the previous parliament had passed – perhaps somewhat surprisingly and clearly courageously – an electoral law which introduced a 5 per cent threshold for parties and an 8 per cent threshold for alliances. The effect was a major: with 20 per cent of the votes, the Democratic Left Alliance (SLD) obtained 37 per cent of the seats (171 out of 460); with 15 per cent of the votes, the Peasant Party (PSL) obtained 29 per cent of the seats (132). There had been unquestionably a movement towards these parties since 1991, as, together, they had then obtained 21 per cent of the votes only, the SDL alone having increased its support from 12 to 20 per cent. But, while over a third of the votes were left unrepresented because they were dispersed among parties and alliances which did not pass over the threshold, the two parties of the new coalition benefited from a massive bonus.

Governmental instability and social unrest did continue, however, and this was fuelled by a number of political scandals, alleged or real, which gave occasion for Walesa to insist on what he regarded as his prerogatives. Thus the Socialist-Peasant Party government formed by Pawlak in October 1993 soon found itself in confrontation with the president. First, the dismissal of the Minister of Finance by the prime minister early in 1994 led to tension because Walesa claimed that it was the president's right to approve of some of the key ministerial appointments, namely defence, interior and finance. A few months later, in October 1994, Walesa asked for and indeed obtained the dismissal of the Minister of Defence. In January 1995, he threatened to veto an income tax bill. A month later he demanded the resignation of the prime minister. Pawlak complied and was replaced, a few months before the end of Walesa's term, by the speaker of the *Sejm*, Olesky.

The second presidential election of democratic Poland took place in November 1995. It resulted in the victory of the socialist candidate, Aleksander Kwasniewski, over Lech Walesa, with 52 per cent of the votes, in a contest which attracted, interestingly, a 65 per cent poll, thus showing that turnout at presidential elections was appreciably larger than other contests. The election of Kwasniewski resulted in a degree of 'normalisation' in the relationship between president and prime minister, as the new president did not, at any rate as much as Walesa, make strong claims to intervene in governmental affairs.

Meanwhile, governmental difficulties were far from over. Almost as soon as he took office, the new president was confronted with an alleged scandal involving the prime minister, as, on leaving his post in order to place the office in the hands of the new head of state, on the basis of the practice started by Walesa, the outgoing Minister of Internal Affairs of the Oleski cabinet claimed that the prime minister had been a Soviet spy. The charge was subsequently dropped for lack of evidence, but Oleski did have to resign and Kwasniewski nominated Wlodzimierz Cimoszewicz, deputy speaker of the *Sejm*, to replace him.

The opposition was reorganising itself at the time and, as was noted in the opening paragraph, an alliance of 25 parties of the right and centre-right, subsequently to group a further 11 parties, formed Solidarity Election Action (AWS). That reorganisation proved effective at the general election which took place in September 1997. A minuscule loss of votes resulted in defeat for the SDL-PSL coalition. In what was once more a low turnout (48 per cent), the 1993–97 coalition obtained 34.4 per cent of the votes against 35.8 at the previous election; the Peasant Party did lose heavily (8 per cent out of a little more than 15), but this was compensated by a gain of 7 per cent, to 27 per cent, of the Democratic Left Alliance (SLD). The small overall decline of the outgoing two-party coalition was sufficient for that coalition to lose its huge majority and for the AWS (which obtained 34 per cent of the votes) to become the largest parliamentary group with 201 seats; the SLD lost seven seats although, as was noted, it had gained votes since 1993. In the process, the proportion of unrepresented voters dropped from 35 per cent in 1993 to 14 per cent in 1997.

The president on the advice of the leader of the AWS, Marian Krzaklewski, appointed as prime minister Jerzy Buzek who constituted a coalition of the AWS and the Freedom Union (UW), which had obtained 13 per cent of the votes and 60 seats. The post of Minister of Finance went to Leszek Balcerowicz, the leader of the UW. The programme of the government was one of rapid integration in NATO and the EU externally and, internally, of accelerated privatisation and of reform of governmental structures, the most spectacular of which was the creation of a smaller number of regions (16) instead of 49 provinces.

Cabinets since 1990

Between the parliamentary election of 1991 and 2000, Poland has had six prime ministers and seven cabinets. The July 1989 Mazowiecki cabinet and the January 1991 Bielecki cabinet are not included as they related to a parliament which had not been freely elected and, in the first case, to a president, Jaruzelski, who represented the old order.

The six prime ministers and cabinets were:

- J. Olszewski (PC), four party coalition, November 1991 to July 1992
- H. Suchocka (1) (UD), seven-party coalition, to July 1992 to April 1993
- H. Suchocka (2) (UD), five-party coalition, April to October 1993
- W. Pawlak (PSL), left two-party coalition, October 1993 to March 1995
- J. Olesky (SLD), left two party coalition, March 1995 to February 1996
- W. Cimosczewicz (SLD), left two-party coalition, February 1996 to October 1997
- J. Buzek (AWS), right two-party coalition, from October 1997

All these governments have also included independents.

Cabinet instability has therefore been substantial, at least up to 1997. This has been due mainly to internal divisions among the parties, groups and movements which emerged from Solidarity, these divisions in turn having stemmed from the fundamental ambiguity of Solidarity itself. The actions of Walesa, both when he was president as well as before, have to be considered in the light of the ambiguity of the movement which he had created. The difficulties experienced by AWS since 1997 have also been in part the consequence of the fact that it was an umbrella organisation: it is a tribute to the ability of Busek that he should have been able to hold the coalition between the AWS and the Freedom Union for two and a half years and that he should have also succeeded in maintaining the unity of the AWS throughout the period.

The size of Polish cabinets has varied. The Mazowiecki 1989–91 government had 23 ministers as did the governments of Mrs Suchocka of 1992–93. In between, the Olszewski government of 1991–92 was much the smallest of all post-communist Polish governments, with 17 ministers. Since 1993, the cabinet has had 20 ministers under the Socialist-Peasant coalition and, under the AWS-UW coalition, 23 ministers up to March 99 and 17 ministers afterwards. There have generally been three deputy prime ministers and occasionally between one and three ministers without portfolio. There are also 'deputy ministers' (junior ministers) who do not belong to the cabinet. The deputy prime ministers have been in part appointed *ad hominem* and in part in relation to a variety of departments, such as agriculture, internal affairs or justice. The Minister of Finance has always held such a post. Women have rarely become ministers. There were none in the 1991 Olszeweki government; there were three in the 1997 Buzek government, a maximum so far. One woman, Mrs Hanna Suchocka, was prime minister; she returned to office as Minister of Justice with the centre-right government of 1997.

The ministerial posts in the 1997 Busek cabinet were: Deputy prime minister and Minister of Finance; Deputy prime minister and Minister of Internal Affairs; Agriculture; Treasury; Foreign Affairs; Defence; Justice; Education; Transport and Maritime Economy; Communication; Environmental Protection, Natural Resources and Forestry; Culture and Arts; Health and Social Welfare; Labour and Social Policy; Economy; Without portfolio, for the Security Services; Chairman of Committee on European Integration; Chairman of Centre for Strategic Studies; Chief of Chancellery; Chairman of Committee on Scientific Research.

Cabinet structure

The Constitution

At the 'Round Table' which took place early in 1989, a rudiment of a Constitution was agreed upon and this led to approval of amendments to the 1952 Constitution. In October 1992, the *Sejm* adopted what came to be known as the 'Little Constitution'. This document was finally superseded after a series of unsuccessful proposals had been made and after the Constitution had been approved by the people, on a 43 per cent turnout, in 1997.

The Constitution states that Poland is a unitary democratic state, the legislative power being in the hands of the two-chamber parliament and the executive power being vested in the president and the Council of Ministers. Parliament is elected by the people for four years and the president for five (renewable only once). There is a Constitutional Court, whose members are elected by the lower house of parliament, the *Sejm*. The president of the Bank of Poland is also elected by the *Sejm*.

The theory and practice of the Polish Constitution remain partly clouded in ambiguity about the extent to which the system is semi-presidential or not. A crucial element appears to have been the fact that the president is elected by universal suffrage. That provision was introduced by the *Sejm* in 1990, not as a permanent arrangement, but as a means to cope with the curious situation arising from the 'semi-free' election of 1989, which had resulted in what was clearly an undemocratic outcome. Yet, once introduced, the provision proved untouchable because it was manifestly popular. We noted that presidential contests were the only elections after 1989 at which 60 per cent or more of the electorate voted. The situation parallels the one which developed in France after 1965. Parties in parliament did not dare to propose openly the abandonment of the election of the president by universal suffrage for fear of the reactions of the population.

Yet a system based on a president elected by universal suffrage is not necessarily semi-presidential, as the majority of Western European cases show and as some Eastern European examples, in particular those of Bulgaria and Slovenia, also indicate. Moreover, French experience since the mid-1980s and Finnish experience since the 1990s show that semi-presidentialism needs both favourable circumstances and the strong will of the president for the head of state to be able to use to the full the powers which the Constitution gives the holder of the office and indeed to go beyond the text of the Constitution where this text is silent or ambiguous. Thus Walesa's strong will and a certain weakness on the part of his opponents explain why the Polish head of state managed to succeed in insisting on his right to agree on who is to hold some of the key ministries even in a period of what the French call 'cohabitation'. The Constitution merely states that the president heads the armed forces and represents the state in foreign affairs.

As a matter of fact, the only truly substantial power of the Polish president which is out of the ordinary is the power of veto. If a bill is vetoed by the president, the parliament can only overcome this action by passing the text again by a three-fifths majority. The other prerogatives of the president are to appoint the prime minister (but the Constitution does not say that the head of state has the power of dismissal), to appoint a number of members of the top judiciary and to dissolve parliament, but only if parliament has rejected three successive names proposed by the president.

The other provisions of the Constitution indicate that the system is parliamentary. The cabinet (the 'Council of Ministers') is presided over by the prime minister, not by the president. The prime minister must obtain the confidence of the *Sejm* and cannot remain in office if he is censured by the *Sejm*. The 1997 Constitution restated the procedure of the constructive motion of no-confidence; the cabinet falls only if the *Sejm* votes a motion, by a majority, which includes the name of the subsequent prime minister. The right of dissolution is almost entirely linked to the constructive motion of no-confidence since 1997. Moreover, it is no longer permissible for the president to dissolve parliament as Walesa did in 1993, when the second Suchocka cabinet was defeated by a vote of censure. The Polish system of government is unquestionably parliamentary.

Cabinet life

Political characteristics

Formation of cabinets

As was noted earlier, the process of formation of cabinets was often difficult, in part because of the fragmented nature of the party system, even after its relative 'rationalisation' from 1993 onwards, and in part because of the efforts made by Walesa to play a key part in political life. The very large number of parties of the 1991–93 parliament accounted for the difficulties encountered in the formation of the Olszewski and Suchocka governments.

Difficulties did not cease in 1993 as in shown by the fact that it took over a month for the Pawlak cabinet of October 1993 to be constituted after the general election of the previous September. Since then, however, and up to 1997, the appointment of prime ministers and of governments has been more rapid. The replacement of Pawlak by Olesky was 'automatic', in a sense, for it resulted technically from the vote of a constructive motion of no-confidence in March 1995 in which the name of Olesky was given, as the procedure required.

The role of the president

There was a marked difference between the role of the presidents played in the selection of prime ministers. Walesa took the initiative, even though he was not always ultimately successful and thus he attempted to appoint Pawlak in 1992 but failed and he had to recognise that Mrs Hanna Suchocka would be the only candidate who could command a majority. He did succeed in appointing Pawlak after the 1993 election, but, after having quarrelled with him, had to accept Olesky, who commanded a majority in the *Sejm*. Kwasniewski, on the contrary, did not see that it was his role to select prime ministers of his own choice. The appointment of Cimoscewicz, who had been Minister of Justice in the Pawlak government, was designed to calm the situation at the beginning of 1996; the appointment of Busek was merely the ratification of the choice made by the newly formed AWS-UW coalition after the September 1997 election.

The role of parties

Political parties have also played a major part in the formation and life of cabinets. This is perhaps not surprising, given the fragmented nature of the Polish party system. It is also not surprising that all governments should have been coalitions, in the 1990s at least; it is indeed questionable as to whether even the AWS minority government which emerged in 2000 as a result of the break-up of the AWS-UW coalition should not be described as a coalition, since, as we noted, the AWS is an alliance of a large number of parties.

Admittedly, at times, especially under Walesa, the role of parties was one of responsiveness rather than one of initiation, but it was always important. Thus Pawlak was in effect blocked by the centre-right and centre parties in the *Sejm* in 1992 and Mrs Suchocka was the agreed candidate of these parties: Walesa had to accept. Thus, while Pawlak, who was the leader of the smaller Peasant Party (PSL), was accepted as prime minister by the new Socialist-Peasant Party coalition which won the 1993 election, the difficulties between Walesa and Pawlak gave the Socialist Party the opportunity to select Olesky as their candidate in the context of the constructive motion of no-confidence of March 1995. Finally, the choice of Busek as prime minister of the AWS-UW coalition was entirely due to the parties of that coalition and in particular to the part played by the chairman of the AWS, Krzaklewski, who wished the prime minister to be a 'technician' (Buzek had been a researcher in chemistry) rather than a 'real' politician.

Turnover of ministers

The rate of turnover of cabinets and of ministers has been relatively high in Poland. There were seven cabinets for a period of somewhat over eight years and, including prime ministers, 107 persons occupied governmental posts during that period. This means that cabinets lasted on average little over one year. Given that the number of cabinet ministers oscillated, as we saw, between 17 and 23 posts, given also that some ministers came to office more than once, the members of government were in office on average for about a year and a half (1.48 years). This average suggests that the turnover of ministers is no higher than in but even lower other countries of the region.

Both the duration of cabinets and the duration of ministers in office tended to increase throughout the 1990s. Including prime ministers, 45 different persons occupied government posts during the first legislature, which lasted 22 months, 44 during the second, which lasted four years, and 28 during the first 27 months of the third legislature. On average, those who were ministers during the first legislature were therefore in office for 11 months, those who were in office during the second, 18 months and those who were in office during the first 27 months of the third, 22 months. In practice, there was almost a complete change of the holders of portfolios between the Olszewski and Suchocka governments (only two ministers remained in office). However, nearly half, that is, eight, of the ministers of the Pawlak government of 1993 remained in office under Olesky and half (eleven) of the ministers of the Olesky government remained in office under Cimoszewicz. There was only one change in the Busek government between October 1997 and March 1999. At that point, in an effort to streamline decision making, ministers without portfolio ceased to be members of the cabinet and eight deputy ministers were dismissed, while there was a sizeable reshuffle affecting four ministers; there were also four more ministerial changes in the early part of 2000 before the coalition eventually collapsed.

Administrative characteristics

The Polish cabinet meets regularly once a week on Tuesdays and the prime minister may also convene extraordinary meetings. Meetings are chaired by the prime minister or, in the absence of the prime minister, by a deputy prime minister designated by the prime minister. Attendance at meetings includes, beyond the ministers (the chairmen of the Scientific Research Committee and of the European Integration Committee have ministerial rank), the secretary of the Council of Ministers, the president of the Court of Auditors, other persons specified in statutes as well as persons designated by the prime minister. Representatives of bodies concerned with a specific item of the agenda may be invited to attend with respect to that item. The prime minister may also allow ministers to be assisted by an adviser in relation to matters of a highly technical character.

Meetings of the cabinet are prepared by the secretary general of the cabinet who draws up the draft agenda, submits it to the prime minister for approval and circulates it to the members of the Council of Ministers at least five days before the date of the meeting. Drafts of texts to be discussed by the Council must be submitted to the secretariat, which is responsible for the distribution of these texts to members of the Council no less than seven days before the meeting at which the discussion of the text is due to take place. The decisions of the Council of Ministers are typically taken by consensus, although votes may occur. A majority of the members of the council of ministers must be present for decisions to be valid.

Administrative support for the government and its members is provided by the chancellery, which is directed by the head of the chancellery. The chancellery is in charge of the implementation of the decisions of the council of ministers, of the publication of statutes and regulations, of the relations between the Council of Ministers and parliament and generally of all the activities in which the prime minister is involved. The secretariat of the government is part of the chancellery, as is the political staff ('cabinet') of the prime minister.

There are three formally constituted cabinet committees of the Polish government, the Economics Committee, the Social Committee and the Committee on Defence Affairs. These committees are composed of members of the government appointed by the prime minister and their chairmen are appointed and dismissed by the prime minister. The secretariat of these committees is provided by the chancellery.

Texts to be discussed by the Council of Ministers may not reach that body without having first been examined and in principle approved by one of these committees. The drafts must then be submitted to and passed by the legal committee of the chancellery. The European Integration Committee (which is chaired by a member the Council of Ministers with the rank of minister) has also to give an opinion on the draft's conformity with European Union legislation before the text can be sent for decision to the Council of Ministers.

Cabinet decision-making

According to the Constitution, the cabinet, not the president, is in charge of the executive. The president has a limited part to play while that of the prime minister is substantial. Apart from a limited right of dissolution and a role in emergencies and in some appointments, the veto is the only constitutional power which the president has with respect to home affairs, while the powers in relation to foreign affairs are larger. The president thus formally signs treaties and is a guardian of the sovereignty and security of the state, being advised in this respect by the Council of National Security. The president is also the head of the armed forces. However, as we saw, the first president of democratic Poland, Walesa, did intervene in home affairs as well, by using the right of veto and by demanding – with some success – that a number of key ministerial posts be filled with persons whom he approved.

The prime minister, however, is constitutionally the leader of the government: the prime minister does indeed appoint and dismiss the ministers. While Walesa did intervene markedly in this respect, the right of appointment and dismissal of ministers by the prime minister was not challenged by his successor, the role of Kwasniewski being confined to giving formal sanction to what were in effect decisions of the prime minister. Yet, in practice, unquestionably up to 1997 and even to a large extent since then, the effective position of the Polish prime minister has not been a dominant one. This has been due in large part to the fact that none of the incumbents has been the leader of the most important party of the majority, at first because such a party did not really exist and later because this was not regarded (by the president or by the relevant party and in some case by both) as opportune.

Thus the first two prime ministers, Olszewsky and Suchocka, were squeezed between the *Sejm* and Walesa. Their role appeared essentially to try and placate these two 'masters'; their margin of manoeuvre was consequently rather small. The third prime minister, Pawlak, was a party leader, but he was the leader of the Peasant Party, which was the junior partner of the coalition. Walesa was no doubt hoping to be able to exercise considerable influence over him, but that hope proved unfounded, not because of the prime minister's own strength, but because of the pressure of the larger Socialist Party both in the *Sejm* and in the government. In the end, the prime minister had to go but his successor, Olesky, who had been speaker of the *Sejm*, was regarded as a compromise candidate who would reduce tension. He was therefore not strong enough to exercise real power over his cabinet. Since Olesky fell from office as a result of an alleged scandal, the main aim was to restore confidence in the executive and the choice went to someone whose reputation for impartiality was high. Cimoszewicz was in practice probably stronger than any of his predecessors but he did suffer from the fact that he was not the party leader and therefore could not – or did not wish to – impose his decisions on the cabinet.

The seventh prime minister, Buzek, was selected by the AWS leader, Krzaklewski, on the grounds that the distinction between the 'political' and the 'managerial' or 'technical' leadership of the country should be kept separate,

Krzaklewski being adamant to continue to control the AWS which he had brought together with great difficulty and major political flair. He therefore chose Buzek who, being known primarily as a scholar, was not expected to move out of the role which had been expected to be his. In the event, Buzek did exercise leadership even in the political field. Yet the power he had in the cabinet as leader of the government remained somewhat subdued, not just because his base in the AWS was not truly solid but because he was confronted in the government with the very strong, indeed potentially dominating, influence of Minister of Finance Leszek Balcerowicz, who eventually decided in 2000 to break the coalition. The fact that Buzek not only kept the coalition together for nearly three years but also subsequently succeeded to remain at the head of the minority AWS government is a tribute to his political as much as his managerial talent, although it remains true that he did not exercise a forceful leadership.

Overall, the evolution of the Polish executive in the decade following the end of communism has been substantial. From a situation in which the government was very shaky, lacking any consistent party base and in many ways subjected to the desires of the president to play a major part in policy making, a rather stable executive has emerged. This is so, even if the head of the executive has not as yet been able to exercise the kind of strong leadership which has been characteristic of many Western European prime ministers in the second half of the twentieth century.

5
Czech Republic

Ferdinand Müller-Rommel and Zdenka Mansfeldová

Cabinet setting

Czech Republic developments since 1989

Czechoslovakia was founded in 1918 and occupied by Germany in 1939, although it continued to keep a *de jure* existence. In 1946, at the first (and last) free post-Second World War election for over forty years, the Communist Party emerged as the strongest party in the country. After the communist takeover in February 1948 the communist-led government established the Czechoslovak People's Republic and aligned itself to the Soviet Union.

The first free election since 1946 was held in June 1990. It was based on proportional representation, with a 5 per cent threshold. The parliamentary term was to be four years, but it was agreed to limit the first electoral period to two years during which new federal and republican constitutions would be drafted and the party system become consolidated.

Voter turnout in the first national elections was extremely high. In the Czech Republic, 96.7 per cent of the population voted for 16 parties and movements which competed for 75 seats in the Chamber of People and for 101 seats for the second Chamber of Nations in the Federal Assembly. The Civic Forum Alliance (OF), which consisted of several civil and political rights groups, came first with 53.1 per cent of the votes and 68 seats in the People's Chamber and 49.9 per cent of the votes and 50 seats in the Chamber of Nations; the communists came second with 14 per cent of the vote.

After the election, Calfa restructured his government. The Civic Forum (OF) had nine ministerial appointments out of sixteen, thus holding 56 per cent of the cabinet posts. Four ministerial posts went to the Slovakia counterpart of the OF, Public Against Violence (VPN). Overall, the coalition of OF and VPN held an absolute majority in the CSFR Federal Assembly and re-elected Václav Havel as president of the CSFR in July 1990.

In the election to the Czech National Council, held together with the federal elections, the Civic Forum (OF) obtained 49.5 per cent of the votes and 127 of the 200 seats in the Council. The new Czech cabinet, headed by

Petr Pithart, had 21 ministers. Ten were held by the OF while eight went to independents. Thus the Civic Forum was by far the strongest party in the 1990 federal and republican elections.

Yet a division between two wings quickly emerged in the OF, one being conservative orientation, the other broadly liberal. In February 1991, the Civic Forum did split. Václav Klaus, who had become Finance Minister in the new CSFR government, led one group, Jirí Dienstbier, Foreign Minister of the CSFR and Pavel Rychetsky, deputy chairman of the CSFR government, the other. While Klaus proposed to reorganise the Civic Forum into a 'normal' political party with individual membership, permanent officials and a fixed party organisation, his opponents strongly supported the movement character of the Forum. In April 1991, Klaus decided to set up a Civic Democratic Party (ODS). The Civic Movement (OH) became the second political entity which originated from the OF, while smaller political groupings also split from OF, the Civic Democratic Alliance (ODA) and two social-democratic groupings.

The split within the Civic Forum led to a polarisation between right and left while the centre declined. This development had an immediate impact on the stability of the CSFR cabinet. Some former OF ministers became members of the newly founded ODS while others supported the OH movement. Both factions did agree to remain in the coalition up to the next election, the Czech cabinet became less homogeneous.

Meanwhile, Czech-Slovak tension grew in 1991. Members of the Federal Assembly at first agreed on a framework for three constitutions to be jointly and simultaneously drawn up before the 1992 elections but later on in the year the federal parliament failed to agree on a draft. Intense cabinet discussions were held between Czechs and Slovaks, from which the federal parliament was excluded. President Havel suggested a referendum on the issue, knowing from public opinion surveys that the majority of the citizens in both the Czech and the Slovak parts of the country would support a federal state structure, but the majority of deputies in the Federal Assembly refused.

The constitutional debate continued in 1992. Representatives from Slovakia advocated the formation of two highly autonomous states on a confederal rather than on a federal model but this was strongly opposed by the Czechs. It was then agreed to postpone the issue until after the 1992 elections.

In early 1992, the Federal Assembly modified the electoral law and made it more difficult for party alliances to gain seats in parliament. The threshold remained at 5 per cent for parties, but alliances of two or three parties would need to obtain 7 per cent of the votes and alliances of four parties or more 10 per cent to be entitled to participate in the allocation of seats for parliament. This rule was obviously to the advantage of larger parties, but it was also likely to reduce the fragmentation of the party system and thus to lead to greater stability, which was essential during the discussions that were to take place about the break up of Czechoslovakia.

The June 1992 federal election led directly to the division of Czechoslovakia into two sovereign states. On the Czech side, the newly founded conservative ODS under Klaus gained 85 out of 300 seats in the Federal Assembly and became the largest party in parliament. The Movement for a Democratic Slovakia (HZDS) became the second strongest group with 57 seats.

The election of the president of the Czech federation, held a few weeks after the parliamentary elections, ensured that the future of Czechoslovakia was no longer viable. President Havel failed to receive the majority of the vote in the Federal Assembly in two rounds. His candidacy was effectively blocked by the HZDS in parliament. After a symbolic declaration of independence by the Slovak parliament in July, President Havel announced his resignation as president of Czechoslovakia. In such a fluid situation, the two leading parties formed an interim coalition government, which had the task to dissolve the CSFR. After Havel's electoral defeat as presidential candidate, the ODS did agree to dissolve the CSFR and to create two sovereign republics. The arrangements between the ODS and the HZDS focused on three issues – the transformation of the federal institutions into the new two sovereign states, political co-operation between the Czech Republic and Slovakia and the future economic co-operation between the two states.

In November 1992, the necessary three-fifths majority of the members of the Federal Assembly agreed, but by a margin of three votes only, to abolish the existing federal constitution and to form two sovereign states. It was also agreed that by 31 December all federal structures would be dissolved. The two new republics came into existence on 1 January 1993.

In January 1993, the Czech national parliament elected Václav Havel as first president of the independent republic. Five months later, the Chamber of Deputies agreed to establish a Constitutional Court composed of 15 judges appointed for a ten-year term.

Cabinets since 1993

In the Czech Republic, executive power is in the hands of the prime minister and the cabinet. Between 1993 and 2000, the Czech Republic has had three prime ministers and four cabinets:

- Klaus (ODS), four-party composition, January 1993 to July 1996
- Klaus (ODS), three-party minority coalition, July 1996 to December 1997
- Tosovsky (Ind), three-party caretaker minority coalition, January 1998 to July 1998
- Zeman (CSSD), one-party minority coalition, since August 1998.

The composition of the first government of the new Czech Republic was basically the same as that of the previous Czech cabinet except for the defence and transport departments, which were set up after independence. The government was led by a centre-right coalition consisting of the Civic Democratic Party (ODS) of prime minister Klaus, the Christian Democratic Union-Czechoslovak People's Party (KDU-CSL), the Christian Democratic Party (KDS), and the Civic Democratic Alliance (ODA).

The first Klaus coalition cabinet had eighteen ministers, among whom nine were from the ODS, four from the KDU-CSL, three from the ODA, and two from the KDS. Thus, after a merger between the ODS and the KDS, the new party had 62 per cent of the seats in cabinet and controlled 38 per cent of the seats in parliament. The KDU-CSL had 21 per cent of the seats in cabinet and controlled 7 per cent of the parliamentary seats, while the ODA, with also 7 per cent of the parliamentary seats had 15 per cent of the ministerial portfolios. Overall, the governing coalition controlled 52 per cent of the seats in parliament.

During 1993–96, the Klaus cabinet was fairly stable. One minister resigned in 1993 and four in 1994, but the large majority of ministers stayed in office for over three years. The government introduced a new currency, improved its relations with the European Union, privatised large segments of state property and reduced inflation.

At the 1996 general election, the ODS obtained almost exactly the same proportion of the votes as in 1992 (29.6 per cent), but, because a number of small left-wing parties united within the Czech Social Democratic Party (CSSD), the ODS lost eight seats in the Chamber of Deputies, although it remained the largest party with 68 out of 200 seats. The Social Democratic Party made substantial gains and, with 26.4 per cent of the votes, gained 61 seats in parliament. The Czech party system was thus moving from a multiparty system with one dominant party to a multiparty system with two dominant parties one on the left and the other on the right of the political spectrum.

After the May 1996 national elections, Prime Minister Klans formed a minority government. The strength of the Civic Democratic Party (ODS-KDS) decreased in cabinet as well as in parliament. While it held only 50 per cent of the cabinet posts and 34 per cent of the seats in parliament, the ODA and the KDU-CSL had about the same level of electoral support as in 1992, but had proportionally more seats in cabinet, where their representation increased to 25 per cent each.

The neo-liberal economic policy of the conservative government and of the Civic Democratic Party in particular was not as successful as it seemed to be in the first part of the 1990s, however. In June 1997, the ruling coalition parties won a vote of confidence in the Chamber of Deputies by the narrowest of margins (101 against 99), thanks to the vote of an independent to whom the prime minister promised not to privatise banks and large-state owned companies without a vote in parliament. The support for the cabinet had thus sunk to the lowest possible level.

The fiscal crisis that occurred in the spring of 1997 and that led to an economic crisis, resulted from a number of financial scandals. The composition of the cabinet was markedly affected. In late 1997, the Foreign Minister resigned on the grounds that there was a lack of communication and poor management within the centre of government and the ODS and a financial scandal within Klaus's party erupted a few weeks later, which resulted in internal divisions within the party. As a result, the eight ministers from the two junior coalition parties (KDU-CSL and ODA) handed in their resignation directly to the president without informing the prime minister. Social tensions also grew. At least 60,000 people took part in a demonstration in Prague organised by the trade unions against the government's economic policy. This led finally to the resignation of Klaus in November 1997. A month later, president Havel appointed Josef Tosovsky, former governor of the Central bank to be the new prime minister.

The third cabinet under Prime Minister Tosovsky had 15 ministers. President Havel appointed five independet ministers, three ministers from the ODA, three from the KDU-CSL and four from the ODS, which subsequently split to form the US. This caretaker cabinet remained in office for six months only.

In January 1998 President Havel was re-elected for a second and final five-year term, but only with difficulty. In the first ballot, he was supported by 91 deputies out of 200 and by 39 senators out of 81 only. However, neither of his two opponents received enough votes to participate in the second ballot and Havel thus won as the only candidate, but he obtained only 99 votes in the Chamber of Deputies and 47 in the Senate.

The second general election after the division of federation was held in June 1998, two years before it was due, because of the resignation of the Klaus cabinet in December 1997. The result was remarkable in two ways – the number of parties represented parliament was reduced from six to five and the Social Democratic Party (CSSD) became the largest party in parliament, having won 74 seats out of 200, although the centre-right bloc consisting of the ODS, the KDU-CSL and a newly founded US made out of former members of the ODS had a slim majority with 102 seats.

President Havel appointed the leader of the CSSD, Miloš Zeman, to be prime minister. The new government had eighteen ministers, all of whom were members of the CSSD, except for the Minister of Justice, who was an independent. The CSSD had thus a very large majority of seats in cabinet, but controlled only 37 per cent of the seats in parliament. However, together with the ODS, which tolerated the CSSD minority cabinet, the government held 68 per cent of the seats in parliament, on the understanding that the ODS, although not represented in the cabinet, enjoyed a strong, albeit indirect, influence on cabinet decision-making.

The ministerial posts in the 1998 Zeman cabinet are deputy prime minister and Minister of Employment and Social Affairs; deputy prime minister responsible for the co-ordination of ministries of Foreign Affairs, Interior and Defence; deputy prime minister responsible for economic policy; deputy prime minister responsible for Legislative Affairs; Foreign Affairs; Defence; Regional Development; Health; Culture; Agriculture; Trade and Industry; Interior; Environment; Justice; Transport and Communication; Finance; Education, Youth and Sports; Cabinet Office.

With one exception, none of the new ministers had any experience of running a government department. Prime Minister Zeman obtained the confidence of parliament on his programme by 73 votes for to 39 against, one CSSD member being absent and, following an agreement between Klaus and Zeman, the deputies of the ODS left the chamber in order to ensure a government win. The members of the Communist Party, the KSCM, abstained. The minority Zeman cabinet was to last over two years and was still in office by the end of 2000.

Cabinet structure

Constitutional framework

The new Constitution of the Czech Republic came into force on the same day the Czech Republic was founded. The Czech Republic is a parliamentary system with a weak president and a strong prime minister. The president is the head of state, but the government controls the executive. It is accountable to the national parliament, which holds the legislative power. Independent courts exercise judicial power.

The president is elected by a joint session of both houses of parliament for a five-year term and may not serve more than two consecutive terms. The presidency is non-partisan. The president appoints the prime minister and, on the prime minister's recommendation, appoints the ministers and accept the resignation of the government. Furthermore, he or she appoints the justices of the Constitutional Court, the president and vice president of the Court of Accounts, the members of the board of the Czech Central Bank, the heads of diplomatic missions, the judges and the generals. As in most other countries, he or she represents the state internationally, ratifies treaties and is the supreme commander of the armed forces.

Yet these powers remain limited. The president needs, for instance, the counter-signature of the prime minister to appoint or dismiss ministers and, for other appointments, the counter-signature of a minister is required. The president convenes sessions of parliament, but has no power to initiate laws. He or she may veto legislation, but an absolute majority of deputies can override that veto. In reality, the president of the Czech Republic may be influential when there is a high degree of party fragmentation and there is therefore no majority against a presidential veto. Havel was thus more influential during the second and the third minority cabinet than during the fourth when the second strongest party in parliament supported, albeit passively, the minority Social Democratic government.

The power of the president to dissolve the Chamber of Deputies is also markedly circumscribed. It is limited to three situations. One of these is somewhat peculiar and occurs if the presidential candidate for prime minister fails twice in parliament and a vote of confidence for a nominee of the speaker of parliament is also rejected in parliament. Second, the president may dissolve the Chamber of Deputies if a bill, which has been declared a matter of confidence by the cabinet, has not been discussed in parliament for a period of three months. Finally, the president may dissolve the Chamber of Deputies if it has been inquorate for three months.

The prime minister directs the activities of the government which takes its decisions collectively. A new cabinet must present its programme and win a vote of confidence in the chamber of deputies within 30 days of its appointment. Confidence is obtained even if only a relative majority of deputies votes for it. This made it possible for the Zeman government to win after the members of Klaus's party had left the chamber. Hence, the vote of confidence for the minority governments in the Czech Republic was only possible after single or several party factions have left the parliament prior to the vote on the programme.

According to the new Constitution, legislative power is exercised in a bicameral parliamentary system. The existing Czech National Council was transformed into the Chamber of Deputies (lower house) retaining the 200 members of the old parliament. The structure and the Act on Elections to the Senate (upper house) was adopted in 1995 only. The upper house was to consist of 81 members at first to be elected in single-member constituencies on a two-ballot majority basis. Senators were to be elected for six years, with one-third retiring every two years.

The total number of days during which parliament is in recess cannot exceed 120 each year. Ordinary laws are adopted by a relative majority, but constitutional amendments must obtain in each of the two houses a three-fifths majority of the members present. The president has no right of veto, even suspensive, on constitutional amendments. Members of the cabinet may attend sessions of either house as well as sessions of the committees; they must attend when requested to do so. Members of parliament have the right to question ministers in respect to the matters relating to their department. The Chamber of Deputies can pass motions of no confidence in the government and a request for such a motion must be signed by at least 50 members. An absolute majority is required for the motion to be approved.

Cabinet life

Political characteristics

Cabinets in the Czech Republic have been coalitions. Even the 1998 single-party minority government signed an agreement with the opposition party, which agreed to support the Social Democratic cabinet. Party leaders have usually been members of the cabinet. Thus party interests have been well reflected in the cabinet decision-making processes.

Negotiations for the first cabinet coalition took place immediately after the 1992 federal elections. The ODS negotiated with the Slovak HZDS on the formation of a coalition government. During these talks, the difference in the positions of the two parties on the future of Czechoslovakia became obvious. While the HZDS was in favour of a sovereign Slovak state, the ODS asked for a clear definition of the powers of the federation. This was refused by the Meciar government. Neither the Czech nor the Slovak leading political elite were really interested in maintaining the union but they did agree on the composition of the federal cabinet, however. This was headed by J. Strásky and had ten ministers, four from the ODS, four from the HZDS, one from the KDU-CSL and one independent. This cabinet was called 'the government of liquidation', being from the very beginning a temporary cabinet. It lasted up to the dissolution of the federation.

After the 1996 general election the formation of a new Czech government proved difficult, as the former centre-right coalition had only 99 out of 200 seats. As has been noted, minority governments are not constitutionally ruled out, but any cabinet must win a vote of confidence on its programme within 30 days. After lengthy negotiations with the parties which had previously been part of the coalition, Klaus signed an agreement with the KDU-CSL and the ODA, but he still had to look from some support elsewhere and he turned to the opposition Social Democratic Party (CSSD). The arrangement was that CSSD deputies would leave the chamber when the vote on the motion of confidence would be called. In the interest of the country, the main opposition party allowed the centre-right coalition to be in office without having to support the programme of that coalition.

Klaus reduced the number of ministries from 18 to 15. Eight of these, including the post of the prime minister went to the ODS-KDS and four seats went to each coalition partner. Four of the ministries, Legislative Affairs, Economy, State Control, and Privatisation, were abolished while a Ministry for Regional Development was created. Eleven of the sixteen ministers had already been in the cabinet.

A coalition agreement signed in June 1996 concerned mainly the allocation of ministers in the cabinet, amendments to their jurisdiction and the allocation of positions in parliament. The smaller coalition parties gained substantial benefits during the negotiations and the KDU-CSL and the ODA, which had only 15 per cent of the seats in parliament, obtained 50 per cent of the cabinet seats. The ODS lost its majority in the cabinet.

In 1998, Tosovsky offered four ministries to the ODS. All four designated ministers wanted to accept the offer, but they were not allowed by the party to participate. They then joined a new party under the name of Union of Freedom (US). The caretaker cabinet thus included seven independent ministers, four ministers from the newly founded US, three ministers from the ODA and three minister from the KDU-CSL.

At the 1998 election, the Social Democratic Party became the largest in parliament, but the three centre-right parties still had a majority of the seats. The prime minister appointed by Havel, Zeman, had therefore a difficult task. Even combined with the Communist Party (KSCM), he could count on only 98 seats only in parliament and for historical reasons he did not intend to accept the votes of that party.

To the surprise of president Havel, the ODS signed a so-called 'opposition contract' whereby the ODS would support a CSSD minority government. The agreement established procedure specifying what the relations would be between the two parties and laid down the terms and conditions of the formation of a minority cabinet of CSSD and conditions under which the cabinet would be tolerated by the ODS. The CSSD agreed that the opposition party would have the chairmanship of both the upper and the lower houses of parliament, the chairmanship of the control bodies of the lower chamber, the Commission for the Control of the Intelligence Service, the Commission for the Control of Military Protection Intelligence, the chairmanship of the Budget Committee and the presidency of the Court of Accounts. In exchange, the ODS agreed not to support any motion of no-confidence against the CSSD minority government.

Turnover of ministers

During 1993–99, the Czech Republic had four cabinets, three prime ministers and sixty ministers. The average duration of cabinets was 15 months and that of ministers 18 months. This suggests instability, but this was true only of the second and the third cabinets, which together were in office for 12 months only. However, the first and the fourth cabinets have been stable. The first cabinet lasted 39 months and the average ministerial duration was 32 months. The fourth cabinet was still in existence after over two years and there had been only three ministerial changes by the end of 1999.

Prime minister Klaus, who was in office for four years after the declaration of independence of the republic appointed a total of 34 ministers for 18 departments in the 1993–96 legislature and 15 ministrers in the 1996–97 legislature, three of whom changed posts while the other twelve resigned; in 1997 alone, eight ministers resigned. One of the strongest Czech ministers has been the Minister of Agriculture, Josef Lux, who stayed in office during both Klaus cabinets and served in the Tosovsky caretaker cabinet in the same post.

During the six months of that caretaker government, only the Environment Minister resigned. In the 1998 government, the number of cabinet posts increased from 15 to 18, only to decline later to 17.

Administrative characteristics

The Czech cabinet meets once a week. It consists of the prime minister, the deputy prime ministers, and the ministers. The governor of the Czech National Bank, the president of the Czech Statistical Office, and the president of the Court of Accounts may attend cabinet meetings, but without a vote. The prime minister may also invite experts to the meetings. The president of the republic may attend cabinet meetings, ask for reports from the cabinet and its members and discuss with the cabinet or its members matters which are under their jurisdiction. The president may not, however, intervene in the executive process.

The prime minister calls and chairs the cabinet meetings, which deal on average with 20 to 30 policy items and last between five and six hours. If the prime minister is absent or unable to attend for any reason, the meeting is summoned and chaired by a deputy prime minister. The quorum is constituted by a majority of ministers and, to be adopted, resolutions have also to be passed by a majority of ministers; the Minister of Finance has no right of veto. In case of absence, a minister may be replaced by a senior state official, who is allowed to participate in cabinet discussions, but not to vote.

Cabinet decision-making

Although the prime minister holds overall political responsibility for cabinet decisions, policy proposals are prepared by the four deputy prime ministers. The deputy prime ministers decide which proposals require inter-ministerial consultation. The prime minister and the deputy prime ministers receive technical and organisational assistance from the Prime Minister's Office (PMO), which, in June 2000, had a staff of 492, of whom 80 were directly concerned with the co-ordination of cabinet proposals. The head of the PMO is appointed by the cabinet on the proposal of the prime minister.

The co-ordination of proposals initiated by the departments is organised by the state secretaries. In some cases, these set up inter-ministerial meetings or ad hoc committees whose function is to draft proposals for the cabinet. In 2000, the government registered 12 inter-ministerial councils and commissions. The members of the committees are appointed by ministers and usually consist of civil servants, state secretaries and ministers; external experts may be invited. One exception is the Economic and Social Council, which has an equal representation of trade unions, employer associations and the government.

As in most other countries, the implementation of policy decisions is the responsibility of each department. In order to guarantee a more effective and efficient inter-ministerial communication on policy implementation, all ministries have the same vertical organisational structure, which consists of a legislative unit, a personnel unit, an organisational unit, an economic and financial unit, and a unit for European integration.

Since 1994 special attention has been given to proposals relating to European Union laws. During the first Klaus government, the cabinet established a standing committee headed by the prime minister. The committee consisted of three deputy prime ministers and the ministers for Trade and Industry and the Minister of Employment and Social Affairs. In addition, the governor of the Czech National Bank and the president of the Czech Office of Statistics attended the meetings.

In 1995, the government decided that each new cabinet proposal had to state its adequacy within EU norms and about the departments involved. For this purpose a special information technology system was set up in each department. The Minister of Justice was responsible for overall co-ordination as far as the implementation of EU laws was concerned. Externally, the Minister of Foreign Affairs co-ordinated the relations of the Czech Republic with the EU. The first deputy prime minister is officially in charge of negotiations with the EU.

In sum, cabinet decision-making in the Czech Republic is highly formalised. The prime minister and the minister concerned must sign all proposals submitted to cabinet. Although cabinet decisions are taken collectively, the prime minister usually does not intervene in the sphere of activity of individual ministers, who enjoy a wide autonomy. The desire of ministers to obtain autonomy for their departments and thus to achieve higher status in the cabinet and in the nation reduced, however, the profile of the cabinet as such. The Czech cabinet is therefore more a loose board of political managers than the apex of the political system which it was once regarded as being in parliamentary democracies.

6
Slovakia

Ferdinand Müller-Rommel and Darina Malova

Cabinet setting

Slovak developments since 1990

Like the Czech Republic, Slovakia grew out of the former Czechoslovakia and was formally established on 1 January 1993. In the first freely held election to the Slovak National Council, which took place in June 1990, anti-communist movements and parties won the majority of the seats. At the state level, these groups were organised in the Public Against Violence (VPN) parliamentary party, which held a dominant position in the new Slovak parliament as well as in the government. Overall, the VPN gained 48 per cent of the parliamentary seats and one of its members, Vladimir Mečiar, was appointed prime minister. He appointed VPN ministers to 12 of the 23 cabinet posts. In 1991, he was forced to resign as prime minister due to his nationalist and anti-free market stance. Consequently, he left the VPN, and founded – together with several ministers and many members of parliament – the Movement for a Democratic Slovakia (HZDS).

The HZDS participated in the 1992 state and national elections and became the dominant party in the Slovak part of the country. Under Mečiar's leadership, the Slovak National Council approved by 113 votes to 24 with 10 abstentions a declaration of Slovak sovereignty and, on 1 January 1993, the Czech Republic and Slovak Republic became sovereign states. The HZDS-dominated Slovak National Council remained in power and was renamed the Slovak national parliament.

Cabinets since 1993

From 1993 to 2000, Slovakia was governed by three prime ministers in five cabinets. These were

- Mečiar (1) (HZDS), two-party majority cabinet, January 1993 to November 1993

- Mečiar (2) (HZDS), two-party minority cabinet, November 1993 to March 1994
- Moravčík (APR), five-party minority cabinet, March 1994 to December 1994
- Mečiar (3) (HZDS), three-party majority cabinet, December 1994 to October 1998
- Dzurinda (SDK), four-party majority cabinet, from October 1998.

Immediately after independence, Michal Kováč, the HZDS candidate was elected by parliament as president of the new Slovak Republic.

The divisions among the political parties during the presidential election lead to severe internal conflicts within the governing party. During the early part of 1993, four HZDS ministers and one minister from the Slovak National Party (SNS) left the cabinet. Mečiar lost his majority as a result and he had to start to negotiate with the SNS on the formation of a new coalition government. This resulted in the formation of a new cabinet in which the SNS held a post of deputy prime minister and the Ministry of Education and Science. Yet the new coalition held only 49 per cent of the seats in parliament.

Conflicts within that minority coalition soon erupted. Early in 1994, six SNS deputies left to form the National Democratic Party, while the Foreign Affairs Minister and a deputy prime minister from the HZDS resigned from the cabinet and formed a new party, the Realist Political Alternative (APR), which ten HZDS members of parliament proceeded to join. As a result of this, the support for the governing parties declined to 38 per cent. In March 1994, parliament voted a motion of no confidence in Mečiar's cabinet by 78 votes out of 82, the HZDS and the SNS having abstained. Mečiar resigned.

A new coalition was hastily formed to avoid further conflicts. It consisted of five parties from the Left, the centre and the right – the Party of Democratic Left (SDL), the Christian Democratic Movement (KDH), the Realist Political Alternative (APR), the Alliance of Democrats (AD) and the National Democratic Club (NDK). These parties together held 46 per cent of the seats. The coalition needed further support, which could be obtained from the 14 deputies of the two Hungarian parties. The new prime minister, Moravčik, who had been foreign minister in the Mečiar government, offered these parties the right to send representatives when the cabinet was dealing with minority issues. This gave the cabinet a majority.

Parliament immediately passed a bill to organise an early general election, which was scheduled for September-October 1994. Meanwhile, the government was successful in speeding up privatisations and in tackling inflation; it also established closer links with the European Union and closer ties with Hungary. Yet, these developments did not prevent the highly populist leader of the HZDS, Vladimír Mečiar, to increase the support for his party. However, although having become once more the largest party in parliament, the HZDS, did not obtain an absolute majority, even together with its junior partner, the Slovak National Party (SNS). Various attempts to form a broader coalition were unsuccessful: but the Association of Slovak Workers (ZRS), which had originally not shown any interest in participating in the government, eventually joined the HZDS-SNS coalition after long negotiations on their representation in cabinet, as the ZRS made its participation conditional on obtaining a number of ministries and in particular the ministry of Privatisations. In the end, the ZRS, which had only 13 seats in parliament, received four cabinet posts and the SNS, with nine seats, had two cabinet posts. The new three party coalition thus had 56 per cent of the seats in parliament.

All three parties supported a policy of more state control and governmental intervention in the privatization process. They opposed the influx of foreign capital. Privatization was to take place under the leadership of the former managers of the state-owned companies. They also preferred to sell companies instead of privatising by means of 'vouchers': in July 1995, parliament replaced 'vouchers' by government bonds. The government was very cohesive: no minister was dismissed and only four of them resigned during the four years of the legislature.

The fourth Slovak cabinet came, however, under pressure in mid-1996. Protests erupted against the government's economic, cultural and education policies. The prime minister was attacked for having an authoritarian leadership style and the government was attacked for not respecting fully the human and language rights of the Hungarian minority. Mečiar retaliated by making major changes in the cabinet: the ministers of the Interior, Economy and Foreign Affairs were replaced. At the same time, however, a number of civic movements founded 'Charter 97', whose purpose was to monitor the treatment of civil rights in Slovakia.

In the spring of 1998, repeated attempts were made to elect a new president of the republic, but no candidate obtained the required three-fifths majority in parliament. The opposition parties claimed that Mečiar deliberately prevented the election of a new president to increase his own power, since, according to the constitution, the cabinet takes over the powers of the president when the president's term expires if the position is not filled. Kovác retired in March 1998 and Mečiar did indeed take over a number of presidential powers, one of his first decisions being to dismiss 28 ambassadors of the country.

The second general election since independence was scheduled for September 1998. Four months previously, parliament passed a number of amendments to the electoral law, initiated by the HZDS and the SNS parliamentary parties which were designed to reduce the strength of the opposition parties. The electoral alliances which these had formed were in effect rendered useless, as the new provisions of the law stated that each party in any alliance would have to pass the 5 per cent threshold in order to be allocated seats. This was directed against an alliance of five small parties, the Slovak Democratic Coalition (SDK) of which two were not expected to reach 5 per cent of the votes. It was directed also against three small Hungarian parties brought together under the label Hungarian Coalition Party. These two alliances had therefore to merge into two parties, which required difficult and lengthy negotiations during the election campaign.

In addition to the newly founded SDK and the Hungarian Coalition Party (SMK), a new catch-all populist party was formed under the name of Party of Civic Understanding (SOP), which looked for support among left-inclined voters of Eastern Slovakia and among disillusioned HZDS voters. Together with the Party of the Democratic Left (SDL), these three new opposition parties met prior to the election to discuss their campaign strategies as well as possible post-election coalition arrangements.

In the event, the four opposition parties did win the election with 58 per cent of the votes and obtained 93 of the 150 seats in parliament. The government was formed by Mikuláš Dzurinda, the leader of the Slovak Democratic Coalition (SDK). The new prime minister increased the number of cabinet posts from 18 to 20. Nine of these went to the largest party, the SDK, and six to the second party, the SDL. Three posts, those of Human and Minority Rights and Regional Development, the Environment and Construction and Public Works went to the Hungarian minority parties and two, European Integration and Privatisation, to the SOP. With 62 per cent of the seats, the four-party government had a comfortable majority in parliament.

The ministerial posts of the Dzurinda government were four deputy prime ministers; Foreign Affairs; Finance; Defence; Economy; Privatisation; Agriculture; Transport, Posts and Telecommunication; Interior; Justice; Labour, Social Affairs and the Family; Construction and Public Works; Health; Education and Science; Environment; Culture.

The ruling coalition proposed to parliament, which approved it, a constitutional amendment providing for the popular election of the president. It was agreed that the election should take place rapidly, since Slovakia had been without a head of state since March 1998.

At the first ballot, Rudolf Schuster, the chairman of the governing SOP, obtained 47 per cent of the and Vladimír Mečiar 37 per cent, none of the eight other candidates having scored even 10 per cent. Schuster was then elected president at the second ballot with 57 per cent of the votes – the governing coalition had retained strong popular support.

Cabinet structure

Constitutional framework

The new Constitution of Slovakia came into force on 1 January 1993, the day of Slovak independence. According to the Constitution, Slovakia is a unitary state and a parliamentary republic in which the government proceeds from the political representation in parliament.

Parliament is very powerful. It is composed of a single chamber of 150 members, elected by universal suffrage for four years by adults of 21 years and over on a proportional representation basis. On becoming a minister or president, a member of parliament must give up his or her seat but retains the right to participate in parliamentary proceedings.

A three-fifths majority of the members (90) is required to censure the president, to adopt or amend the Constitution and to declare war (Article 84).

The constitution defines the cabinet as a collegial body. A majority of members constitutes a quorum and decisions must be taken by an absolute majority of members. Ministers are collectively and individually responsible to parliament. Thirty days after being appointed by the president, the prime minister has to present a government programme to parliament and ask for a vote of confidence. Parliament may at any time pass a vote of no-confidence in the government or in a minister. The Constitution further states that the prime minister organises government activity, may dismiss members of the cabinet and may ask parliament to vote on a motion of confidence in the government.

The president is the head of state. He or she is appointed for five years and may be re-elected only once. The election of the president was originally held by parliament and since 1998 it has been by popular vote. Parliament can still remove the president by a majority of three-fifths if he or she is engaged in activities directed against the sovereignty and territorial integrity of the state or aiming at undermining the democratic constitution of Slovakia.

The Constitution does not specify that the president shall be non-partisan. However, as the head of state needed originally a three-fifths majority in parliament to be elected, it seemed to follow that the holder of the office should be seen not to belong (any longer) to a political party. As in the case of the Czech president, the president of Slovakia is part of the executive but has little political power. He or she ratifies international treaties, accredits ambassadors and appoints rectors, university professors and generals. As in most other parliamentary democracies, the president is commander-in-chief of the armed forces. He or she appoints and, if a vote of no confidence has been passed, dismisses the prime minister. The president may dissolve parliament if it rejects the government's programme three times within a six-months period. He or she may attend cabinet meetings, but may not formally submit any proposals to the executive. He or she may, however, send bills back to parliament for reconsideration. The president signs all bills and decrees and, of parliament so decides, calls a referendum to take place.

Parliament has the totality of the constitutional and legislative power. It votes the law, decides on international agreements. Parliament can also oblige the cabinet as a whole or individual ministers to resign if it votes a motion of no-confidence, proposed by at least 30 members, is adopted by an absolute majority. Parliament can require the attendance of ministers at its plenary sittings or at its committee meetings.

Cabinet life

Political characteristics

Slovak cabinets have always been coalitions. There have been five cabinets since independence and these have reflected the party composition in parliament, but this party composition has in turn affected the duration of the process of governmental formation. The formation process goes through several phases. Once selected, the prime minister has to negotiate with the leaders of the potential coalition about the composition of the cabinet. The duration of the cabinet formation process has varied from one week (in March 1994) to ten weeks after the 1994 elections. In 1998 the new prime minister needed eight weeks to formed a new cabinet.

The duration of the process depends on the political conditions at the time of the constitution of the government. There was massive turmoil at the beginning of 1994. Immediately after the second Mečiar cabinet had been completed, President Kováč used his constitutional right and presented 'a report on the state of the Republic' to parliament. He emphasised the need for a broadly-based coalition and for an early election. He also strongly criticised Mečiar's political methods and policies. This led to a vote of no confidence.

A new coalition cabinet under Jozef Moravčík was formed in March 1994 to avoid a further political crisis. This cabinet, which consisted of five parties, established a coalition council to facilitate co-operation among the governing parties. At first, the council, which was composed of party leaders, was asked to set up a preliminary cabinet agenda. It was used later to exchange political views after cabinet meetings and before parliamentary sessions in order to facilitate the passage of legislation.

The composition of parliament was even more fragmented than before after the 1994 election. Only seven political groups officially had seats in parliament, but these represented 16 political parties and movements, brought together within eight parliamentary 'clubs', as the Hungarian Coalition Party formed two such 'clubs'. The coalition building process became highly complex. There was first an attempt to form a broad coalition between the HZDS, the KDH and the SDL. The KDH and SDL party leaders rapidly withdrew from the coalition talks because of deep disagreements with the HZDS. Subsequently, despite efforts by the Hungarian Coalition to form an alliance with the KDH, the SDL and the Democratic Union, while relying on the parliamentary support of the ZRS, differences in the political programmes of these parties became too large and the scheme was abandoned.

Since the Constitution does not determine precisely the procedure to be followed in relation to the selection of the prime minister, the president waited for the results of the coalition negotiations, noted that they had failed and asked Vladimír Mečiar to become prime minister. The only straightforward coalition which then emerged consisted of an alliance between the HZDS and the SNS, but these two parties did not have a majority. The deadlock was broken by the ZRS deciding to support the ZDS-SNS government without even having agreed to a joint coalition pro-gramme. In this way, Mečiar's coalition could count on a comfortable majority of 83 seats out of 150 in parliament: but it took six weeks for the agreement to be signed by the three parties, an agreement which was inci-dentally rather vaguely framed. During the following four years, regular meetings of the party leaders took place, but no Coalition Council was formally established.

After the 1998 elections the process of cabinet formation was rendered easier because of the composition of the previous government. What had hitherto four opposition parties, the Slovak Democratic Coalition (SDK), the Party of Democratic Left (SDL), the Hungarian Coalition Party (SMK), and the Party of Civic Understanding (SOP) formed a 'democratic round table'. This included, apart from the parties, labour unions, a third sector group constituted of the top organization of voluntary associations and the Union of Towns, an organization representing local authorities. Immediately after the election the SDK began discussions in view of the formation of a new government with the SDL, the SMK and the SOP. Although these negoti-ations were difficult, a cabinet was formed within a month after the selection of the new prime minister. All the coalition partners agreed on a pro-Western orientation in foreign policy, including the seeking of membership of the EU and of NATO. The government formulated a detailed coalition agreement and established the Coalition Council, which came to be used for regular meetings of cabinet members: the decisions taken by the Council have been binding on the cabinet.

Turnover of ministers

Since independence was declared in 1993, Slovakia had five cabinet govern-ments and three prime ministers. Among them, Mečiar stayed in office for exactly five years (60 months). From January 1993 to March 1994, he was responsible for the first phase of Slovakia's transition. His prime ministership was interrupted by Moravčík who remained in office only nine months before Mečiar returned and led the government for 45 months. He was replaced by Dzurinda in September 1998.

During 1993–2000, 71 different persons occupied a position in the cabinet. Their average duration in office was 24 months, well above that of ministers in most other post-communist Eastern European governments. The duration in office of ministers in the Mečiar governments was particularly high. In order to obtain a majority in parliament, Mečiar had to reshuffle his cabinet in April 1993 after eight parliamentary deputies left the HZDS. The ministers of Foreign Affairs, of Economy and of Privatisation were replaced. A second major reshuffle took place in August 1996 when the ministers of Foreign Affairs, of Economy and of the Interior were replaced. Overall, there were only 14 resignations or dismissals among the 71 ministers. Five of these occurred during the first ten months after independence.

There were 18 members, including the deputy prime ministers, in the first and second Mečiar cabinets. These positions were held by 23 different individuals. During the short leadership of prime minister Moravčík, from March to December 1994, no ministerial changes occurred apart from Kovác, who was deputy prime minister and had already served in the first two Mečiar cabinets. All the other sixteen ministers were in office for the first time and none of them had any ministerial experience.

The next government was the long Mečiar cabinet which began in late 1994 and lasted 45 months. It was the most durable which Slovakia had known since 1989. Only five ministers were changed during that period. The 1998 Dzurinda cabinet has also been rather stable, but two ministers resigned during its first year in office.

Administrative characteristics

The cabinet consists of the prime minister, deputy prime ministers and ministers. The number of the deputy prime ministers has varied over time and tends to reflect the number and strength of the coalition parties in the cabinet.

According to the cabinet's standing rules adopted in 1995, secretaries of state may attend cabinet meetings instead of the minister concerned, but they have no vote. The heads of government secretariats, the Prosecutor General, the chairman of the Statistical Office, the chairman of the Antitrust Agency and the governor of the National Bank also attend cabinet meetings. In addition to this core of decision makers, the director and the heads of a number of departments of the government secretariat are present. Several civil servants and special advisers of the prime minister may be asked to take part; cabinet members have also the right to invite experts who drafted policy proposals which are on the cabinet agenda. The number of persons who attend cabinet meetings is therefore rather large and is on average as high as 40.

In constitutional terms, the cabinet and the prime minister are relatively weak in comparison to parliament. It is even difficult for the prime minister to take action against ministers, since these are effectively appointed by the political parties in the coalition. The prime minister in Slovakia does not have in reality the freedom to 'hire and fire'. He may formally have the right to reject the ministers selected by the coalition parties, but, in practice, prime ministers depend too much on their coalition partners to be able to do so. The situation changed somewhat after 1993 as the Constitutional Court decided that the president could take the decision to dismiss a minister if the prime minister made such a request.

The cabinet has set up a variety of councils, committees, commissions and representative bodies, but these have only an advisory function. Committees are ad hoc bodies dealing with specific problems, while commissions have a long-standing character, as for example the commission on legislation. In 1998, the government established ten short-term advisory bodies, among them the committees on national minorities, on European integration, on the mass media, the committee to fight anti-social activities and the committee for the completion of the construction of the highway system. There are altogether 33 different councils, committees and commissions. The cabinet also appointed 22 cabinet representatives in charge of dealing with the reform of the state administration, with the Romany minority, with construction, etc.

The government secretariat plays an important role in supporting the cabinet decision-making process. It consists of 14 units, namely political analysis, economic policy, government legislation, social and spiritual development and minority issues, European integration, defense and security, foreign assistance, information, government agenda, the rationalisation of the state administration, personnel, foreign relations and protocol, control and monitoring, and the economy. In addition the prime minister's as well as the deputy prime minister's secretariats belong to the government secretariat. In 1998, it employed 269 staff members and has thus more staff than the ministries of Privatization (135), Education (266), Health (205), Culture (175) and Construction (186). As their counterparts in the ministries, most employees are civil servants, but 30 per cent are political staff. The government secretariat is headed by a director who is appointed by the cabinet on the proposal of the prime minister. The director is in charge of guiding and controlling the activities of the secretariat and is thus responsible for the overall performance of the government. He or she may appoint and dismiss the heads of the units after consultation with the prime minister.

The secretariat fulfils the administrative tasks connected with the programmatic, organisational and technical aspects of governmental activities.

It is responsible in particular for the preparation of the cabinet agenda and for the organization of cabinet meetings. It has acquired since the late 1990s an important role with respect to matters relating to the accession of Slovakia to the European Union, as it manages the administrative problems involved in the negotiations with the EU.

Cabinet decision-making

The prime minister or, in his or her absence, a deputy prime minister chairs the cabinet meeting. Regular cabinet meetings take place weekly, normally on Wednesdays, but urgent or special meetings may be called if required.

Committees play little part in cabinet decision-making in Slovakia. This may account in part for the length of the meetings. They have tended to last around six hours and sometimes longer under Dzurinda. They lasted much longer – up to 12 or even 14 hours – under Mečiar.

The agenda of cabinet meetings is planned on an annual basis and is prepared by the cabinet agenda unit of the government secretariat. Members of the cabinet as well as all governmental institutions may propose items for the agenda. The agenda is distributed to members at least five days before the meeting takes place.

The fact that the decision-making process is not highly structured led the Dzurinda cabinet to have on Mondays at 08.30 an informal meeting – a working breakfast – during which the prime minister discusses with the deputy prime ministers the agenda of the cabinet meeting and any other important matters. There was no such inner cabinet under Mečiar.

Two formal requirements have to be followed in order to submit a proposal to cabinet. There has to be an interministerial scrutiny undertaken by the deputy prime ministers; proposals may also be discussed within cabinet committees and commissions as well as with non-governmental organisations when appropriate. Moreover, all proposals must include an estimate of the financial implications and this estimate must have been agreed by the Minister of Finance.

As in most countries, the cabinet meeting is split into two parts, the first for formal decision-making, at which items are approved without discussion, and the second, in which policy issues are debated. The minutes of the meeting record all cabinet decisions as well as the names of the ministers who are responsible for the implementation of these decisions. The minutes also indicate the time span allowed for implementation and the costs involved. The minutes are distributed to all cabinet members, to the heads of most government departments, to the members of parliament, to the president and to anyone who is directly concerned with a particular policy proposal.

The implementation of cabinet decisions is examined on a quarterly basis by the control and monitoring department of the government secretariat. The head of the secretariat is entitled to find out how the implementation process is progressing and to ask for reports by the relevant department about the stage which policies have reached.

The Dzurinda cabinet has tended to take its decisions on a consensual basis. Policy proposals have been discussed until the ministers agreed. Voting has rarely taken place. It has been suggested that the leadership style of that prime minister has been rather weak. Dzurinda appears to have been without a clear vision and to have been more a 'chairman' than a 'chief' (Farrell). This contrasts sharply with the style of Mečiar who has tended to play the part of 'father of the nation'. Mečiar would pick up crucial issues and ask the ministers for comments; it was even reported that he occasionally insulted ministers who were unable to provide satisfactory answers to his questions. Nonetheless, cabinet decision-making was (formally) collective. Voting took place, although the result turned out generally to be along the lines of the prime minister's position.

Mečiar's very strong leadership has markedly shaped cabinet decision-making in Slovakia. He led the cabinet for five of the first eight years of the country's independent existence, while Moravčík was prime minister for nine months only and Dzurinda from October 1998. Mečiar was a strong leader who was able to discipline ministers. He was a 'chief'. He did not need an inner cabinet to prepare the cabinet agenda. He carefully considered the policy positions of the various parties and factions represented in the cabinet. If a crucial issue could not be solved at the meeting, the matter was sent back to the party-based Coalition Council. The secret of his ability to remain prime minister for so long lies in the unusual way in which he combined a very strong leadership with a willingness to devolve matters when he felt that this was politically required.

Overall, the relative stability of Slovak cabinets can be explained by the personality and the leadership style of Mečiar. He established formal or informal coalition agreements among the governing parties and set up Coalition Councils, in order to maximise party interests in cabinet decision-making.

7
Hungary

Ferdinand Müller-Rommel and Gabriella Ilonszki

Cabinet setting

Hungarian developments since 1989

The new Republic of Hungary was proclaimed on 23 October 1989, 33 years after Soviet troops intervened in Hungary and installed a Soviet-supported government. Compared to most other countries in Central-Eastern Europe, Hungary had long and stronger economic and political ties with several Western European countries, above all Austria. The economic and the political reform process started early as a result.

In 1989, several new political parties were founded and old parties reconstituted. Among them, the most prominent were the centre-right Hungarian Democratic Forum (MDF), the liberal Alliance of Free Democrats (SzDSz), set up by dissident intellectuals from several unofficial opposition groups, and the Independent Smallholders' Party (FKgP), which had been a dominant party in Hungary's first postwar election of 1947. In addition, the Social Democratic Party (MSzDP), which had merged with the Hungarian Communist Party in 1945 to form the Hungarian Workers' Party, was reconstituted.

As a result of by-elections in July 1989, a member of the opposition party (MDF), who had defeated the candidate of the leading Communist Party (HSWP), entered parliament for the first time since 1947. In three other by-elections MDF candidates had been more successful than HSWP candidates. Faced with these new challenges, the HSWP dissolved the party and created a new Hungarian Socialist Party (MSzP), committed to multiparty democracy and to an efficient market economy.

In October 1989, the national parliament approved an amended Constitution defining Hungary as an independent democratic state based on the rule of law. All powers were to belong to the people, which they would exercise through their elected representatives. The Constitutional Court was also established. The Presidential Council was abolished and was replaced by a president; the speaker of parliament, Matyas Szürös, was appointed as interim president.

The first free general election since 1947 was held on the basis of two ballots in March and April 1990. At the first ballot electors had to vote for a single constituency candidate and for a party list. Out of more than 50 parties and groupings, 28 contested the election at constituency level but only 12 at national level; the 4 per cent threshold reduced the number of parties represented in the new parliament to six. On a 65 per cent poll, the centre-right Hungarian Democratic Forum (MDF), led by Jozsef Antall, emerged as the strongest single party, closely followed by the liberal Alliance of Free Democrats (SzDSz), and the agrarian Independent Smallholders' Party (FKgP). Only five of the 176 single-member constituency seats were filled at the first ballot. At the second ballot on 8 April, the MDF won 114 out of 176 seats with 41 per cent of the votes; meanwhile, with 30 percent of the votes, the Free Democrats obtained only 35 seats from the single member constituencies.

Josef Antall, the party leader of the MDF, became prime minister of the first three-party coalition government of the new Hungarian Republic. The major aims of the new government were to withdraw from the Warsaw Pact, to become a member of the European Union and to turn the country into a Western-type market economy. To this effect, the government outlined a four-year plan designed to restructure and privatise the economy in 1991, to decrease inflation and introduce convertibility in 1992, to stabilise the economy in 1993 and to return to economic growth in 1994.

A major change in the composition of cabinet took place in 1993 when Antall died after 43 months in office. He was replaced by the former Minister of the Interior, Peter Boross, also a member of MDF. At the same time, the MDF elected a new party leader, Sandor Lezsak, thus dividing the prime ministerial and the party leadership positions.

The conditions under which the second general election took place in May 1994, differed markedly from those of 1990. To begin with, the party system was by then better established. Moreover, the political leadership in all parliamentary parties was more experienced: political campaigning was therefore more professional, in particular with respect to the use of the media by the parties when presenting their programmes. There were also some changes in the electoral system – the threshold had been raised from 4 to 5 per cent and members of some public autonomous agencies, such as the National Insurance Board, became barred from standing for parliament.

The 1994 election resulted in major changes in party strength, although the same six parties were represented in parliament. The Hungarian Socialist Party (MSzP) won an absolute majority (54 per cent), having obtained 209 of the 386 seats. The Alliance of Free Democrats (SzDSz) obtained about 20 per cent of the votes and 70 seats, while the former governing MDF obtained only 12 per cent of the votes and 37 seats. The junior coalition partners in the former centre-right government FKgP and KDNP (Christian Democratic People's Party) won respectively 26 and 22 seats.

Although the MSzP could have formed a government alone, public opinion polls indicated that the majority of Hungarians were not in favour of a single-party socialist government. The MSzP thus started discussion with the Free Democrats (SzDSz), the second strongest party in parliament, with a view to forming a coalition. It took 40 days to finalise the accord. The new government was to be led by Gyula Horn of the MSzP, who was formally appointed prime minister by parliament by 265 votes to 93 and one abstention. The new coalition government could count on a two-thirds majority and could therefore introduce constitutional changes if it so desired.

The third democratic general election took place in May 1998. At the first ballot, Hungarians voted in 20 regional lists as well as in 176 single-member constituencies. With over nine candidates on average per constituency, only one of these 176 seats was filled outright. The election was surprising on various counts. First, the result had been uncertain until the end. Second, the winner at the first ballot (the socialist MSzP) was not to be the overall winner. At the first ballot, the MSZP obtained 32.9 per cent of the votes and the Young Democrats (FIDESz-MAP) 29.5 per cent, while the MSzP candidate was ahead in 113 constituencies and the FIDESz-MPP candidate in 43 only. This appeared to give hope to the Young Democrats. The campaign intensified between the two ballots; turnout even marginally increased from 56 to 57 per cent.

Co-operation strategies developed between the opposition parties. The FIDESz-MPP and the MDF agreed on joint candidatures for the second ballot; the Independent Smallholders' Party (FKgP) withdrew its candidate in 69 constituencies and the Young Democrats in 19 in order to increase the chances of defeating the socialists.

These tactics enabled the Young Democrats to overtake the socialists and to obtain 148 seats, while their main opponents obtained 134; but the difference between these two parties was much smaller than had been the case between the main contenders at the two previous contests. The Christian Democrats (KDNP) disappeared as a parliamentary party while the Hungarian Justice and Life Party (MIEP) entered parliament with 14 members. The Free Democrats (SzDSz) lost the election. The party had had 92 seats in 1990 and 69 in 1994; it obtained only 24 in 1998. The junior coalition partner of the socialist–liberal coalition paid a high price for having participated in the previous government.

The results of that general election suggested that liberal democracy was consolidated in Hungary. There had been a change in government for the third time and the party system has remained stable. National parties received more than 91 per cent of the regional list votes. The two largest parties (the socialists and the centre-right Young Democrats) dominated the scene with over 60 per cent of the votes, an indication that fragmentation has decreased; meanwhile, the centre-right MDF and the liberal SzDSz had become small parties.

Cabinets since 1990

Between 1990 and 2000, Hungary had four cabinets and seventy cabinet ministers. With the exception of the seven-month Boross government of 1994 constituted after the death of Prime Minister Antall, cabinets in Hungary have been stable. The four cabinets were

- Antall (MDF), majority coalition government, May 1990 to December 1993
- Boross (MDF), caretaker government, December 1993 to July 1994
- Horn (MSzP), majority coalition government, July 1994 to July 1998
- Orbán (FIDESz-MPP), majority coalition government, from July 1998.

A first three-party coalition government was constituted in May 1990. It comprised the centre-right Hungarian Democratic Forum (MDF), the Independent Smallholders' Party (FKgP) and the Christian Democratic People's Party (KDNP). Together, these three parties had 60 per cent of the seats in parliament. In line with the electoral result, the MDF received the majority of the cabinet posts (52 per cent), followed by the FKgP (19 per cent) and the KDNP (5 per cent). Four cabinet seats were given to persons with no party affiliation, among them the ministers of Finance and International Trade and two ministers without portfolio. The FKgP obtained the ministries of Labour and of Agriculture and two ministries without portfolio, while the KNDP had the ministry of Social Welfare.

After Prime Minister Antall's death, the second caretaker cabinet was led by Prime Minister Borass. He filled the post of Minister of Interior by the MDF parliamentary party leader. The Boross government remained in office for seven months only, as the general election was scheduled for May 1994.

After the 1994 election, the distribution of seats in cabinet reflected the strength of the MSZP in parliament. Eleven portfolios went to socialist ministers and only three to the SzDSz. These were of the Interior, whose incumbent was also deputy prime minister, of Transport and of Education and Culture. In contrast to 1990, when there was neither an outline of the principles nor a plan of the detailed operation of the coalition, a document was published on which the co-operation between the parties would take place. It included a description of the general characteristics of the activity of the coalition and a list of specific tasks in eleven policy areas. This document and the coalition itself were formally approved at MSzP and SzDSz congresses respectively with 98 per cent and a 81 per cent of the votes.

The fourth cabinet was formed after the 1998 general elections. The new cabinet included three parties, the Federation of Young Democrats (FIDESz-MPP), the Independent Smallholders' Party (FKgP) and the Democratic Forum (MDF). These parties together held 54 per cent of the seats in parliament. At the age of 35, the prime minister, Viktor Orbán, of the Federation of

Young Democrats, was the second youngest politician in the post. The coalition with the FIDESz-MPP and the MDF was quickly arranged, but, as the two parties held 42 per cent of the seats only, the Smallholder Party (FKgP) had to be invited to join as well. The coalition agreement was signed in June 1998.

Party strength in parliament reflected the distribution of cabinet posts. The MDF received one ministry only (Justice) while the FKgP obtained the ministries of Agriculture and of Environmental Protection and a ministry without portfolio concerned with the co-ordination of EU funds. The FIDESz-MPP took ten cabinet posts (71 per cent of the total). A number of non-career politicians, albeit affiliated to a party, were appointed to the cabinet; thus half the cabinet members were not parliamentarians.

The ministerial posts of the 1999 Orbán cabinet have been similar to the posts in the last German cabinet under *Bundeskanzler* Helmut Kohl. The Orbán cabinet consisted of the following ministerial posts: Minister Leading the Prime Minister's Office; two ministers without portfolio; Interior; Foreign Affairs; Defence; Finance; Agriculture and Rural Development; Justice; Economic Affairs; Environmental Protection; Transport, Telecommunications and Water Management; Education; National Cultural Heritage; Health; Social and Family Affairs; Youth and Sports.

Cabinet Structure

Constitutional framework

The Constitution states that Hungary is a unitary state and a parliamentary democracy. Political power is divided between parliament, the president of the republic and the government. The unicameral parliament is composed of 386 members elected for a four-year term. Parliament may require the prime minister (but not single ministers) to resign, but only if a constructive vote of no-confidence, including the name of a new prime minister, is adopted.

Proposals regarding, among others, the constitution, referenda, the electoral law or citizenship need to be adopted by a two-thirds majority. The Constitution also specifies that members of parliament may not hold the post of president of the republic, of ombudsman, of president of the national audit office, posts of judge, prosecutors or civil servants, be members of the armed forces or of the police.

The president is the head of the state, is elected by parliament for five years and may be re-elected once. He or she represents Hungary, signs international treaties, accredits ambassadors and exercises the right of pardon in individual cases. The president decides on the date of the parliamentary and local elections, may propose the holding of a referendum and decides in citizenship cases.

The government is composed of the prime minister and of the ministers who are jointly responsible to parliament. The constitution lists the main responsibilities of the government, which are in particular to protect the constitutional order, to direct and co-ordinate the work of the ministries and other state authorities and to protect the rights of citizens. The constitution gives the prime minister a strong position: the prime minister is the only member of government to be elected by parliament and to be responsible to parliament for cabinet decisions.

Cabinet life

Political characteristics

The four cabinets which succeeded each other between 1990 and 2000 have been characterised by a number of important differences, both in form – legal, procedural or institutional – and in substance. What remained stable were the constitutional setting and the coalition government format. As pointed out earlier, constitutional rules have had an impact on cabinet formation and on cabinet life: the prime minister is the leader, not the first among equals. The parliamentary majority is constitutionally restricted in a number of fields in which a two-thirds majority is required. The president's appointment powers are also restricted. Presidents may appoint ministers only on the recommendation of the prime minister. Moreover, the government format also remained fairly stable and cabinets have lasted, except for the Boross 1994 government. The process of formation of these three cabinets was somewhat different, however.

In 1990, the three coalition parties controlled 60 per cent of the seats in parliament. The first coalition was thus oversized but by the end of the legislature the parliamentary support for these coalition parties had fallen to about 50 per cent. Prime Minister Antall had therefore been right to set up a large coalition on the assumption that party stability and consequently the parliamentary majority could not be taken for granted in the early phase of a democratic system. One segment of the FKgP did drop out of the coalition while several MDF members of parliament left their party. Moreover, the two larger parties of the coalition represented only 37 per cent of the votes. Even if the third party was included, the coalition represented only 44 per cent of the voters, as a result of the strongly majoritarian characteristics of the mixed electoral system. To increase the legitimacy of the first government the co-operation of the three parties was required.

When the first government was formed there was no time for coalition bargaining. Perhaps the most important consequence of the electoral process was the fact that an agreement was struck between the largest party, the MDF, and the second largest party, the SzDSz, which became part of the opposition. That agreement determined the policy fields which would require a two-thirds majority. The government and the opposition party also agreed on the implementation of the constructive motion of no confidence on the German model. However, there was no coalition agreement between the governing parties; there was merely a written document signed by several leading personalities, including the prime minister and some members of the FKgP. This document mentioned a number of important policies and in particular the reprivatisation of land.

In 1994, the situation was different. The socialist MSzP had more than 50 per cent of the seats and yet formed a two-party coalition. A detailed coalition compact was prepared, but that document could not hide the fact that the SzDSz could be dispensed with in the oversized coalition. Thus, the SzDSz was a prisoner of the coalition and did not draw any significant benefits from participation.

The coalition agreement between the two parties was over 200 pages long. It determined

- the working rules and the institutional safeguards for the coalition
- the structure of the government
- the principles of the government programme
- some information on the negociation process.

The coalition partners agreed to set up the Coalition Reconciliation Council (CRC), consisting of the prime minister, the deputy prime minister, the leaders of the coalition parties, the parliamentary party leaders of the coalition parties and one additional politician appointed by each party. The CRC was to clarify contentious issues between the coalition partners, decisions being taken on a consensual basis.

The coalition agreement and the creation of the CRC had the effect of reducing the role of the prime minister by comparison to what had been the case in the 1990 government. In the first two-and-a-half years of the government, numerous intra-coalition conflicts occurred which received substantial publicity and the CRC met frequently. Gradually, it came to meet rather less. It had twenty meetings in 1994, fourteen in 1995 and eight in 1996. The deputy prime minister, who belonged to the junior coalition party, but was not its leader, was in the chair. In April 1997, after the party leader of the SzDSz had to resign in connection with a political scandal and the deputy prime minister was elected party leader to replace him, the character of the CRC began to change and its importance diminished. Decisions were increasingly taken within the government itself. In the absence of party-centred public debates and of CRC meetings publicised by the media, the working of the government became smoother. The impact of the junior coalition partner on cabinet decision-making decreased, with negative consequences for the electoral prospects of the SzDSz at the 1998 election.

At that election, the FIDESz-MPP became the largest party although it controlled only 38 per cent of the seats in parliament. An electoral agreement had been made with the MDF (it ran common candidates in several constituencies), but the bad electoral performance of the MDF (which obtained 4 per cent of the seats only) forced FIDESz to ask the FKgP to join the coalition. A minimum winning coalition was formed in the process. There were difficulties, however, principally due to the FKgP which was a divided organisation. It had split several times during the 1990–94 legislature; its leader had been attacked for his occasional demagoguery; and the party had attracted a right-wing radical electorate in addition to its traditional rural following. The MDF, however, was too small to have a significant impact on cabinet formation, despite the fact that the party selected for the post of Justice Minister the only female member of the cabinet who was also one of the most popular politicians in the country.

The coalition parties in the 1998 government did not prepare a detailed accord. FIDESz signed an agreement with both the MDF and the FKgP in which ministerial portfolios were distributed among the parties but where the aims and workings of the government were described in general terms.

There was a further difference between the 1998 and the previous coalition formation processes in relation to junior ministers. These had so far been appointed in such a way as to enable the parties to exercise a kind of political control over each other in the various ministries. In the 1998 government, both full minister and junior minister in a given ministry belonged to the same party.

Finally, coalition discussions in the Orbán cabinet were more informal. The FIDESz-MPP and the FKgP leaders both emphasised that personal talks were more valuable than the formal arrangements of the previous government. Leaders of the three parties met during weekends, including with their families, to discuss political issues.

Duration of ministers

On average Hungarian ministers remained in office for over three years, which is appreciably more than ministers in most other Central and Eastern European countries. Yet there has been a substantial amount of reshuffles in each government. Under Antall, seven posts, namely Justice, Defence, Foreign Affairs, Economic Affairs, Social Welfare and two ministers without portfolio, were held by the same incumbent for four years, but changes did occur in other ministries. The Minister of Finance has been replaced twice. Antall also dismissed the ministers of Labour and of Agriculture and one minister without portfolio.

The composition of the government was then naturally entirely changed after the 1994 election when the socialist-liberal coalition came to power. During his tenure, the new prime minister, Horn, did replace a number of ministers. There were altogether eleven ministerial changes over the four years.

The 1998 Orbán centre-right coalition was more stable and two changes only occurred in the first eighteen months of its existence. The Minister of Economic Affairs was replaced by a more 'business-oriented' person while a FIDESz-MPP member was placed in charge of the Ministry of National Cultural Heritage in lieu of a member of the smaller SzDSz.

Administrative characteristics

In Hungary, the word 'cabinet' is used to refer to what are in effect committees of the government which prepare and co-ordinate those decisions that the government will eventually take. These 'cabinet committees' are technically advisory. Four types of such 'cabinet committees' have developed over the years.

First, is the 'inner cabinet' which meets before the full cabinet meeting and provides one last opportunity to fine tune proposals. Under Orbán, it has consisted of the prime minister, the minister of National Security, the Minister at the Prime Minister's Office, the Minister of Agriculture and Rural Development and the Minister of Justice, these last two ministers being the party leaders of the FKgP and of the MDF. In the Orbán cabinet, this inner cabinet has become a place where the top politicians of the coalition parties met with two FIDESz-MPP politicians who were not merely important ministers but were closely linked to the prime minister and indeed founder-members of the party.

Second, is the 'government cabinet', which meets on Fridays and has a preliminary consultative role; it also decides the agenda of the next government meeting. Its members are the prime minister, the Minister of Foreign Affairs, the Minister of the Interior, the Economic Affairs Minister, the Minister of National Security, the Minister of Finance, the Minister at the Prime Minister's Office, the Minister of Agriculture and Rural Development and the Minister of Justice.

Third, is the 'national security cabinet' which consists of six members, the ministers of the Interior, Foreign Affairs, Defence, National Security and Justice and the head of the Prime Minister's Office. The minister of the Interior leads this 'cabinet'. It co-ordinates national security questions and prepares government decisions on these issues.

Fourth, the Economic Affairs Minister heads an 'economic cabinet', which includes among its members the ministers of Agriculture and Rural Development, of Finance, of Transport, Telecommunication and Water Management. As a general rule, important economic issues have to be discussed in this 'economic cabinet' before being placed on the agenda of the government meeting.

All four 'cabinet committees' may send back submitted policy proposals for revision. They may also ask the departments concerned to clarify policy initiatives before proposing to place them on the agenda of the government meeting.

Beyond these four 'cabinets committees', there are weekly meetings of the administrative state secretaries. These meetings play an important part in inter-ministerial communication and in the overall process of decision making. The administrative head of the Prime Minister's Office chairs the meetings. Every matter on the agenda of the government meeting must be discussed and approved by this body and this means that the administrative state secretary prepares the agenda of the government meeting. Without the approval of that committee, policy proposals may be scheduled on the government's agenda only if the prime minister agrees.

The official government meeting takes place once a week, usually on Thursday mornings. The meeting lasts three hours on average. The meeting, which is chaired by the prime minister, includes all the ministers, with or without portfolio. The permanent observers are the Head of the Prime Minister's Office and, from that Office, the junior minister, the administrative state secretary and the administrative state secretary in charge of legal issues. The government spokesman and the president of the Central Statistical Office also attend. None of these has the right to vote. Votes are rare. If there is equality, the prime minister has the casting vote.

The meeting is prepared by the Prime Minister's Office, which co-ordinates the work of the four 'cabinets' and of the 'administrative state secretary' group. This Office also records the decisions taken. Resolutions, guidelines and decisions are published within eight days after the government meeting. The Office prepares a monthly report on the extent of implementation of government decisions. If a policy is not implemented, the Office must provide a written statement giving the reasons for this failure.

Cabinet decision making

There has not so far been any systematic analysis of decision-making processes of the Antall cabinet, but it seems that the level of institutionalisation was low during that government. The first prime minister of post-communist Hungary saw himself as the country's senior statesman; he was strong and his ministers were weak. Indeed, the relatively long duration in office of some of the members of that cabinet is in this case an indicator of their weakness.

Prime Minister Gyula Horn was a former Hungarian Communist Party bureaucrat who no longer had a political vision. He was pragmatic and viewed the government as a company, which had to function efficiently. His cabinet was as a result highly institutionalised. Most ministers in that cabinet were professionals with an efficient managerial style. Collective decision-making was high.

This collective decision-making approach was continued in the next cabinet, but the new prime minister, Orbán, had a dominant personality, in a context in which there were no strict coalition rules; the government was successful in adjusting political practice to constitutional opportunities. Orbán focused on reforming the Hungarian economy by means of new forms of governmental management and the 'centre of government' was reorganised. One reform concerned the Prime Minister's Office (PMO), which was structured on the German model. Four departments were set up, dealing respectively with the economy, social policy, interior and justice, and foreign and security affairs. As in Germany, the Office was to 'mirror' the ministries and cabinet proposals from the ministries had to be vetted by the relevant department of the Office before coming on the cabinet agenda. Thus the Office co-ordinated the activities of the ministries, elaborated government strategies and supervised the implementation of government decisions. Besides, the prime minister initiated a training programme for ministers, at which members learnt how to prepare policy proposals and how to act most effectively in cabinet meetings. Finally, the Minister of Economic Affairs was given a dominant role instead of the Minister of Finance.

Formal decision-making takes place at the government meeting itself and given the extent to which proposals have been prepared before, unexpected debates rarely occur, however. In particular, coalition party leaders have many opportunities to air their opinions. Yet, despite this close relationship between parties and government, the support of the parliamentary parties cannot always be taken for granted. Some government bills are occasionally defeated. This occurred, for example, in the final vote on the law designed to change rules relating to general medical practice and on the proposal of the Ministry of the Interior to introduce cumulative penalty points for traffic offences.

In sum, the character and the function of the Hungarian cabinet have changed significantly during the 1990s. In 1990, the first Hungarian government was based on a strong prime minister dealing with weak ministers and weak coalition partners without any written or set rules. It then became restructured in 1994 as a result of a detailed agreement implemented by means of a Coalition Reconciliation Council (CRC).

During the third cabinet (1994–98), steps were gradually taken to establish a 'chancellor' democracy in which the prime minister dominated. The Constitution did give superior status to the prime minister since the holder of that post appoints and dismisses ministers without parliament being involved. Meanwhile, the Prime Minister's Office acquired substantial influence during the last phase of the Horn cabinet and was further strengthened under the Orbán government. Thus the Hungarian cabinet has tended to move from being a 'political' to being a 'technical' institution in which a final check is made about the main lines of governmental policy.

8
Slovenia

Ferdinand Müller-Rommel and Slavko Gaber

Cabinet setting

Slovenian developments since 1989

The Republic of Slovenia declared independence on 25 June 1991 after having been part of the Federal Republic of Yugoslavia since 1919. Even before this date, Slovenia was never an independent state.

During the 1970s and the 1980s, Slovenia was the most prosperous part of the Yugoslav Republic. In January 1989 a newly founded 'extra-parliamentary' opposition party (Democratic Alliance) called for a drastic reduction in Slovenia's contribution to the federal budget. They also asked for a sovereign autonomous Slovene state with a new constitution and a parliamentary democracy including free multiparty elections. Later during the year, these requests (and several other) became amendments in the Slovenian assembly's three chambers and were adopted with only one vote against and one abstention among the 256 deputies present – most of them being members of the Slovenia League of Communists (SLC).

In February 1990, the Slovene communists called an extraordinary congress in which they adopted a resolution, stating the end of their relationship to the Federal League of Communists in Yugoslavia (LCY – the federal ruling party). It was also decided to co-operate with all democratic organisations in Yugoslavia. Furthermore, the delegates renamed the former SCL party as 'Party of Democratic Renewal' (LCS) with its own membership, programme and statute. The new programme was drawn up along social democratic lines for the coming multiparty elections to the republican Assembly in Slovenia April 1990.

During the election campaign, six centre-right oriented parties formed an alliance under the name of DEMOS (Democratic Opposition of Slovenia). Programmatically, the party alliance tried to avoid criticism of the communist past. Issues of political pluralism, democracy and the republic's future within the Federation of Yugoslavia dominated the electoral campaign. As was the case with the Lega Nord in Italy, DEMOS refused to subsidise the economies of the southern republics. Instead, they advocated a new Yugo-slav confederation in which Slovenia would have full sovereignty and economic independence including a separate currency.

Overall, DEMOS obtained 55 per cent of the votes and 47 seats in the Slovene main assembly. The strongest challenger to the alliance during the electoral campaign had been the Party of Democratic Renewal (LCS) which emerged as the largest single party in the chamber and obtained 17 per cent of the votes and 14 seats. Among the 17 parties which competed in the election, eight gained parliamentary representation. The turnout was 83 per cent of the around 1,500,000 electorate.

The new Slovene assembly elected Lojze Peterle, chairman of the Slovene Christian Democratic Party (SKD) as the new president of the Slovene executive. The composition of his government was approved on the same day.

A separate direct election for the Slovene presidency was also held in April 1990. In the second round, Milan Kučan of the ruling Party of Democratic Renewal (LCS), formerly the leader of the Slovene League of Communists, obtained 58.4 per cent of the vote and became president of Slovenia.

At the federal state level, Borisav Jovic of Serbia took over as president of the Yugoslav Collective State Presidency in accordance with the system of annual rotation of that office. He rejected the legitimacy of Slovenia's declaration of sovereignty and suggested instead that each component of Yugoslavia would be entitled to request the right to secede from the Socialist Federal Republic of Yugoslavia (SFRY) only provided the majority of the citizens of a republic voted for such a request. In addition, he argued that the SFRY assembly, after consulting the views of all other republics, would have the final decision.

In response to Jovic's threat, the Slovene assembly adopted a further amendment to the Constitution, allowing it to assert its control over the Slovene defence force. This resulted in a severe conflict with the Secretariat of National Defense and the Serb-dominated military command. In October 1990, military police moved into Slovene territorial defence force headquarters. However, the Slovene territorial defence forces had already successfully removed weapons from the reach of the Yugoslav Army. In January 1991, the SFRY presidency ordered the federal army to disarm all paramilitary groups.

The ruling DEMOS coalition parties then initiated a referendum regarding secession if the six republics were unable to agree on a common plan for the restructuring of Yugoslavia. This proposal was approved unanimously by the assembly and ratified by the people almost unanimously. The turnout was 93.5 per cent and 89 per cent of the voters endorsed Slovene independence.

In early 1991, several rounds of talks took place between representatives of the six republics under the auspices of the federal presidency. They failed to achieve any agreement on Yugoslavia's future constitutional structure. Thus Slovenia began to take concrete steps towards secession. First, the republic planned to abolish gradually the federal government's powers over Slovenia.

Second, it created its own currency as well as a separate banking and taxation system. Third, it took steps to obtain recognition from foreign powers. Fourth, it allowed Slovene conscripts to serve in the Slovene Territorial Defence units or the Slovene police force rather than in the federal forces.

Six months after the referendum, Slovenia declared independence from the SFRY on 25 June 1991. In response, federal troops occupied Ljubljana airport, blockaded the borders and bombarded radio and television transmitters. The European Community was asked to arrange a ceasefire, which forced the federal troops to begin withdrawing from Slovenia. After three months of unsuccessful talks Slovenia's independence was recognised by Yugoslavia in October 1991. Two months later a new Slovenian Constitution was promulgated and Slovenia received international recognition shortly afterwards.

Cabinets since 1993

After independence, the first free election took place in December 1992. Between 1992 and spring 2000, Slovenia has had four cabinets and only one prime minister:

- Dronovšek (LDS), five-party majority cabinet, January 1993 to April 1994
- Dronovšek (LDS), three-party majority cabinet, April 1994 to January 1996
- Dronovšek (LDS), two-party minority cabinet, January 1996 to February 1997
- Dronovšek (LDS), three-party majority cabinet, February 1997 to April 2000.

Slovenia's first presidential and parliamentary elections since independence took place in December 1992. At the presidential election, Milan Kučan, standing as an independent, was re-elected as president for a five-year term with 64 per cent of the vote. At the parliamentary election, 25 parties and coalitions competed for the 90 seats of the National Assembly whose term was four years. Seats were to be distributed on a proportional representation basis with a 3 per cent threshold, but two seats were reserved for the Hungarian and Italian ethnic minorities.

On a 86 per cent turnout, the Liberal Democracy of Slovenia (LDS), led by the president of the Slovenian executive council, Janez Drnovšek, came to be the largest party with 22 seats; it was followed by the Christian Democratic Party (SKD), which obtained 15 seats, by the United List of Social Democrats (ZLSD) which won 14 seats and the extreme right-wing Slovenian National Party (SNP) which gained 12 seats. The small parties which were represented were the Social Democratic Party of Slovenia (SDSS) which gained 3.3 per cent of the vote and four seats in parliament, The Greens (ZL) with 3.7 per cent of the vote and five seats, and the Slovenian People's Party (SLS) which received ten seats.

In its electoral campaign, the Liberal Party had stressed the need to introduce economic reforms, despite its past as a communist youth movement. Its members and voters were predominantly young, belonged to the middle class and supported a combination of free enterprise and social justice. The SKD had similar views to those of the German CDU. It supported traditional conservative and religious values and was strongly in favour of EU and NATO membership; the majority of its voters lived in small towns and rural areas. The ZLSD was an alliance of several left-wing parties, including the post-communist Party of Democratic Renewal. The ZL was a member of Socialist International, had a strong youth movement and close ties to unions as well as to the Workers' Party and the Social Union. The party's programme stressed traditional social democratic issues, including the demand of a strong welfare state. Subsequently they tried to adopt an image close to that of the 'third way'. Most ZL voters live in large towns. The SNP is a right-wing populist party strongly opposed to EU membership and to the concessions made to Italy about the possibility to buy land in Slovenia. The Greens have been from the very beginning more reformist than some of their counterparts in Western Europe; they have not been opposed fundamentally to the current political system but adopted a pragmatic approach to political change. The SLS was a conservative party supported by farmers. It requested more political power for local government and held a critical view about the impact of the EU on Slovenian agricultural policy.

Five weeks after the election, the new prime minister, Janez Drnovšek of the LDS, formed a majority coalition government consisting of four parties: the LDS, the Christian Democrats (SKD), the United List (ZLSD) and the Social Democrats (SDSS), while the Green Alliance had one minister in the cabinet but was not a member of the coalition. The coalition held a comfortable majority of 60 out of 90 seats in parliament.

The first Drnovšek cabinet lasted only 15 months. In March 1993, the prime minister dismissed the Minister of Defence, Janez Jansa, after reports of illegal military police interference in civilian matters. The Social Democratic Party (SDSS), of which Jansa was president, withdrew from the coalition. The deputy prime minister and Foreign Minister, who was also the president of the Christian Democrats (SKD), parliament's second largest group, announced that his party might also leave the government.

The disagreement within the coalition and the blackmail potential of some coalition parties strengthened the desire of prime minister Janez Drnovšek, who was also chairman of the LDS, to merge the Liberal Democratic Party (LDS) with the Democratic Party (DS), the Greens-Ecological Party (ZS) and the Socialist Party and form a new Liberal Democracy of Slovenia (also LDS). The merger increased the total number of centre-oriented LDS deputies to 30 out of 90 in the National Assembly. Drnovšek subsequently reshuffled the cabinet in April 1994 to include the new LSD, the Christian Democratic Party (SKD) and the United List of Social Democrats (ZLSD).

In January 1996, Prime Minister Drnovšek was forced to reshuffle his cabinet again after the United List (ZLSD) withdrew from the government. The new coalition consisted of only two parties, LDS and SKD, which together held only 45 out of 90 seats in parliament. This minority government lasted until February 1997.

The second post-independence election to the National Assembly was held in November 1996. The result brought two broad blocs of almost equal size in competition for the formation of the cabinet. On the one hand, there were left centre parties consisting of parts of DEMOS, of the former but renewed Communist Party and the former youth alliance. On the other hand, a so-called new Slovenian Spring Alliance consisting of the SKD, the SLS and the SDS tried to re-establish DEMOS. Electoral blocs could not be set up under the Slovenian proportional representation system, however.

None of the two blocs obtained a majority at the election. The centre-left LDS, the largest party in the outgoing parliament was returned with 25 seats, having lost five seats. Since the SKD changed fronts and joint the Slovenian Spring Alliance, former prime minister Drnovšek needed to look for alternative coalition partners. He suggested a five-party government coalition consisting of the LDS, the United List of Social Democrats (ZLSD), the new Democratic Party of Pensioners of Slovenia (DESUS), the Slovene National Party (SNS), and the two representatives of the Hungarian and Italian minorities. This coalition had 45 seats in parliament, the other 45 seats being held by the Slovenian Spring Alliance. However, one SKD member of parliament announced his defection from the party and became an independent. He declared he would vote for Drnovšek, who was thus elected prime minister by 46 votes to 44 in January 1997. In late February, the Slovene People's Party (SLS) agreed to leave the Slovenian Spring Alliance and join a coalition together with the LDS and Democratic Party of Pensioners (DESUS). The new government of Janez Drnovšek was formed after three months of negotiations and was subsequently approved in national parliament by 52 votes out of 90. LDS, SLS and DESUS together held 49 seats in the chamber.

The second presidential election was held in November 1997. Eight candidates stood but the outgoing President, Milan Kučan, was re-elected in the first round with 55.6 per cent of the votes, followed by Janez Podobnik (SLS) with 18.4 per cent.

Cabinet structure

Constitutional framework

The Slovenian Constitution was adopted in December 1991. According to the Constitution, Slovenia is a unitary state, it has a bicameral parliament consisting of the National Assembly and of the National Council and a president directly elected by universal suffrage for a period of five years and who may be in office for only two consecutive terms. The 90 members of the National Assembly are directly elected and exercise legislative power. The National Council's main power consists in having the right to veto bills passed by the National Assembly.

The president is the head of state and the commander-in-chief of the armed forces. His powers are limited and mostly of a representative nature. The president may not issue decrees to implement legislation nor has he or she the power to appoint and dismiss the prime minister or dissolve parliament at will. The president does not have the right to initiate legislation or direct decision-making processes. In return, the president is not responsible for the decisions taken by the executive. Being directly elected, the president has primarily a role of national integration, with a stabilising effect for the political system, especially under conditions of complex and variable party coalitions.

The president proposes the prime minister to the National Assembly, after consultation with the major political parties. The vote is then elected by secret ballot and, to be elected, the prime minister needs to obtain an absolute majority of the members of the National Assembly. If this does not occur, the president may suggest another or even the same candidate within 14 days to the National Assembly. But candidates for the post of prime minister may also be nominated by parliamentary parties or by ten or more deputies of the National Assembly. If there is more than one nomination, the National Assembly has to vote first on the candidate proposed by the president.

Cabinet ministers are appointed and dismissed by the National Assembly on the proposal of the prime minister. The constitution specifies, that the prime minister is responsible for the unity of the government, leads and guides the government administratively and co-ordinates the work of the departments. Ministers are individually responsible for their department and collectively responsible for overall governmental policy. The prime minister and the ministers have to defend their actions in front of the National Assembly.

A motion of no confidence in the prime minister and in the ministers has to be presented by at least ten members of the National Assembly. If passed, the government has to resign. The National Assembly may also pass a vote of no confidence in individual ministers. The prime minister may also ask the National Assembly for a vote of confidence in the government. If there is not an absolute majority in favour of of the government, parliament must, within 30 days, either elect a new prime minister or pass a confidence vote in the outgoing government, otherwise the president can dissolve the National Assembly and call for an early election.

Cabinet life

Political characteristics

The formation and the duration of cabinets varied over time. The first government, which consisted of five parties, lasted only 13 months. In this cabinet the LDS held 32 per cent, the SKD and ZLSD each 27 per cent and the SDSS and ZS each had 7 per cent of the posts. The second and the fourth 'surplus' majority government were composed of only three parties and lasted for over twenty months. In the second cabinet, the LSD held 50 per cent of the cabinet seats while the SKD and ZLSD each held 25 percent of the portfolios and in the fourth cabinet, the LDS held 50 percent and the SLS 44 per cent of the ministerial portfolios.

Overall, the LDS as well as SKD have been the dominant political forces in the three cabinets which were in office during 1993–97. They held between 60 and 100 per cent of the cabinet posts and controlled between 41 and 54 seats of the 90 seats in the National Assembly. In 1993 and in 1996 the two parties agreed to form a grand coalition with the left-wing party (ZLSD), which included representatives from the former communist party. The ZLSD held 25 per cent of the cabinet seats and 15 seats in the National Assembly.

After the conservative SKD joined the 'Slovenian Spring Party Alliance' during the 1997 election, it was no longer willing to enter into a coalition with the liberal LDS. Thus, the LDS for the first time after independence formed a coalition with two parties which have not served in government previosuly, the Slovenian People's Party (SLS) and the Party of Pensioners (DESUS), the latter having split from the left-wing alliance (ZLSD) and having originally refused to participate in the government. Thus the fourth cabinet consisted of two major and one minor party. The LDS and the SLS held 94 per cent of the cabinet seats, while DESUS had only one minister without portfolio.

With the exception of the third government, which only lasted 12 months, Slovenian governments have been 'surplus' majority coalitions. The existence of these consensus-oriented cabinets has been one of the key factors for the successful way in which Slovenia introduced economic reforms and piloted negotiations with the European Union.

Over time, the negotiations on coalition agreements became gradually better organised; coalition agreements have become more sophisticated and the allocation of ministerial posts more systematic. Negotiations leading to coalition agreements have also taken longer. The first government was appointed by parliament in 38 days, the second in 50 days and the third in 97 days after the election. Coalition agreements include a detailed list of policy fields associated to the various ministries as well as formal arrangements about the procedures to be followed in cabinet.

Turnover of ministers

In Slovenia a total of 47 different persons have occupied a post in cabinet. The average duration of ministers from January 1993 to July 1999 was 25 months, six months more than the average duration of cabinets. Among the 15 ministries, six ministers held the same ministerial portfolio during 1993–97, among them the ministers of Finance, Education, Transport and Communications, Agriculture, and Health.

The first ministerial reshuffle occurred in 1994, after the ministers of Internal Affairs, of Justice, of Labour, Family and Social Affairs resigned; the Foreign Minister resigned in protest against the decision of the prime ministers to recruit new ministers for these posts.

A second major reshuffle occurred in January 1996 when the United List of Social Democrats (ZLSD) withdrew from the government. Prime Minister Drnovšek replaced only three (out of the four) former ZLSD ministers. Two of these came from his own party (Culture and Labour) and the third (Science and Technology) from the conservative coalition partner (SKD).

The fourth Slovenian government was constituted in February 1997 after the second general election. As the parties in government had changed, the prime minister replaced all but three ministers, the Finance Minister, the Education Minister and the Minister for Social Affairs and Labour. From 1997 to July 1999 the turnover was very low, with only four out of 19 ministers having changed, but these held important posts. The Defence Minister tendered his resignation. His successor had been in office for eight months only and resigned following an accusation of corruption. The Minister of the Interior lost a vote of no confidence in the National Assembly by a margin of 49 votes to 20 and resigned, while the Minister of Education and Sports resigned for personal reasons.

Compared with other Central European countries, Slovenian cabinets have been rather stable. This is due in part to the stability of the prime minister who was re-elected three times to the post. As chairman of the Liberal Party, he succeeded in making the party change its programme several times and this enabled the party to remain the largest in the cabinet. Moreover, the Finance Minister, Mitja Gaspari, remained in office from 1993 as the prime minister did. This was particularly important given the introduction of economic reforms and of the negotiations with the EU about the country's future membership.

Administrative characteristics

The Slovenian cabinet is the central policy-making institution of the republic. It consists of the prime minister, the cabinet ministers (including those without portfolio), and the secretary-general of the government. A representative of the secretariat of the government is in charge of legislative procedures, a senior staff member of the government Public Relations and

Media Office and some members of the President's Office may be invited to attend cabinet meetings.

The prime minister chairs the cabinet. In his absence, cabinet meetings are chaired by the deputy prime minister, except on matters relating to votes of confidence and to the appointment and dismissal of ministers. In the absence of a minister, the state secretary or another senior official from the department concerned represent the minister in cabinet, but without a vote. Only the prime minister and the ministers may vote. To be passed formally, decisions must be approved by an absolute majority of member of the cabinet, including the prime minister. Thus, the cabinet is a collegial body which supervises the work of all ministries.

Cabinet meetings are convened once a week, usually on Thursdays and there may be special meetings in case of urgency. The cabinet may also take decisions on certain issues by correspondence.

The work of cabinet is co-ordinated by the Prime Minister's Office (PMO). A secretary-general, who is responsible to the government and appointed and dismissed by the government, is in charge of the office. He or she has the same powers as ministers in their departments. The PMO staff provides predominantly administrative support to the government. As in the German *Bundeskanzleramt*, the PMO staff carries out expert-analytical, organisational, managerial and administrative-technical tasks. However, staff members do not give political advice to the prime minister.

The PMO is the size of a large ministry, which indicates the importance of its political role and the decision-making process of the Slovenian cabinet system. With 153 employed persons in 1997, it had more employees than the Ministry of Culture (53), the Ministry of Economic Affairs (57), the Ministry of Health (58), the Ministry of Justice (65) to name but a few. Only the finance ministry (317), the foreign ministry (381) and the ministry for interior and defence employed more persons than the PMO.

The cabinet meeting agenda is prepared by the PMO and is based on the proposals made by the prime minister and approved by the cabinet. That agenda proposal is circulated to cabinet members seven days before the meeting. Usually, only those issues which have been fully discussed among the ministries and the PMO are included on the agenda. However, the prime minister may add urgent issues to the proposed agenda.

Proposals for cabinet are drafted within the individual departments. When preparing the draft of a bill, departments are required to co-operate with the PMO and the government Office of Legislation. They must send drafts of proposals to the Office of Legislation at least five days before submitting these proposals to the PMO or at least fifteen days prior to a cabinet discussion of these proposals.

In submitting proposals, departments must fulfil a number of formal requirements. They must, for instance, state which aspects of the government programme a proposal is meant to cover and which ministries have been consulted for co-ordination. They must also give detailed information on how and when the proposal will be implemented as well as on the financial implications of the proposal. In addition to these formal requirements, each submission must include data documentation and an expert assessment of the proposal. Finally, the document must be signed by the minister concerned.

To prepare cabinet decisions, several inter-ministerial committees have been set up, most of them being ad hoc. However, with the fourth government coming to office in 1997, two permanent cabinet committees have been created – a committee on economic affairs and a committee on state and public affairs. These meet on Tuesdays, two days before the weekly cabinet meetings. They have between 12 and 15 members and include ministers, state secretaries and some top civil servants.

Draft proposals must be submitted to one of the two interministerial cabinet committees. Members of the committee are allowed to request changes. Once the committee agrees on the proposed draft, it is forwarded to the PMO, which schedules it for a cabinet meeting. In principle this should not be before the session of the cabinet of the following week.

All decisions taken in cabinet are recorded in the minutes which are distributed to cabinet members by the secretary-general of the government office, who also controls the implementation of cabinet decisions within ministries. On request of the prime minister, individual ministers may have to report on the implementation of policy decisions taken by the cabinet.

Cabinet decision-making

During the first years, Prime Minister Dronovšek adopted a decentralised approach to co-ordinate cabinet decision-making. This resulted in severe problems. As departments were relatively autonomous in terms of policy formulation, two many projects were launched and the govenrment was overloaded. First, the government was thus simultaneously confronted with decisions concerning the reform of the banking system, of public administration, of health care, of the social care system, of the educational system, with proposals for privatisation and the stabilisation of economy, with the need to building up its international relations, and with the integration of refuges from former Yugoslavia.

Second, the co-ordination of policy decisions in government became more difficult as a result of the changes of politically strong ministers.

Third, ministers had more political power in their respective departments but cared less for the decisions taken by their colleagues. Some co-ordination did take place in the committees, in which ministers participated collectively, however. Thus wage policy, educational policy, social policy, cultural questions, problems relating to transport, energy and environment, privatisation, refugees, and citizenship regulations led to prolonged discussions in committees. In the fields of economy, foreign affairs (mostly European) and national security, an ad hoc body set up by the prime minister met from time to time when it was necessary to speed up decision making.

Fourth, the size of the staff serving the government increased continuously. There were special advisers for foreign affairs, economy, public relations, national security, relations with parliament, for example. They advised the prime minister on issues with their purview of individual ministers, thereby weakening decentralisation to an extent.

After 1996, cabinet decision-making became more centralised. The new 'minimum winning' coalition stood for more programmatic homogeneity in the coalition. A de facto more consensus-orientated decision-making process developed. Political parties rather than individual ministers became the key actors. As a result, government administration and party politics became more intertwined. For example, negotiations on issues such as privatisation, pension reform, and pre-accession negotiations with the EU were extremely time consuming for the governing parties and the administration. Yet it was considered that these consensus-orientated negotiations were consistent with the strategy of 'open government' and coincided with popular demands.

Several decisions, which previously had been discussed in cabinet committees came on to the cabinet agenda, however. There was thus more 'space' for decisions which were not based on formal procedures and proper expert consultation. In several cases, ministers with wide expert knowledge in their own portfolio lost influence to 'political managers' among political parties and to government officials.

In June 2000, a new cabinet was elected by parliament with one vote of majority. Thus, after eight years of Dronovšek cabinets, the new Prime Minister, Andrerj Bajulk, formed a cabinet consisting of 16 ministries. The post of the deputy prime minister was given to the president of the Social Democrat Party of Slovenia (SDSS) who also held the position of Minister of Defence. Under the new leadership, the former administrative structure of cabinet changed significantly at the symbolic level. Prime Minister Bajuk allows, for instance, the president of the newly formed SLS and SKD Slovenian Peoples Party to participate in cabinet meetings. In addition, two committees were created to systematically prepare the cabinet sessions. Thus, cabinet decision-making became more efficient and more effective.

Part 2

The Balkans

9
Romania

J. Blondel and I. Penescu

Cabinet setting

Romanian developments since 1990

Democratic politics began rather uneasily in Romania. On 22 December 1989, Ceauşescu fled from Bucharest and on the very same day, the National Salvation Front (NSF) was set up, with Ion Iliescu as its chairman. On 26 December, Iliescu was appointed interim President of Romania and Petre Roman Prime Minister. Rapidly, the nature of the NSF changed from being an umbrella organisation to becoming a political party and indeed to becoming *the* dominant political party. Competitive elections were announced for May 1990 and these were expected to favour markedly the NSF, because it enjoyed manifest advantages and in particular could benefit from the resources of the state and from a commanding position in the media, while the opposition was very divided. The NSF seemed likely to perpetuate the communist system under another name, as was to occur in some of the states that emerged from the Soviet Union.

Iliescu was indeed popular, especially in the provinces, even if there were to be some doubts about the extent to which the massive 85 per cent of the votes which he received at the presidential election was truly fair. Meanwhile, the NSF obtained 65 per cent of the votes and 263 of the 385 seats in the lower house, with the party of the Hungarian minority party, the Hungarian Democratic Union of Romania (HDUR) coming second with 7 per cent of the votes;[1] the rest of the electors cast their ballots across a large number of parties.

As a result of the 1990 election, Romania had ceased to be a full single-party system but it appeared to be dominated by a 'charismatic', yet also rather ruthless leader supported by a dominant party. Indeed, the government began to embark in a policy of repression of dissent. Demonstrators who protested against what seemed to have been 'irregularities' in the election and who had occupied Bucharest University were forcefully dispersed by miners whom the president had called to defend the new regime against its opponents.

This mode of behaviour led to loud criticisms abroad. An effort was made to change the image, especially on the economic front. Prime Minister Roman announced privatisation measures but little was done in this respect. Indeed, the economic situation deteriorated in 1991 and unemployment and inflation soared. Demonstrations multiplied, in particular of miners, this time against the government. Having lost the support of Iliescu, Roman resigned in September 1991.

Meanwhile, parliament had adopted a new Constitution which established a semi-presidential system and retained the unitary character of the state. As a result, the Hungarian Party (Hungarian Democratic Union of Romania – HDUR) voted against the project in parliament. The Constitution was nonetheless approved by the people in December 1991 by 77 per cent of the votes.

Indeed, the fall of Roman corresponded to a move away from a 'hegemonic' party arrangement towards a pluralistic form of rule. In September 1991, Iliescu appointed Theodor Stolojan as prime minister. He was an economist who had been deputy minister of finance after the fall of Ceauşescu and who was widely regarded as a reformer. There was to be an era of 'national openness'; the government was indeed to be a 'small' coalition, including three small parties besides Iliescu's NSF.

Moreover, while the most important opposition parties were beginning to unite under the umbrella label of 'Democratic Convention' (and to win many larger cities at the local elections), divisions between Iliescu and Roman led to the break-up of the NSF. The Roman faction retained the original name while the Iliescu faction became the Democratic National Salvation Front (DNSF). Moreover, two nationalist parties emerged on the scene, 'Romania Mare' (Great Romania – PRM), led by Corneliu Vadim Tudor, and the Romanian National Unity Party (RNUP), led by Gheorghe Funar.

The Constitution stipulated that a presidential and a general election had to take place a year after the ratification of the basic law. The campaign of the summer of 1992 was more evenly balanced and the media coverage fairer than a year earlier. Support for Iliescu and his party declined. The outgoing president was forced to a second ballot, having obtained 47 per cent of the votes only at the first, while the candidate of the Democratic Convention, Emil Constantinescu, who was president of Bucharest University, had 31 per cent and the leader of the Romania National Party, Gheorghe Funar, 11 per cent; Iliescu did win the second ballot with 61 per cent of the votes against 39 per cent for Constantinescu. In parliament, the DNSF did come first, but with 28 per cent of the votes only and 117 seats out of 328; the conservative opposition obtained 20 per cent, Roman's NSF 10 per cent and the Hungarian minority party, the HDUR, 7 per cent.

As the Democratic Convention was unwilling to participate in the government alongside the DNSF, the president appointed another independent, also an economist, Nicolae Vacaroiu, to form the government. That prime minister remained in office for four years despite its minority support in parliament. The life of the Vacaroiu administrations was not without problems, however. The government sought and obtained, occasionally with difficulty, the support of other parties, especially small parties of the left. Thus the Socialist Labour Party (PSM) was also included in the formal coalition agreement signed in 1994. The two small nationalist parties were present in the government, the PNUR for almost two years, from late 1994 to the autumn of 1996, and the PRM for eleven months between January and November 1995. In a social context which was often tense, the parliamentary base of the government was never firm.

Support for the centre-right opposition increased in the population during the period, as was shown by the result of the local elections which took place in early 1996. At the presidential elections which took place in November of that year, Iliescu was defeated at the second ballot by Constantinescu, who obtained 54 per cent of the votes. At the general election held concurrently, the Democratic Convention took 122 of the 328 seats of the lower house while Iliescu's DNSF gained only 91. The centre-right thus came to power but it was to be defeated decisively four years later at the election of December 2000 after four years during which three prime ministers in succession had experienced major difficulties among their supporters while massive demonstrations and major strikes occurred repeatedly. The first prime minister of the centre-right, Victor Ciorbea, resigned after little more than a year in office in March 1998. His successor, Radu Vasile, a vice-president of the senate and secretary-general of the Christian Democrat Party, to which Ciorbea also belonged, was not able to control either the political or the economic situation. The Christian Democratic Party having theatened to leave the government, the president dismissed Vasile in December 1999. The prime minister first refused to resign on the grounds that the decision to dismiss was unconstitutional. He subsequently gave in but was also expelled from his party. The president appointed the governor of the National Bank, Mugur Isarescu, to be the new prime minister. Although the new government appeared to be more successful economically and politically more popular, the candidate of the centre-right at the presidential election came fourth at the first ballot of the 2000 presidential election. Iliescu was re-elected, but his direct competitor was Tudor of the nationalist Romania Mare.

Cabinets since 1991

Romania has had six prime ministers and ten cabinets between 1991 and 2000. These cabinets were

- P. Roman (NSF), April to September 1991[2]
- T. Stolojan (coalitior), DNSF and three small parties), October 1991 to November 1992

- N. Vacaroiu (1) (DNSF), included also six independents, November 1992 to August 1993
- N. Vacaroiu (2) (coalition), DNSF, PSDR, independents, August 1993 to August 1994
- N. Vacaroiu (3) (coalition), DNSF, PSDR, RNUP, independents, August 1994 to August 1996
- N. Vacaroiu (4) (coalition), DNSF, PSDR, independents, August to November 1996
- V. Ciorbea (Democ. Conv.), four-party coalition, December 1996 to March 1998
- R. Vasile (1) (Democ. Conv.), six-party coalition, April 1998 to November 1998
- R. Vasile (2) (Democ. Conv.), five-party coalition, November 1998 to December 1999
- M. Isarescu (Democ. Conv.), five-party coalition, December 1999 to December 2000

There has therefore been substantial cabinet instability in Romania, but also, except between late 1992 and late 1996, prime ministerial instability as well. The instability of Romanian cabinets and of the ministerial personnel has to be traced back to the dominant part played by Iliescu and of the party he controlled throughout the first half of the period. The configuration of the parties was very unbalanced in the early 1990s. Moreover, although the 1996 election suggested that Romania had some of the characteristics of a two-and-a-half party or of a two-coalition system, the system was in reality based on rather fragile arrangements on both right and left. The centre-right Democratic Convention has been a restive alliance of several parties rather than one party; the National Salvation Front, in its first dominant incarnation and even in its second, reduced format consisted in an amalgam of individuals and factions or in a confederal arrangement based on a substantial number of political 'chiefs'. Iliescu succeeded for a while to keep that combination together, but Roman's challenge broke the 'charm', so to speak, and Iliescu, helped successively by Stolojan and even more by Vacaroiu, had to manipulate parliament. Roman's decision to leave the National Salvation Front did result in the end of the period of the dominant party.

The size of the Romanian cabinet varied rather erratically from 18 to 24 members during the period. There were 21 ministers under Roman in 1991 and 19 ministers under Isarescu in 2000, the largest size being reached under Ciorbea and the first Vasile government, while the number of members of the Stolojan and Vacaroiu cabinets was intermediate. The very first Roman government, which was set up in December 1989, had 25 members, but it followed an executive of about twice that size. In 1988, the Romanian Council of Ministers had included, besides the prime minister, ten deputy prime ministers and 28 ministers, as well as seven chairmen of committees and 15 secretaries of state. Roman's government was much slimmer from the start, the many industrial ministries (14 in 1988) having been immediately abolished and the cabinet resembling therefore a Western cabinet. Indeed, Roman's government turned out to be smaller than several of the cabinets which came afterwards.

The ministerial posts in the 1999 Isarescu cabinet were deputy prime minister; deputy prime minister, Foreign Affairs; deputy prime minister, Justice; deputy prime minister, Health; Agriculture and Food; Culture; National Defence; Education; Finance; Industry and Trade; Interior; Labour and Social Protection; Local Public Administration; Public Works and Physical Planning; Youth and Sport; Transport; Water, Forestry and Environmental Protection; National Minorities.

There were deputy prime ministers in the first two governments of the post-communist period, but the practice had been abandoned with the Vacaroiu administration until it was revived in the 1999 Isarescu government. There was a minister without portfolio during the last few months of the Roman government, but the practice was not followed subsequently. Meanwhile, there were secretaries of state in various departments (in particular defence and finance) throughout much of the period, and some of the holders of these posts, but not all, graduated to full ministerial status afterwards. The administrations of Ciorbea and Vasile also appointed ministers 'delegate to the prime minister' in a number of fields (Europe, information, minorities). This practice was not continued by Isarescu in 1999.

Cabinet setting

The Constitution of 1991

As was noted earlier, parliament adopted at the end of 1991 a Constitution, the main purpose of which was to maintain the unitary character of the state. The Constitution also retained the republican character of Romania, despite efforts made by the exiled former king, Michael I, to see the question of the monarchy raised at a referendum. The matter appeared to have had little resonance in the population.

Structure of the executive

The Romanian Constitution established a semi-presidential form of government, in many ways imitated from the French model. The president enjoys several powers while the government needs the confidence of both chambers to remain in office. The president is elected by popular vote for a period of five years, renewable only once. There is provision for two ballots and as in France, if no candidate obtains half the valid votes at the first ballot, a second ballot takes place among the top two candidates. There is no vice-president.

The president selects the prime minister, but this must be from among parliamentarians. There is uncertainty as to whether the president has also the power to dismiss the prime minister, since the Constitution does not specify the matter. Thus Vasile refused for a few days to be dismissed in December 1999. The matter was solved pragmatically as the outgoing prime minister was prevailed upon to resign. The president is said to chair the Council of Ministers 'on matters of national interest with regard to foreign policy, the defence of the country, the maintenance of public order...' (Chapter 2, S. 6). In a similar vein, the president chairs the 'Supreme Council of National Defence'. The president may veto laws and ask for a second deliberation by parliament; above all the president can submit to referendums draft bills 'concerning the main problems of state policy' (same clause) and can dissolve parliament.

Meanwhile, the prime minister and the ministers are in charge of governmental policy, but the prime minister has a special position. The prime minister proposes the names of the ministers to the president for approval; the prime minister 'leads the government and coordinates the activities of ministers' (Chapter 3, S. 5). It is the prime minister who presents the programme of the government to the lower house.

The system remains ultimately parliamentary in that the cabinet must obtain the confidence of parliament within five days of the appointment of the prime minister. However, as over the position of the president and of the prime minister, there are provisions in the Romanian Constitution with respect to the relationship between government and parliament which directly originate from the French 1958 Constitution. First, the document specifies limitatively, as does the French document, the fields which are to be covered by a an act of parliament. Second, a piece of legislation linked to a vote of confidence is deemed to be passed, also as in the French case, if the lower house does not adopt a motion of censure. To pass, a motion of censure must be supported by an absolute majority of the members of the assembly. The system is thus both partly parliamentary and partly semi-presidential; it is also tilted in favour of the executive in general and of the prime minister in particular. The existence of restrictive provisions relating to the power of parliament probably accounts to an extent for the relative longevity of the Vacaroiu prime ministership.

Cabinet life

Political characteristics

Formation of cabinets

The duration of the process of formation of cabinets has been short. There never seems to have been major difficulties in the selection of prime ministers and of the members of the cabinet.

The role of the President in selecting prime ministers

This state of affairs seems largely due to the major part which the president, whether Iliescu or Constantinescu, has played in the selection of the prime ministers. The choices of Roman, Stolojan and Vacaroiu have been Iliescu's. As a matter of fact, Vacaroiu was non-party and he was selected to find a solution to the problem posed by the result of the 1992 election at which Iliescu's party non longer had a majority. The task which Iliescu gave him was therefore to attract the support of various political groups. He succeeded in doing so and operated a complex game during the following four years.

Constatinescu was clearly less fortunate in his choice of prime ministers, since he had to select successively three different persons to the post in as many years. In all three cases, the choice was his, but only in the third case, that of the appointment of Isarescu, who was governor of the National Bank, was the decision of the president less constrained by party intervention.

The role of parties in cabinet formation and development

After the November 1996 election and the coming to power of the Democratic Convention, parties have come to play a significant part in the selection of the prime minister. Both Ciorbea and Vasile were key persons in the largest party of that 'confederation', the Christian Democrat Party. They were selected by President Constantinescu for that reason. Only the major economic difficulties of the country combined with the proximity of the election succeeded in giving once more to the president a major part in the selection of prime minister Isarescu in 1999.

In the course of the 1990s, Romania had, as mentioned previously, governments wholly or principally composed of members of the party of Iliescu (NSF, then DNSF, then PSDR) and governments composed of members of the Democratic Convention. Only two cabinets, that of Roman in 1991 and the first of Vacaroiu, were wholly of one party. The subsequent cabinets under Iliescu were coalitions. The first Vacaroiu cabinet was single-party but was a minority cabinet and it was followed by a coalition after a few months. All of the centre-right cabinets which came to office after the 1996 election were coalitions, and uneasy coalitions at that. Thus the fluidity of the party system had a direct effect on the stability of coalitions. The role of parties in the Romanian government thus remains somewhat limited, as individuals in the parties or small groupings in the larger parties or alliances are able to play a major part in either keeping governments in office or in toppling prime ministers.

Turnover of ministers

The rate of ministerial turnover has been high in Romania since the end of communism, paralleling in a sense the high turnover of cabinets – 116 different persons occupied cabinet positions between April 1991 and

December 1999 (119 if new ministers in the Isarescu cabinet of December 1999 are taken into account). Allowing for variations in the size of cabinets during the period, the average duration of the ministers who served in these cabinets was 1.32 years only, by no means an outstanding performance.

There were few variations over time in the rate of turnover of ministers. The 'culture of the reshuffle' has been widespread, although it was very slightly more prevalent when Iliescu was in office than afterwards as the average duration of ministers was 1.3 years under his presidency against 1.4 years afterwards. The only cabinets that were not reshuffled were those of Roman of April 1991, which lasted six months, of Stolojan, which lasted a year, of the fourth Vacaroiu government, which lasted three months, and of the second Vasile government, which lasted 18 months. The others were more or less substantially reshuffled, particularly those of Vacaroiu, who appointed four new ministers in 1993 and in 1994, five in 1995 and nine in 1996, and of Ciorbea, who appointed ten new ministers between December 1997 and March 1998. It may be that the propensity to reshuffle has started to diminish. The conservative governments have been more remarkable by changes of prime ministers than by changes of ministers, at least since Vasile came to office.

The end of cabinets

Only three cabinets out of the ten which had ended by 2000 'naturally', so to speak, in all three cases because an election had taken place. These were the Stolojan government in 1992, the fourth Vacaroiu government in November 1996 and the Isarescu government in 2000. Roman resigned in September 1991 because of strong disagreements with Iliescu; two of the Vacaroiu cabinets ended in order to allow new parties in while a third ended because one party, the right-wing RNUP, left the government. The Ciorbea and second Vasile cabinets ended because the prime minister had become unacceptable to one or more of the parties in the Democratic Convention coalition, while the first Vasile cabinet ended because one small party decided to leave the government. Thus government crises were more due to the search for a stable majority under Iliescu, especially after 1992, and to the apparent inability of Christian Democrats and Social Democrats to find a satisfactory prime ministerial leader under Contantinescu.

Administrative characteristics

The Romanian cabinet meets on Thursdays. Meetings were long under Ciorbea and in the first Vasile government; they were reduced to three hours in the second Vasile government. Meetings are in practice chaired by the prime minister, although the Constitution, stated that the president chairs the meeting on matters relating broadly speaking to foreign affairs and defence. The Constitution also adds that president may do so on other matters on the request of the prime minister. In practice, these provisions are not implemented as at least President Constantinescu did not attend. Attendance at the meetings includes, beyond the ministers, those state secretaries who are designated as 'members of the government', the government secretary-general, advisers to the prime minister and officials of the General Secretariat who record the deliberations. Other secretaries of state may attend meetings in place of the minister, but they do not have the right to vote.

Meetings of the cabinet are prepared by the secretary general of the cabinet who draws up the agenda, which has to be approved by the prime minister, although, in practice, the agenda tends to be communicated to the prime minister only shortly (i.e. two days) before the meeting. To be included, items must be communicated to the secretary-general one week in advance. The agenda is finalised on Mondays at a meeting attended by several officials and chaired by the government secretary-general. Additions to the distributed agenda are frequent. Under Ciorbea, agendas could include as many as sixty items. Before being included, these items must have gone through an elaborate procedure, which was codified in a document issued in December 1997. That document specifies, for example, the ministries which need to be consulted (Finance, Justice, Council for Reform). In the case of draft legislation, the Directorate for Analysis and Legal Advice of the General Secretariat must examine the bill and formulate an opinion on the text relating to its intrinsic legal qualities and its compatibility with the governmental programme in general.

The secretariat of the government is thus entrusted with important tasks of co-ordination. Alongside the secretariat, the prime minister has at his disposal his cabinet, a special directorate and a group of counsellors, all coming together under the general label of chancellery of the prime minister, that is to say the Prime Minister's Office. There are also a host of other institutions which are attached to the 'centre of government', for instance the Department of Public Information, the office of the government Spokesman for Relations with the Press and the Department of Local Public Administration. Overall, however, it does not seem that the Romanian government is particularly well co-ordinated. There is fragmentation resulting from the proliferation of central offices and indeed competition between these various offices. This state of affairs is further complicated by the fact that some ministers are placed in charge of these central offices and these offices become semi-independent ministries rather than a genuine part of the 'centre of government'.

There are no formally constituted cabinet committees of the Romanian government but there are a large number of 'inter-ministerial' committees headed by a secretary of state. These committees do not appear to be very efficient, however, and more often than not interministerial communication is nominal rather than real. The government is aware of these problems and an emphasis is placed on improving interministerial communication and consultation.

Cabinet decision-making

President and prime minister

As mentioned previously, the Constitution of 1991 specifies that the prime minister 'shall lead the government, coordinate the activities of ministers ...' (Chapter 3, S. 5), after having stipulated (Chapter 3, S. 1) that 'the government ensures – at a national level, under the control of the Parliament and under the Constitutional provisions – the setting forth and implementation of home and foreign policy, in accordance with its governmental programme'. Thus the president's constitutional role in policy making is limited, while that of the prime minister is substantial. In practice, however, the first two presidents of post-communist Romania have exercised considerable influence, although to a different extent and for different reasons.

Iliescu did interfere markedly in the affairs of the state, hence the difficulties he had with Roman who resigned because he disagreed with the president over policy. The appointment of Vacaroiu after the 1992 election was aimed at ensuring the continued involvement of the head of state in political affairs, because Vacaroiu was a 'technical' prime minister whose main role was to 'manage' his ministerial colleagues as well as parliament, rather in the way a British prime minister of the second half of the eighteenth century was appointed by the king to manage parliament. Constantinescu has acted differently, partly because the parties of the centre-right coalition were more adamant and able to intervene but, over time, he has been prepared (or obliged) to become more involved in policy development – the apparent failures of the coalition indicated that there was an urgent need for improvement, especially in the light of the then coming general election at the end of 2000. In the case of both presidents, however, as in the case of the semi-presidential French Fifth Republic, on which the Romanian arrangements were modelled, the intervention of the head of state was based on informal authority over prime minister and government, not on formal powers.

The prime minister is formally the co-ordinator of governmental action, and he proposes the names of the members of the government to the president; he also proposes their dismissal (Chapter 2, S. 6). However, as mentioned previously, post-communist prime ministers have been relatively weak, either, under Iliescu, because, with the exception of Roman, they were effectively 'men of the president' or, under Constantinescu, because they were, except for Isarescu, markedly dependent on the way they were viewed by the leadership of the parties of the coalition.

The role of the cabinet

The cabinet appears to play a substantial part in decision-making and this has been so especially under Ciorbea and Vasile, given the level of conflict characterising the conservative coalition. Indeed, it seems that there is over-centralisation of power in the government as a whole, at any rate formally, if not always informally, given the relatively limited co-ordinating capacity of the agencies which work broadly under the aegis of the prime minister. This results in overload at the centre and relatively limited efficiency overall. Yet this has not led to the setting up of an inner cabinet which might be in a position to settle difficulties among ministers. In the early 1990s, there was an 'executive bureau' comprising the prime minister, the ministers of state and the ministers of Justice, Defence and Interior, but this structure disappeared subsequently only to be re-established by Isarescu, this time under the name of 'executive council'. At least within the centre-right coalition, the representatives of the various parties in the government have been too strong, at any rate under Ciorbea and Vasile, to be prepared to yield regularly either to the prime minister or to a small inner group.

Yet, despite the conflicts which have characterised Romanian cabinets, decisions appear to be taken in the end consensually if not necessarily amicably. Votes are not taken, nor does the prime minister have to exercise his right of veto. The need to live together has made it impossible for the various parties to go beyond a demand for the resignation of the prime minister, a demand which has been granted by the president, out of necessity, in two occasions. Romanian cabinets have therefore some way to go before they become truly efficient and succeed in finding an adequate equilibrium between the overall role of the cabinet and the prerogatives of individual ministers.

Notes

1   Before 1991, the legislature was the National Assembly. The Constitution adopted in November 1991 instituted a two-chamber parliament, with a Chamber of Deputies and a Senate.
2   A Roman cabinet was set up for the first time in December 1989, just after the fall of Ceaușescu, but the first multiparty general election took place in May 1991.

10
Moldova

J. Blondel and S. Matteucci

Cabinet setting

Moldovan developments since 1990

In 1998, the general election resulted in an upset whereby the Communist party became the largest in the country. This followed an earlier upset at the presidential election of November 1996 when the first president of Moldova since independence, Mircea Snegur, was defeated at the second ballot by Petru Lucinschi, hitherto speaker of parliament and first secretary of the Communist Party since November 1989. Moldova had come to have a competitive system, but parties were volatile and coalitions difficult to build until, in February 2001, the communist party won an absolute majority of seats in Parliament; its leader, Vladimir Voronine, was elected President of the country by Parliament in April 2001.

Moldova declared itself independent from the Soviet Union on 27 August 1991, a few days after the coup by which the Old Guard attempted to stop Gorbachev's reforms, although a number of moves in the direction of Moldovan statehood had taken place earlier. These moves had been initiated partially by Lucinschi and even more by Snegur, then chairman of the Supreme Soviet of Moldova. In particular, the issue of language and alphabet had been resolved in favour of the Moldovan language (in effect Romanian) and of the Latin script as early as August 1989, following the creation of the pro-Romanian Popular Front of Moldova (PFM) in May 1989. Other moves occurred after the February 1990 semi-competitive elections for the Supreme Soviet at which the PFM took a large number of seats. In the course of the following three months, a tricolour flag, which was a modified version of the Romanian flag, was adopted; sovereignty was declared and the communist government of Petr Paskar was defeated by a vote of censure. He was replaced by Mircea Druc, who belonged to the Popular Front. Finally, in September 1990, Snegur was appointed as president of Moldova by the Supreme Soviet, which was to call itself parliament (*Sfatul Tarii*) in the subsequent May.

Meanwhile, the new republic (in which about two-thirds of the population are ethnic Moldovans) had come to be confronted with the issue of secession, both in the Gagauz area, in the south-west, mainly populated by orthodox Christians of Turkish origin, and in the 'Transdniestr Republic', along the left bank of the Dnestr river (Nistru in Romanian), mainly populated by Russians and Ukrainians. This last problem was to be the key issue of Moldovan politics, above the issue of reunion with Romania and even above the extremely serious economic difficulties faced by the country. Transdniestr had meant war; it had meant subsequently uneasy peace only. The area was to continue to be ruled by a president and a government that did not recognise that they were part of Moldova.

President Snegur consolidated his position. He was popularly re-elected unopposed – obtaining 98 per cent of the votes – in December 1991. He did have some difficulties in parliament, however. His first prime minister, Mircea Druc, was defeated by a vote of no-confidence in May 1991; his second, Valeriu Muravshi, who was regarded as more moderate on the issue of links with Romania, resigned little over a year later, in June 1992. It took two months for his successor, Andrei Sangeli, to form a new coalition but that prime minister was to remain in office for four years.

The Moldovan parliament also experienced difficulties in adopting a constitution, largely because of lack of agreement about the extent of autonomy to be given to the Gagauz area and to Transdniestr. By October 1993, with an electoral law having been passed, parliament was persuaded to dissolve itself in order to enable the first truly competitive election to be held. The Constitution was adopted by the new parliament in July 1994, after the people had confirmed by a referendum held in March of that year its desire to see the continued independence of Moldova from Romania.

The February 1994 general election resulted in a victory for the Agrarian Democratic Party (ADP) which Petru Lucinschi led at the time and which obtained 43 per cent of the votes and 56 of the 104 seats of the parliament, which had been reduced from the 366 seats that it had had previously both under communist and post-communist rule. The Constitution adopted in mid-1994 stated that parliament would have 101 seats. The Socialist Party (formerly Communist Party of Moldova), first banned but subsequently re-legalised, came second with 22 per cent and 28 seats; the Peasant and Intellectual Bloc obtained 9 per cent of the votes and 11 seats; but the pro-unification Popular Front of Moldova, renamed Christian Democratic Popular Front (CDPF), obtained only 8 per cent of the votes and 9 seats. Lucinschi became speaker of the new parliament.

The Sangeli government was maintained by Snegur after the election, based as it was primarily on the ADP, of which President Snegur was then one of the leaders. The ADP increased in strength again at the local elections of April 1995, when it obtained 62 per cent of the votes. This was to be the peak of the party's support, a peak from which it fell rapidly to almost complete disintegration. The issues of language and unification with Romania were to prove intractable for the ADP. The party was strongly in favour of continued independence; indeed, it was even lukewarm about the formal recognition that Moldovan was the same language as Romanian (which it is).

This was regarded by Snegur as too soft a line on links with Romania. He left the Agrarian ADP and formed his own party, the Party of Revival and Accord of Moldova (PRAM), taking with him 11 members of parliament. Snegur seemed to become increasingly authoritarian. He was forced to re-instate in early 1996 the Minister of Defence whom he had summarily dismissed, as the Constitutional Court judged his action to have been illegal. Snegur also declared himself in favour of the presidential system (which had been introduced in Georgia in 1994 after parliamentarism had been pre-viously in force) and announced that he would attempt to establish that system if he were re-elected. Perhaps because of this and other somewhat unorthodox moves, Snegur was defeated at the presidential election of November 1996. He obtained 39 per cent of the votes at the first ballot against Lucinschi's 28 per cent, and lost the second round by a 54–46 per cent margin. With the end of Snegur's tenure that of the Sangeli government also came to an end.

The new president chose a non-party economist, personally devoted to him, Ion Ciubuc, to form the government in January 1997. Almost imme-diately, however, president, prime minister and government entered in conflict with parliament. To attempt to overcome these difficulties, a new party, the Movement for a Democratic and Prosperous Moldova (MDPM), headed by the speaker of parliament, Dimitru Diakov, was set up to support the president, but this had little effect. Indeed, with the general election of March 1998, Moldova came to have a four-party system. While the Agrarian ADP was wiped out, the Moldovan Communist Party (MPC) became the largest party with 30 per cent of the votes and 40 members of parliament. It was followed by Snegur's PRAM associated with the Democratic Conven-tion of Moldova (DCM) which obtained 19 per cent of the votes and 26 seats, by Lucinschi' MDPM which gained 18 per cent and 24 seats and by the Christian Democrat Popular Front (CDPF), which obtained 9 per cent and 11 seats. Ciubuc was re-appointed as prime minister with the task of forming a government based on the three non-communist parties of the parliament and which formed an 'anti-communist' alliance known as the Alliance for Democracy and Reforms. But that cabinet lasted under one year – the prime minister resigned in February 1999 in a tense social climate. Meanwhile, Petru Lucinschi, as Snegur before him, was endeavouring to introduce the presidential system by referendum, but the electors rejected the proposal in the summer of that year. He had earlier experienced great difficulty in finding a successor to Ciubuc and, when this successor, Ion Sturza, was found, his government lasted under one year. It then took a further six weeks for a new cabinet, headed by Dumitru Draghis, who had been deputy minister of Economy and Reform in the Sturza government, to be constituted in December 1999. That government marked the return of the Communist Party to office, in coalition with the Christian Democrats; the party gained full control in February 2001.

Cabinets since 1990

Moldova has had five prime ministers and seven cabinets between 1991, when the country became independent, and 2000. These were

- V. Muravshi (Pop. Front of Moldova), May 1991 to June 1992
- A. Sangeli (1) (ADP),[1] June 1992 to April 1994
- A. Sangeli (2) (ADP), April 1994 to November 1996
- I. Ciubuc (1) (non-party), January 1997 to March 1998
- I. Ciubuc (2) three-party coalition, April 1998 to February 1999
- I. Sturza same coalition, February to November 1999
- D. Braghis two-party coalition,[2] December 1999 to February 2001.

Cabinets were stable under Snegur and unstable under Lucinschi. Sangeli remained prime minister before and after the parliamentary election of 1994 largely because the Agrarian ADP (then led by Lucinschi) had obtained an absolute majority of seats at that election. Lucinschi was faced with a more fractionalised party system, both before – since Snegur and himself had by then created parties of their own – and after the 1998 election. The effect on the duration of cabinets was marked.

The size of the Moldovan cabinet has varied somewhat from one prime minister to another. The Muravshi cabinet was the smallest, with 19 members, while the Sangeli cabinet was the largest, its membership having oscillated between 26 members at the start, 23 members in 1995 and 25 members when it resigned. Subsequent governments were smaller. The 1999 Sturza government had 20 members and the Braghis government 21. The nature of the ministerial departments in the Moldovan cabinet has been the same as in Western cabinets since the country became independent. Posts have practically never been given to women, at least before 1999.

The ministerial posts in the 1999 Braghis cabinet were three deputy prime ministers, one of whom was officially in charge of the economy and reforms; Minister of the Cabinet; Minister of State; Foreign Affairs; Defence; Finance; Justice; Internal Affairs; National Security; Labour; Public Utilities, Territorial Development, and Construction; Transport and Communications; Agriculture; Culture; Education; Environmental Protection; Health; Industry and Trade.

There were ministers in charge of foreign economic affairs and of privatisations in the Sangeli government. These posts have not re-appeared subsequently.

There have always been several deputy prime ministers in Moldovan cabinets. This practice follows the Soviet tradition according to which the prime minister and the deputy prime ministers formed a kind of inner cabinet. In the Sangeli cabinet, deputy prime ministers were not officially assigned a particular area of jurisdiction. In the Muravshi and the Ciubuc cabinets, on the contrary, they seem to have been 'super-ministers' with a broad competence; in the Sturza and Braghis cabinets, this appears to be the case for one of the deputy prime ministers only. All the cabinets from that of Sangeli onwards have also had one minister of state, who is not to be regarded as a second rank minister but as a minister without portfolio. The Sangeli government also included for a while (in 1995) some deputy ministers. Such posts have not been mentioned in the governmental list either before or since, but there have been 'chairmen of state departments'.

The constitution of 1994

Parliament adopted a Constitution for the country in 1994 only but despite the time it took to pass it, the basic law did not provide a solution to the problem posed by the secession of Gagauz and of Transdniestr. The text is silent on the subject of the real powers to be given to decentralised authorities. The Constitution states that Moldova is unitary (Article 1) and that the territory is 'inalienable' (Article 3); all that is subsequently said is, first, that 'the territory of the Republic of Moldova is divided into regions, towns and communities' (Article 110) and, second, that 'the places on the left bank of the Nistru [Dniestr] river, as well as certain other places in the South of the Republic of Moldova, may be granted special forms of autonomy according to special statutory provisions of organic law' (Article 111).

The structure of the executive

The Moldovan Constitution establishes a parliamentary system with only a few traces of semi-presidentialism, although the reality has been somewhat different under the first two presidents. President Snegur has had enough prestige and authority to be highly influential; President Lucinschi has intervened frequently and has indeed wanted to increase the formal powers of the presidency on the grounds that parliamentarism did not function well. He thus asked the people to vote on the matter by way of referendum in the spring of 1999, but, while there was a majority in favour, the turnout was too low for the result to be valid.

In institutional terms, Moldovan arrangements are intermediate between the solutions adopted in Bulgaria and in Romania. Although the document is in some respects closely modelled on the Romanian basic law, it gives the president in particular and the executive in general fewer powers than their equivalents received in Romania. Moldovan presidents are to be elected by popular vote for a period of four years, but, in 2001, Parliament elected the President. The Constitution does not enter into the mechanism of the election but the electoral law states that there shall be two ballots if no candidate obtains half the valid votes at the first ballot. A second ballot then takes place among the top two candidates. There is no vice-president.

The president selects the prime minister, chairs the Council of Ministers when questions of foreign policy, defence or public order are being discussed and the National Defence Council. A semi-presidential element is found in the fact that the president can 'request the people to express in a referendum their wish concerning problems of national interest', a power which was used by Lucinschi in 1999, to little effect in practice (Article 86 (2)). However, the president can dissolve parliament only if parliament has not expressed its confidence in a new government within 60 days since a first request for such a vote had been made or if two requests have been rejected (Article 83 (1)). That clause had not been used by 1999 by either of the two presidents of Moldova.

The government is responsible for the policy of the state, but the prime minister has a special part to play in this respect. First, the prime minister proposes the names of the ministers to the president for approval and indeed for their dismissal; the prime minister also leads the government and co-ordinates the activities of ministers, although he must '[show] respect to [their] functions' (Article 97 (1)). Second, the prime minister 'leads the government and co-ordinates the activities of ministers'. It is the prime minister who presents the programme of the government to parliament, a programme which must be followed by the government subsequently (Article 92 (2)).

The system is therefore fundamentally parliamentary. Indeed, not only does the government have to present a programme which parliament must approve, but the government is said to operate 'under the control of [parliament] and its commissions' (Article 100 (1)). Moreover, unlike the Romanian and French constitutions, the Moldovan text does not restrict the use of the question of confidence, which is 'adopted with a majority of votes'. There is no need for an absolute majority to overthrow a government. While the powers of the president are therefore not negligible, those of parliament are not subjected to the limitations which are introduced in countries where those who draft the Constitution fear that the government might be weak or unstable.

Cabinet life

Political characteristics

Formation of cabinets

The duration of the process of formation of cabinets has been long, except when Snegur re-nominated Sangeli after the 1994 election – an election at which the president's party had obtained a majority of seats. In the other cases, complex negotiations have taken place to form viable cabinets and two months have typically elapsed before cabinets have been constituted and even three months did elapse in 1998 in the case of the second Ciubuc cabinet.

The role of the president

The fact that the process of governmental selection was protracted under President Lucinschi was no accident. He was adamant to establish his right to select prime ministers at will in a context in which his own party was weak and he could not therefore count on substantial support in parliament. Thus the tactic of the president failed but the consequence was that the process of prime ministerial selection and of government nomination was long in all four cases in which Lucinschi was involved in attempting to build the government. Admittedly, the Constitution does give the president the right to select the prime minister, but, while Snegur did so without difficulty, as the parties were not solidified during the first legislature and as his Agrarian party obtained the absolute majority of seats during the second, his successor was not in the same fortunate position, as we noted. Yet President Lucinschi endeavoured to appoint the prime ministers he wanted. This obstinacy of the second president of Moldova has no doubt contributed to the increased instability of governments since that president was appointed and possibly to the subsequent victory of the Communist party.

Presidents have also played a part in the life of cabinets once they have been formed. Both Snegur and Lucinschi have interfered with appointments in the cabinet. As we noted, Snegur was forced to reinstate a Minister of Defence whom he had dismissed; Lucinschi is known to have been fully involved in the dismissal of three ministers. Lucinschi's first prime minister, Ion Ciubuc, did try to disengage himself from presidential pressure, but failed.

The role of parties in cabinet formation and development

During the 1990s, Moldovan governments became more political, less dependent on the head of state and more party-based. Muravschi's cabinet was still in the 'Soviet' mould. Its members were former communists who were also supporters of the Popular Front, that organisation being more in the nature of a grouping of relatively like-minded people keen on their 'Romanian' ethnicity than in that of a political party. Sangeli's cabinet was more political but retained a technical character and was largely dependent on the president in a context in which the legislature did not, at least until the very end, display marked independence from that president. As a matter of fact, parties were still somewhat inchoate. The president either could manipulate them or indeed had a majority in parliament. There was therefore only a relatively limited role of parties during the Sangeli government.

Parties and party leaders started to play a large part with the accession of Lucinschi to the presidency. The formation of the three-party coalition under Ciubuc implied both negotiations within each party and among the three parties and the president. These negotiations related both to the programme and to the composition of the government. Programmatic demands were indeed strongly made, probably because of the limited development of parties at the regional and local levels. The aim was to attract the attention of potential electors. These negotiations, which took place under the aegis of the Alliance for Democracy and Reform (ADR) to which the three non-communist parties belonged, led to a written agreement, although this agreement was not fully respected.

Negotiations relating to the composition of the Ciubuc cabinet resulted in an accord which stipulated that that composition should reflect the relative strength of the parties in parliament. The principle was therefore that the DCM (Democratic Convention of Moldova) of former President Snegur and the MDPM of President Lucinschi were to have twice as many seats each as the Party of Democratic Forces (PDF). Party leaders did not join the cabinet. Some party leaders held the chairmanship of parliamentary committees, on the grounds that these committees can be valuable instruments of pressure on the cabinet.

Indeed, these outside pressures on the government were such that the Christian Democratic Popular Front (CDPF) decided not to join the Sturza government but to support the government without participating in it. The party remained in the ADR coalition but stated that its members would vote only for those proposals which they thought consistent with the general principles of the 'clean hands' programme which had been one of the main planks of the 1998 general election campaign. Similar developments took place in the context of the subsequent government.

Turnover of ministers

Only Sangeli cabinets lasted for a substantial period. The others lasted a year or less. A corresponding contrast can be found in the rate of turnover of ministers. Overall, 96 different persons occupied a position in Moldovan cabinets since independence. If one excludes the Braghis cabinet of late 1999 (which included 13 new ministers), the average duration of ministers was slightly over two years (2.15 years). However, while the average duration of ministers in the Sangeli cabinet was 2.65 years, that of the members of the subsequent cabinets (again excluding the Braghis cabinet) fell to 1.43 years. Despite the fact that half of the Sangeli cabinet was replaced after the 1994 election, but also despite the fact that the Sturza cabinet only had five ministers who did not belong to the second Ciubuc cabinet, the turnover of ministers almost doubled under President Lucinschi from what it was under President Snegur. The prime minister and eight other ministers remained in office for the full four and a half years of the Sangeli government; a further ten ministers were in office from early 1994 (when the new parliament met) to the end of 1996; and all of these remained in the same post while in government. By contrast, only two ministers remained in the same post from 1997 to the end of 1999 (and only one continued in the Braghis government into the year 2000) while a third minister remained in the cabinet from 1997 to 2000, but not in the same post. Marked cabinet and ministerial instability thus characterised the second Moldovan presidency.

The end of cabinets

The end of the Muravshi cabinet can be regarded as constituting the last stage of the transition and as opening the way to at least an embryonic parliamentary system. The end of both Sangeli cabinets was normal, since the first ended when the general election was called and the second when the new president was elected. The end of the first Ciubuc cabinet was also normal since it coincided with the election of a new parliament. From early 1999 onwards, resignations of cabinets did become 'abnormal', however. The second Ciubuc cabinet resigned in February 1999, ostensibly because of the tense social situation which was exploited by the largest party, the Communist Party, then in opposition, but also for three other reasons. First, from outside the government, the leader of the Party of Democratic Forces, a party which was in the coalition, attacked Lucinschi's MMPD on the grounds that that party had obtained funds in exchange for the delivery of favours. Second, relations between the prime minister and the deputy prime minister in charge of the economy, Ion Sturza, who was perceived as a rival candidate for the prime ministership – which was indeed to be the case – were difficult. Third, relations between the prime minister and the president were also strained. It has been claimed that the president forced the prime minister to leave office. Yet the new prime minister did not benefit long from having wrenched the office from Ciubuk. He had to resign after less than a year as his cabinet had lost support from a number of deputies belonging originally to the government parties.

Administrative characteristics

According to the 'law on government' revised in September 1997, the cabinet has to meet 'not less than once per trimester'; in fact the Sturza cabinet met every two weeks. Except when matters of foreign affairs and defence are discussed, as we noted, the cabinet is chaired by the prime minister or, in his absence, by the (first) deputy prime minister. Meetings are held in public.

There are deputy ministers or secretaries of state (of which Braghis was one before becoming prime minister). These have the power to sign documents when the relevant minister is absent. There has never been a minister for minorities, but each party include minority representation among their members. An ethnic Bulgarian was nominated once for a ministerial post, but it was subsequently discovered that this candidate had applied for

Russian citizenship and he was therefore disqualified. However, there is a Department for Ethnic Minorities and Languages, whose director takes part in cabinet meetings.

The structure of cabinet support appears to be still rather rudimentary. Although there are cabinet committees, all of them are ad hoc. There is staff around the cabinet, but the notion of a cabinet office is not clearly delineated. Admittedly, there is a presidential and a prime ministerial staff, each of which is about 80 strong, but the prime ministerial staff is in the nature of a 'chancellery'. It is headed by a member of the cabinet, the Minister of State, and appears to deal primarily with the registration of documents and with protocol matters. Cuts have indeed been made in the size of the office under Prime Minister Sturza in order to render the central government more efficient.

Cabinet decision-making

The cabinet is a collective organ which is expected to take its decision jointly. This seems actually to be the case as ministers try to adopt a common position by consensus. As noted previously, the Moldovan cabinet does not appear to overshadowed by committees, since these are all ad hoc. However, there are other signs which suggest that the role of the cabinet as such may not be truly significant. To begin with, meetings of the cabinet do not appear to be as frequent as elsewhere. Only since the Sturza government do they appear to take place at least every two weeks. Moreover, as has already been suggested in relation to both Snegur and Lucinschi, the role of the president has consistently been significant. The prime minister has also exercised influence. Under Lucinschi in particular, that influence has resulted from the fact that the prime minister is closer to the political parties of the majority and to parliamentarians in general. Thus, on some issues, leaders of the political parties are consulted by the prime minister. This was for instance the case in relation to the privatisation of the Moldavan telecommunication organisation, Moldtelecom. This suggests, on the one hand, that party leaders outside the cabinet but also that some ministers are involved in the decisions taken in the name of the cabinet and, on the other hand, that the prime minister does at least occasionally play a substantial part independently from the president.

The characteristics of Moldovan cabinet life and decision making are thus clearly not fully consolidated. The role of the president is especially not truly delineated and it is unquestionably the case that the second president has been attempting almost continuously to strengthen his position. It is therefore difficult to say whether Moldova is or not, in practice, semi-presidential. Nor is the role of the cabinet as yet satisfactorily defined. While some ministers may occasionally be influential, there does not appear to be a full recognition of the need to give the cabinet a real position in the decision-making process.

There is another side to the picture, however. By and large, the relationship between the executive and the legislature have gradually developed in the direction of a kind of partnership, even if that relationship is at times rather strained. A multiparty system does exist, although it would gain by being simpler and less prone to fractionalisation. The government was based on party coalitions and alternance has taken place during the 1990s. These are positive elements in the political life of a country whose economy is weak and is seemingly condemned to remain weak in the context of the unresolved and apparently insoluble question of Transdniestr.

However, after the elections of 2001, at which the Communist party obtained an absolute majority and as a result of which a communist government was elected, the future of Moldova became highly uncertain. The country seemed to be moving back to a close link with Russia and Ukraine and abandoning its earlier dispositions to become part of the truly pluralistic nations of Eastern Europe.

Acknowledgement

The authors warmly thank Igor Munteanu of the Viitorul Foundation in Chisinau for the major help which he gave.

Notes

1   There were also some independents in these cabinets.
2   The Braghis government has been described as being 'technical' with Communist Party and Christian Democratic Party support. In practice, however, the ministers have been vetted by and indeed belong to these parties.

11
Bulgaria

J. Blondel and S.A. Andreev

Cabinet setting

Bulgarian developments since 1990

To begin with, the change from communist rule took place smoothly in Bulgaria and the transition was even described as a 'gentle revolution'. The veteran communist leader, Todor Zhivkov, in power since 1954 as party chief and since 1971 as president of the republic, was forced to resign when a majority of the members of the Party Presidium led by Petar Mladenov, Foreign Minister since 1971, turned against him in November 1989. Mladenov was then appointed to replace Zhivkov in both offices.

Mladenov was soon confronted with mass demonstrations demanding the end of the single-party system and free elections. He responded at first by appointing as prime minister Andrey Lukanov, a communist leader with a reputation of reformer under the Zhivkov regime who had been removed from the council of ministers in 1987. The opposition, recently united as the Union of Democratic Forces (UDF), was not convinced and demonstrations continued. Mladenov had no alternative but to announce the end of the single-party system and the introduction of free elections. The name of the Bulgarian Communist Party was changed to Bulgarian Socialist Party (BSP). Negotiations began between the former communists and the opposition at the 'round table talks' over a wide range of economic and political issues, including the forthcoming parliamentary elections and the format of the new constitutional assembly.

The election took place in June 1990. The BSP obtained 44 per cent of the votes and an overall majority of 211 seats out of 400 as against 38 per cent of the votes and 144 seats for the UDF, the third place going to the party defending the rights of the Turkish minority, the Movement for Rights and Freedom (MRF), which obtained 24 seats.

Yet, soon after this victory, the BSP suffered a major setback. It was revealed that Mladenov had wanted to send tanks against demonstrators in late 1989. He had to resign in July 1990 and was replaced in August by

Zheliu Zhelev, a philosopher who had probably been the most outspoken dissident and was the leader of the UDF. Having failed to form a coalition including the UDF, Lukanov had an entirely BSP cabinet in which 11 of the 18 ministers were new. As pressure from demonstrators continued and major strikes were planned, however, Lukanov felt unable to rule despite his majority and he resigned in November. In the context of a deepening economic crisis (food queues were long and electricity was rationed, among other problems), and to make it possible to build a coalition including the UDF, the president appointed a non-party prime minister, Dimitar Popov, who had been secretary of the electoral commission. The economic situation began to be tackled and privatisations were started. The Popov government resiged when parliament, having approved a new Constitution, decided to dissolve itself: a second general election took place in October 1991.

The result was indecisive. The UDF came on top with 34 per cent of the votes and 110 seats, but the BSP obtained 33 per cent of the votes and 106 seats out of a total of 240 in the new National Assembly, the remaining 24 seats having gone to the Movement for Rights and Freedom (MRF). On behalf of the UDF, the leader of the Green Party, Filip Dimitrov, was asked by the president to form the government. This was to be a minority administration supported by the Turkish minority. That government was also faced with major labour troubles and tension developed within the UDF. In October 1992, after less than a year in office, the government was abandoned by the Turkish party, which joined forces with the BSP on a motion of censure. Dimitrov resigned. With the BSP unable to organise an alternative majority, Zhelev appointed a technical cabinet, headed by an economic historian, Lyuben Berov, himself leaning towards the left. That government was to last almost two years, up to October 1994, although it did encounter major economic and political difficulties.

Berov's resignation indicated that there was no majority in parliament. Elections had to be called for the third time in little over four years. A caretaker cabinet, led by the head of the Privatisation Agency, Mrs Reneta Indzhova, was appointed and the National Assembly was dissolved. The result was clear-cut. The UDF fell to 24 per cent and obtained 69 seats, while the BSP obtained 43 per cent of the votes and an absolute majority of 125 seats out of 240, the rest going to the Turkish minority party (15 seats) and to a newly created business party, the Bulgarian Business Bloc (BBB) which obtained 13 seats.

The new leader of the BSP, Jan Videnov, was asked by the president to form the government, a government expected to be strong and long-lasting, but this turned out not to be the case. It was to be a 'small' coalition including, alongside seven BSP ministers, two members of the tiny Agrarian Party (BAPU), one member of the ecological party, Ecoglasnost, previously a political club, and eight independents. A programme of economic reforms was announced, including privatisations, to bring Bulgaria closer to Western Europe, but little took place on this score, while, however, controversial measures were passed, in particular with respect to agricultural property. The President used his veto in several occasions, a veto always upheld by the Constitutional Court.

By the middle of 1996, the presidential election campaign began. A primary took place on the UDF side at which Zhelev was defeated. Petar Stoyanov became the candidate of the alliance. On the BSP side, Lukanov, who had remained an influential leader of the BSP, was assassinated in the summer. The conservative wing of the party, together with Videnov's 'circle of friends', promoted Ivan Marazov, who had briefly been minister of culture in 1996. In part as a result, but also because of the growing discontent with the manner in which the government had dealt with the economy, Stoyanov came largely ahead at the first ballot with 44 per cent of the votes, while Marazov obtained 27 per cent only and the Business Bloc leader, Georges Ganchev, 21 per cent. At the second ballot, Stoyanov won 60 per cent of the votes against Marazov.

That result led to a major pressure for the resignation of the Videnov government and for new elections to take place. At an extraordinary congress of the Socialist Party in December 1996, Videnov resigned both as party leader and as prime minister. Parliament subsequently accepted the resignation of the government. The BSP designated the Minister of the Interior, Nicolay Dobrev to replace Videnov, but outgoing President Zhelev refused to nominate Dobrev on the grounds that a socialist cabinet would be unacceptable to the population and would be an impediment to the adoption of urgent measures recommended by the IMF. Stoyanov was inaugurated president on 20 January 1997 and succeeded in convincing the leadership of the BSP to agree to a caretaker government charged with the implementation of IMF-approved economic reforms. Pending new elections scheduled for April, Stoyanov appointed the mayor of Sofia, Stefan Sofiyanski, to form an interim government.

The fourth election in under seven years took place in April 1997 at which the UDF won a resounding victory, obtaining 137 seats out of 240, while The Socialist Party received only 58. Ivan Kostov was appointed prime minister. His government tackled economic problems and was stable for the following four years. Its popularity declined as a result of the reforms, however. At the June 2001 election, in an extraordinary upset, a party founded two months earlier by ex-King Simeon obtained nearly half the seats, thus changing abruptly the configuration of Bulgarian politics.

Cabinets since 1990

Bulgaria thus had eight prime ministers and eight cabinets between September 1990 and early 2000; the cabinet led by Lukanov in September 1990 was not very different from its predecessor, but it has to be regarded as a different administration as it held office on the basis of a parliament democratically elected in June 1990. These cabinets were[1]

- A. Lukanov (BSP), September to December 1990
- D. Popov ('Grand' Coalition), December 1990 to November 1991
- F. Dimitrov (UDF minority), November 1991 to December 1992
- L. Berov ('Technical'), with BSP and MRF support, December 1992 to October 1994
- R. Indzhova ('Technical'), October to December 1994
- Z. Videnov (BSP) plus participation of agrarians, ecologists and independents, January 1995 to December 1996
- S. Sofiyanski (Technical), February to May 1997
- I. Kostov (UDF and PU (BP and BANU), from May 1997

Cabinet instability has therefore been substantial. Political difficulties are emphasised by the fact that periods of party government have alternated with periods of 'technical' cabinets or, in one case, with a 'grand coalition' led by a non-party prime minister. This cabinet instability is somewhat surprising since, almost immediately after the end of communist rule in the spring of 1990, the party system was streamlined to become of the 'two-and-a-half' variety. Yet, as we saw, even majority cabinets, before that of Kostov, encountered major political difficulties as well as and probably because of economic difficulties. Thus the Dimitrov and Videnov cabinets were fairly extensively reshuffled during their relatively short existence (with six new ministers in each case).

Political instability in post-communist Bulgaria seems therefore have been due, not to the number of the significant parties, but to the character of the parties and, even more, to the part played by social groups and movements in weakening the governments and their leaders. The right is ostensibly united in one political body, but the UDF was until the beginning of 1996 an umbrella movement and tensions within it have been severe at times, particularly during the Dimitrov government. On the left, the BSP was also divided between more orthodox and more reformist segments. Meanwhile, pressure from trade unions, students and other demonstrators, perhaps not surprisingly given the weakness of the economy, led to an almost continuous undermining of governments, at least up to the 1997 election. Yet it is remarkable that the two main political groupings, UDF and BSP, were sufficiently structured to resist these pressures and did not break up.

The size of the Bulgarian executive varied little during the post-communist period, at least after the first Lukanov cabinet. With 22 ministers, that cabinet was of about the same size as the last communist cabinets, which had gradually become smaller during the 1980s as a result of a deliberate policy of restructuration. From September 1990 onwards, however, the Bulgarian cabinet had 17 or 18 members, except for the early phase of the Berov cabinet from December 1992 to June 1993, during which the cabinet had 14 members only.

Ministerial posts in post-communist Bulgarian cabinets have been similar to those of Western countries. There have been positions of deputy prime ministers, but these have been given *ad hominem* and not in relation to a post except in the case of the Berov administration when deputy prime ministerships were given to each of the coalition partners. Very few posts have been given to women, the maximum number being three in the 1997 Kostov government; the only woman prime minister, Mrs Indzhova, headed the caretaker cabinet set up in late 1994 to administer the country during the election period.

The ministerial posts in the reshuffled 1999 Kostov cabinet were deputy prime minister; Economics; Foreign Affairs; Defence; Interior; Finance; Education and Science; Justice; Agriculture; Industry; Transport and Communication; Labour and Social Policy; Health; Regional and Urban Development; Trade and Tourism; Culture; Environment and Water; Accession to the European Union.

A minister without portfolio was appointed in a post-communist Bulgarian cabinet only in 1990 and in 1995. There have been deputy prime ministers from time to time, but their number was reduced from three to one in the 1999 reshuffle of the Kostov cabinet. There have never been junior ministers, although the Constitution does allows for the opporunity to do so (Article 108).

Cabinet structure

The Constitution of 1991

In a first phase, in the course of 1990, the communist Constitution was amended to eliminate some of its more objectionable provisions, such as that giving a guiding role to the Communist Party and that establishing the single-party state. Quickly, however, parliament began discussing an entirely new text. This document was approved in July 1991 and it came into force immediately without a referendum. By doing so, Bulgaria produced one of the first democratic constitutions in post-communist Eastern Europe.

The structure of the executive and the role of the president

The new Constitution set up unmistakably a parliamentary system, the Bulgarian executive being wholly dependent on the National Assembly despite the fact that the president is elected by universal suffrage. The regime is not semi-presidential, either in law or in practice. The institution of the presidency is of recent origin and it was created in the aftermath of the 'round table' talks between former communists and opposition in the spring of 1990. Throughout the 1990s, the role of the president has been limited to ensuring that a government be able to function. This role has been smaller than that of the Finnish president under Kekkonen; it has been larger than that of either the Austrian or Irish presidents, but only because, as we saw, the head of state had to intervene in the formation of governments. Moreover, even in the case of the 'technical' cabinet of Berov, the Bulgarian president did not attempt to influence policies in a significant manner.

While, on the first occasion, in 1990, President Zhelev was elected by parliament, the president has since been elected by universal suffrage in accordance with Article 93 of the Constitution. There is provision for two ballots. As in France, if no candidate obtains one half of the valid votes at the first ballot, a second ballot takes place among the top two candidates. The president is elected for five years and can be re-elected only once. There is a vice-president, who is elected on the same ticket as the president and who replaces the president, as in the United States, during the unexpired portion of the term if the president dies, resigns or is incapacitated. There has been some discussion as to whether or not the post should be abolished.

The effective powers of the president are limited. They are those of a parliamentary head of state. He or she appoints the prime minister, but he/she is constrained to choose the leader of the largest parliamentary group; if this designated prime minister fails to form a government 'within seven days' (Article 99), he/she has then to select the head of the second largest parliamentary group, etc. The president does have the power to dissolve the National Assembly, but only if that body fails to approve a government. The only other major power of the president is that of vetoing legislation. To override that veto, an absolute majority of the members of National Assembly is required. The president also appoints four of the twelve judges of the Constitutional Court and several members of the board of directors of the National Bank and of the Media Council.

Meanwhile, it is the prime minister who exercises the leadership of the government. The Constitution does not specify who appoints the ministers, but, since the prime minister is expected to form the government within seven days, as we just noted, it follows that the prime minister is in charge. The government then goes to the National Assembly as a body for a formal investiture. The government must resign if it fails to receive the confidence of the National Assembly. Although most prime ministers of the 1990s resigned without having formally lost the confidence of the Assembly, Dimitrov had to resign in October 1992 after the confidence had been refused. The Bulgarian executive is thus truly parliamentary.

Cabinet life

Political characteristics

Formation of cabinets

The duration of the process of formation of cabinets has varied appreciably. Two governments took a long time to be set up. At the end of 1990, although the Lukanov government remained nominally in office, there was in effect a power vacuum until the moment the prime minister resigned and the Socialist Party came to accept the idea of a 'grand coalition' under a 'technical' prime minister. A somewhat analogous situation occurred in 1996. There was effectively a hiatus of nearly three months between the moment Videnov resigned in December 1996 and the appointment of Sofiyanski in the following February because the Socialist Party was not prepared for a long time to allow for a 'technical' government to be appointed before a new election would take place. However, President Zhelev quickly appointed Mrs Indzhova to lead the government when the Berov cabinet resigned, while the 1991 Dimitrov government, the 1995 Videnov government and the 1997 Kostov government were set up almost immediately and as a direct consequence of the results of general elections.

The role of the president in selecting prime ministers

These variations also broadly explain differences in the part played by the president in selection the prime minister. The selection of Lukanov in 1990 was exceptional in that the president at the time, Mladenov, had exercised his choice on the basis of what was still a pre-transition state of affairs. Moreover, the 'difficult' decisions were made essentially by Zhelev during his presidency, because he found himself having to appoint a 'technical' prime minister three times, when the Lukanov government was disintegrating under strike pressure late in 1990, when the Dimitrov government was defeated in parliament in October 1992 and no obvious alternative party-based cabinet was in sight and two years later when the technical Berov government resigned because of the mismanagement of economic reforms. In all three cases, it was the president who found a way out of the problem or at least who found ways of influencing the political forces in parliament. His successor, Stoyanov, had to exercise the same kind of authority on one occasion only, at the very beginning of his mandate, when he had to convince the Socialist Party to agree to a technical government. Since the spring of 1997, however, the new UDF majority has been stable and led by the same prime minister and the president has not had to intervene in the government-building process.

The role of parties in cabinet formation and development

Since the June 1990 election, Bulgaria has had, as mentioned previously, three cabinets of a non-party technical (Berov) or of a caretaker kind

(Indzhova and Sofiyanski), a grand coalition (Popov), three single-party governments (Lukanov, Dimitrov and Kostov) and one small coalition dominated by a party (Videnov). If the Lukanov February – June 1990 cabinet is excluded as it can be regarded as being still intermediate between the communist and the post-communist periods and as it remained in office for a very short period, the main characteristic of Bulgarian governments is that the parties, and in particular the UDF, did play a large part in the formation and development of these governments. First, on three occasions, the party base and even the composition of the cabinet resulted directly from the election process. Second, in the first two of these occasions, internal complications within the party in power (UDF and coalition partners (MRF) or the dominant party in the case of the Videnov government) led to difficulties in the cabinet and probably ultimately to its downfall. Third, the UDF forced twice a new government on a highly reluctant BSP, which was proving unable to reform itself, in late 1990 by the massive demonstrations which it launched and in early 1997 as a result of the pressure of the newly elected UDF president. Finally, even the small Turkish minority party did play a part when it held the balance of power following the 1991 election. It made it possible for the first UDF government to be set up in November of that year and it forced the resignation of that cabinet a year later by joining its votes in parliament with those of the Socialist Party and the secession of some MPs from the UDF itself. Apart from the two short periods of the Indzhova and Sofiyanski governments, which were in office to prepare the general elections about to take place, the only time when parties were not directly and closely involved with the life of a government was therefore during the two-year 'technical' Berov cabinet, as this government did not have a secure majority and was therefore continuously engaged in ad hoc deals with individual members of Parliament. Thus, by and large, the history of the first decade of post-communism in Bulgaria is one of the rather rapid build-up of 'party government'.

Turnover of ministers

The rate of turnover of cabinets and of ministers has been high in Bulgaria during the first seven years of the post-communist period. The period between May 1997 and December 1999 has been characterised, however, by complete stability. Between June 1990 and December 1999, 126 different persons occupied positions in cabinet, and 115 of these served up to May 1997 and only 17 afterwards (6 had served under previous governments). There were, as mentioned previously, usually 17 or 18 members in each cabinet, except under Dimitrov for a brief period and under Berov, when there were 14 ministers only. The average duration of ministers for the whole decade was 1.31 years, but it was only almost exactly one year between June 1990 and May 1997 and two-and-a-half years from May 1997 to December 1999. The arrival of the Kostov government to power in 1997 constituted a break with instability, which had been substantial under all previous governments. Prior to 1997, two cabinets had lasted almost two years, those of Berov (22 months) and of Videnov (23 months); but these cabinets were substantially reshuffled, largely because there were internal difficulties within the Socialist Party while in office. Thus the duration of ministers in office changed little between 1990 and 1997. The Dimitrov cabinet of 1991–92, which lasted a little under one year, had six new ministers sometime during its tenure, the Berov government had five and the Videnov government six. The Kostov government is therefore not only exceptional in having lasted three years by the spring of 2000, but it is also exceptional in not having been reshuffled at all up to December 1999. There is therefore substantial ground for suggesting that party government arrived in earnest with the coming to power of the Kostov cabinet in 1997.

The end of cabinets

Three cabinets out of the seven which had ended by the spring of 2000 ended because they were set up to administer the country only up to the next election. This was the case of the Popov government in 1991, of the Indzhova government in 1994 and of the Sofiyanski government in 1997. The administration of the election was not the only task of these governments, in particular of the first and third, as both of these were engaged in the stabilisation of the economy in particular and the Popov government was also able to pilot successfully the process of constitution-making. Yet it had been assumed in advance that all three governments would resign after the election had taken place. The four other governments ended prematurely, not only because of external pressure from trade unions, other interest groups and the opposition of the time, but also because these problems were the result of internal party difficulties, while in the case of the Dimitrov cabinet the decision by the Turkish party (MRF) to no longer to support the government was the immediate cause of the downfall of the cabinet. The fact that the Kostov cabinet of 1997 did not suffer from the same difficulties is another indication that the Bulgarian party system appears to have come of age.

Administrative characteristics

The Bulgarian cabinet meets once a week on Mondays. Meetings are chaired by the prime minister or, in his absence, by the deputy prime minister. Attendance at the meetings includes, beyond the ministers, the secretary-general of the government, the head of the staff ('cabinet') of the prime minister, the heads of four of the seven sub-departments of the cabinet office, namely the chancellery, the legal department, the local administration department and the information service. Deputy ministers attend (without a vote) when the corresponding minister is unable to be present. A representative of the president may also attend. Heads of committees, heads of agencies, deputy ministers and heads of departments of ministries can be invited to participate to provide information on certain issues.

Meetings of the cabinet are prepared by the secretary-general of the cabinet who draws up the agenda, but this agenda is expected to be approved in advance, not only by the prime minister but also by all the ministers. The secretariat is responsible for the co-ordination of all seven administrative units of the cabinet office, which have in total a staff of about 250. The prime minister, the deputy prime minister and the Minister for Public Administration are also supported by a 'cabinet' of their own, with both expert and political functions, but these 'cabinets' are small, having only between three and seven members each. Kostov complained that these bodies did not function effectively, especially the ones providing the link between the UDF/PU executive and parliament.

There are no formally constituted cabinet committees of the Bulgarian government, but only informal meetings at which specific problems are discussed. These informal meetings of ministers are important; they take place several times a week and are chaired by the prime minister, a characteristic which underlines their importance. These meetings may reject a proposal or alternatively suggest that a topic be placed on the agenda of the cabinet meeting. However, two of these bodies have in effect become permanent and could be regarded as being committees of the cabinet. These are the Council for Structural Reform and the Council for Education, Science and Culture. These committees are chaired by the deputy prime minister and ministers attend the meetings ex officio.

Decision-making

President and prime minister

The Constitution of 1991 specifies that the cabinet directs 'the implementation of the state's domestic and foreign policy' (Article 105). The president has a limited role while the role of the prime minister is substantial. The president is commander of the armed forces, heads the Consultative National Security Council and has the formal power of signing treaties. This enables the president to have a say in a variety of aspects of foreign policy, but Bulgarian presidents have used this power sparingly. Moreover, the intelligence unit was transferred from the president's office to that of the prime minister in 1995. The role of the president in home affairs has been very limited, except in the case of President Zhelev who was involved in the formation of some of the cabinets.

The prime minister, however, is the leader of the government. The Constitution states that the prime minister 'shall head, co-ordinate and bear responsibility for the overall policy of the government' (Article 108). The same Article also states that the prime minister appoints and dismisses deputy ministers, but not the ministers, who are appointed by the president on the proposal of the prime minister. In practice, Bulgarian prime ministers have on the whole been rather strong, either because they were the leaders of the (main) government party (Dimitrov, Videnov, Kostov) or because, in the case of at least the majority of the technical governments, because they were expected to help to solve difficult economic problems.

The role of the cabinet

Meanwhile, the cabinet appears to play a substantial part in decision making. Even in the Sofiyanski government, despite its brief tenure, members of the cabinet were markedly involved involved. The role of ministers was large in the Popov government, which was a 'grand coalition' of socialists and the UDF and in which the UDF was anxious to ensure that its favoured policies be adopted. Cabinet members played a major part in the governments of Dimitrov and Videnov. Their over-involvement even resulted in the ultimate disintegration of these cabinets. At least some of the ministers appear to have been large in the case of the Berov 'technical' cabinet, as that cabinet was continuously in search of a majority. The influence of cabinet members seemed to have declined in the Kostov government, in which policy making has been more streamlined and the position of the prime minister unchallenged. Informal meetings of ministers appear to have started to take over some aspects of the role of the whole cabinet. Bulgarian cabinets may thus come to increasingly resemble Western European cabinets.

Overall, the swift move of Bulgaria to a system of two or 'two-and-a-half' parties has been remarkable. There may have been problems, not just at the beginning of the period, in late 1990 and in most of 1991, but between late 1992 and early 1995 as well as between late 1996 and early 1997. In each case, the problem was that of 'succession'. Yet, in the end, compromises were found as no political group was willing to go beyond the brink. By the beginning of the twenty-first century, the major political difficulties of the first years of the post-communist period have apparently been overcome. It remains to be seen how the 'monarchical' government will be inserted in these developments.

Note

1 Lukanov had formed a first cabinet before the June 1990 election (from February to June), but his government was altered somewhat after the election in order to take the result into account. Since Dobrev was not able to form a cabinet in late 1996, his name is not mentioned in the list. However, although the Videnov cabinet remained formally in office until Sofiyanski became prime minister, the Minister of the Interior, Dobrev, did assume the functions of prime minister from the end of December 1996 until February 1997.

12
Albania

J. Blondel and L. Chiodi

Cabinet setting

Albanian developments since 1991

There were three phases in the first decade of post-communist Albania. The first began when President Alia, who was of the 'old guard', having succeeded Hoxha in 1985, was confronted with demands for change resulting from the overall collapse of communism in Eastern Europe. His answer was to appoint in January 1990 a new cabinet led by a member of the pre-reformed party, A. Carcani, and designed to bring about reforms in both the economy and politics. Reforms were, perhaps inevitably, slow to come. There was little economic change and political change seemed primarily cosmetic. The Workers' Party, renamed the Socialist Party, attempted to maintain itself in power. While large-scale emigration was occurring, massive protests took place in the capital and elsewhere in the country. Carcani was replaced by Fatos Nano as prime minister in February 1991. This had no effect.

President Alia therefore agreed in June to appoint a coalition government including members of the newly constituted Democratic Party. This government was to calm unrest by drafting constitutional amendments and by preparing free elections. Some constitutional provisions were indeed adopted, although a fully fledged document had to wait – indeed was approved only in 1998. But the free election was scheduled and did occur in March 1992. It resulted in the defeat of the Socialist Party and the victory of the Democratic Party and of its leader Berisha. Thus, there was a change in the power base and a two-party system came about in Albania.

This opened the second phase of post-communist Albania. Parliament elected Berisha to the presidency and he in turn appointed Alexsander Meksi as prime minister. Major economic difficulties came gradually to the fore, which culminated with the massive scandal based on the collapse of a financial 'pyramid' in which large numbers of Albanians had been involved. Confronted with strenuous attacks from the opposition, the government resorted increasingly to illiberal measures, in part on the grounds that many leaders of that opposition had been associated with the old regime. The president dissolved parliament early in 1996 on the basis of a new electoral law slanted against the opposition, which decided to boycott the contest. The government's victory at the polls was pyrrhic. Demonstrations and mass protests gradually came to be on such a scale that the government was wholly unable to maintain order. Revolts in the south of the country in particular resulted in civil war and almost total anarchy.

Unrest only decreased and eventually came to an end as a result of international intervention. Diplomatic pressure by European countries was also exercised on President Berisha and led to him agree in March 1997 to appoint a coalition cabinet able to restore order. That government would also ensure that an acceptable electoral system was adopted and a date for a new election fixed. The general election was announced for the end of June. At that election, the Democratic Party was soundly defeated and the Socialist Party was returned to power. President Berisha eventually resigned. In July 1997, parliament elected Rexhep Mejdani of the Socialist Party to succeed him. Life in Albania gradually (indeed relatively quickly) returned to some kind of normalcy, although the country's institutions had been badly weakened during the crisis.

Since July 1997, Albania has been ruled by mainly socialist governments including a small number of representatives of other parties. The government was first headed from July 1997 to September 1998 by Fatos Nano, the then leader of the Socialist Party which had won a landslide victory at the July 1997 election with 101 of the 155 seats in parliament, while the Democratic Party had obtained only 29 seats. In September 1998, however, the assassination of a prominent Democratic Party politician led to large-scale demonstrations and to what seemed to be an attempted coup by the opposition. Nano resigned and was replaced as prime minister by Pandeli Majko, the then leader of the Socialist Party in parliament; but, having faced in turn major problems within his party, Majko resigned in October 1999. He was replaced by Ilir Meta, hitherto deputy prime minister and also of the Socialist Party.

Cabinets since 1990

Albania had ten cabinets and seven prime ministers between 1991 and 2000. These were

- F. Nano (1) (Socialist Party), February to April 1991
- F. Nano (2) (Socialist Party), April to June 1991
- Y. Bufi (Grand coalition), June to December 1991
- V. Ahmeti (Grand coalition),[1] December 1991 to March 1992
- A. Meksi (1) (Democratic Party), with some participation of Republican party, March 1992 to May 1996

- A. Meksi (2) (Democratic Party), May 1996 to March 1997
- B. Fino (Grand coalition), March 1997 to July 1997
- F. Nano (3) (Socialist Party), plus some participation of small parties July 1997 to September 1998
- P. Majko (same party composition), September 1998 to October 1999
- I. Meta (same party composition), from October 1999

These cabinets have been single party or one-party dominated 'surplus' coalitions (from April 1992 to March 1997 and from October 1997 onwards) during periods of 'normal' or 'peaceful' rule (as well as two short-lived single-party (Socialist) governments at the beginning of the transition period in 1991) and three 'grand coalitions', respectively from June 1991 to March 1992 and from March to June 1997, when massive turmoil occurred. The 'surplus' coalitions were led by the Democratic Party in the first period and by the Socialist Party in the second. The 1992 'surplus' coalition led by the Democratic Party included two members of the Republican Party;[2] the coalitions of 1997, 1998 and 1999 led by the Socialist Party included members of four other parties, three of which had one minister each while the fifth had two ministers.[3] The 'grand' coalitions were composed essentially of Socialist Party and Democratic Party members; the 'grand coalition' of the spring of 1997 did include nine parties, however, but half of its members belonged in equal numbers to the Socialist Party and the Democratic Party, while the other parties had, except for one of them, one minister each only.

The size of the Albanian executive diminished somewhat from December 1991. The last 'pre-democracy' government of Carcani, which had been appointed by Alia in 1990 and remained in office up to February 1991, had 20 ministers. This was a relatively small number by the standards of communist governments elsewhere, but Albanian governments had already relatively few ministers in the 1980s. As in pre-1990 governments, the only ministerial posts not found in non-communist countries in the 1990 Carcani cabinet were those of light industry, of state planning and of state control. These disappeared in the course of the following two years. The Ministry of Light industry ceased to exist in February 1991, the Ministry of State Planning was replaced by the Ministry of the Economy in May 1991 and the Ministry of State Control in early 1992. The second Nano government of 1991 had 23 ministers and the 'grand coalition' cabinet of Y. Bufi of June 1991 had 21 ministers, but all subsequent governments had between 16 and 19 members. From 1992 onwards, the cabinet was wholly similar to a Western European cabinet.

The ministerial posts in the October 1999 Meta cabinet were deputy prime minister, also Minister of Labour and Social Affairs; Foreign Affairs; Defence; Public Order; Public Economy and Privatisation; Agriculture and Food; Finance; Economic Co-operation and Trade; Construction; Transport; Education and Science; Culture, Youth and Sport; Health; Justice; Local Government; Minister of State to the Prime Minister.

Cabinet structure

The absence of a fully fledged Constitution until late 1998

Although several documents had been drafted between 1991 and 1995, Albania had to wait up to the late 1990s to have a Constitution. Provisional arrangements were made in April 1991; a text was then presented by the Democratic Party majority in 1993 but it was not adopted by parliament. A new text was submitted to the people in 1994 but it was rejected. In 1995, the then opposition drafted its own constitutional version but this did not become law either. It had been suggested that there would be a further referendum in March 1998. The referendum did take place in November of that year at which the Constitution was finally adopted. During most of the 1990s, therefore, the executive structure was based on the provisional arrangements of April 1991.

The structure of the executive

Up to 1998, the governmental structure could be regarded as being *de facto* semi-presidential in that the effective power of the president depended more on what the relationship was between president, prime minister and parliament than on formal constitutional provisions. The Albanian regime was peculiar in that it was semi-presidential although the president was not elected directly by the people but by the members of parliament. The provision was kept in the 1998 Constitution – to be elected, a candidate must receive two-thirds of the votes cast. The term of office is five years.

In the 1990s, specifically when President Berisha held the post, the head of state exercised his power by influencing directly the prime minister and the ministers. Berisha, who had founded and was the leader of the Democratic Party, had as strong an influence as that which was once exercised by De Gaulle over his party. Yet the only formal powers of the president were the right of dissolution, a right which the head of state can exercise since 1998 only in a restricted manner reminiscent of the German constitution, appointment of the leadership of the armed forces and the right to nominate the prime minister, who is formally appointed by parliament.

Meanwhile, up to 1992 and since 1997, the prime minister has exercised full leadership of the government. Ministers are appointed and dismissed by the president on the proposal of the prime minister. While the executive is exercised jointly by prime minister and ministers, the prime minister conducts the policy of the state and supervises the administration. There has therefore been since the early 1990s a cabinet in the Western European sense, even though the influence of the president was very large when Berisha was in office.

Cabinet life

Political characteristics

Formation of cabinets

The duration of the process of formation of cabinets has varied appreciably. The grand coalition cabinets of 1991 took much longer to form (several weeks in April–May 1991) than the Democratic Party government which emerged from the general election of 1992 (ten days). Similarly, the (third) Nano government of 1997, the Majko government of 1998 and the Meta government of 1999, all three of which were primarily composed of Socialist Party ministers, were formed in a few days.

The role of the president in selecting prime ministers

The way in which the prime minister has been chosen has also varied appreciably. Basically, the president of the republic played a key part under Alia and Berisha, while the role has been more modest under Mejdani. Yet even the first two presidents had to give in when confronted with massive social unrest. Thus, while Alia chose Nano as his prime minister before the first general election, the choice of Bufi and even more of Ahmeti resulted from the strong popular demand for a multiparty general election in a context of strikes and of an economic crisis. Thus, too, Berisha freely chose Meksi to head the government after the Democratic Party victory of 1992. However, five years later, in 1997, Fino was imposed on him following the virtual collapse of the state and because of international pressure. Mejdani had little choice but to appoint Nano who was then the leader of the Socialist Party after the 1997 election; he was also constrained, but exercised perhaps a little more influence in the selection of Nano's successors, in 1998 Majko, then secretary-general of the dominant Socialist Party, and Meta in 1999, although the first was appointed in an atmosphere of crisis and the second as a result of fierce internal party conflict.

The role of parties in cabinet formation and development

By and large, the role of parties has been relatively modest in the formation of cabinets and during the lifetime of these cabinets, although there have been some differences between the Democratic Party and the Socialist Party. The Democratic Party was ruled in an authoritarian fashion by President Berisha, who was also its founder. Those ministers who did not agree with the president's line were expelled. A number of them set up small splinter parties. President Berisha intervened directly in the life of the Meksi cabinets and played a large part in the reshuffles which occurred during 1992–96.

The Socialist Party has been slightly more influential in the formation of governments in the late 1990s, in part because it has been divided into two main factions, the reformists or 'euro-socialists' and the 'old guard'. The 'reformist' faction came to play a larger role only with the departure of Nano in 1998, as his successor, Majko, was a 'euro-socialist'; but Nano succeeded in defeating Majko at the internal party election and then forced his resignation as prime minister. However, Nano was not able to become prime minister himself again, given his controversial political role in previous years which generated major hostility towards him from among the younger generation of party members, from among foreign partners and from within the opposition. He was therefore obliged to settle for the appointment of Meta.

The role of the small parties has been limited in general, although two of them, the Social Democratic Party and the Republican Party contributed to the collapse of the Democratic Party government in 1997 by joining with the Socialist Party opposition in demanding fair elections. One party, the Union for Human Rights Party, which represents in fact, if not in law, as ethnic parties are illegal, the Greek and Macedonian minorities, has participated in the Fino government which prepared the 1997 election and in the 'surplus' coalitions led by the Socialist Party after that election. These are the only cases of a party representing *de facto* a minority being in government.

Turnover of ministers

With ten cabinets having been in office between 1991 and 2000, it is not surprising that the turnover of ministers should have been high in Albania during that period, in sharp contrast with the near-record longevity of their predecessors under communist rule. From February 1991 to October 1999, 131 different persons occupied a ministerial position. On average ministers remained scarcely over one year in office (exactly 1.21 years).[4]

Variations between the early, middle and later periods, were noticeable, however. Between February 1991 and March 1992, there were three prime ministers and a total of 59 ministers. The average minister stayed in office only about four months, an extremely high turnover to be attributed in part to the difficulties experienced in establishing the new system of government.

Ministerial longevity became higher when the Democratic Party government came to power in 1992. For five years, the country was ruled by the same prime minister, A. Meksi, and during his term of office only 37 different persons occupied a cabinet position, the average duration of these ministers being 2.6 years. Yet substantial reshuffles did take place, the ministers of defence and energy being, with the prime minister, the only members of the cabinet to keep the same position throughout the period. Meanwhile, there were three ministers of agriculture, of industry, of tourism and of labour and two ministers in the other posts. The stability of the cabinet was thus only relative.

There was a return to greater instability during the subsequent period of Socialist rule which followed the June 1997 election. Between then and early

2000, there were three prime ministers, while 33 different persons occupied a ministerial position during a period of less than three years, an average of under 1.5 years.

The end of cabinets

Four cabinets out of nine ended for technical reasons, specifically because an election had been held. This was the case of the first Nano government in 1991, of the Ahmeti government in 1992, of the first Meksi government in 1996 and of the Fino government in 1997. Among the other five governments which had ended their tenure by 1999, two, the second Nano government in 1991 and the second Meksi government in 1997, fell because of 'chaos' in the country, while a third, that of Bufi at the end of 1991, disintegrated because the Democratic Party refused to continue to serve in the 'grand coalition' under that prime minister. The last two cases of cabinet collapse were due directly or indirectly to internal factionalism within the Socialist Party, although this was more marked in the case of the fall of Majko in 1999, as, in the case of the resignation of the third Nano government in 1998, the opposition to that leader was much greater outside the party than inside. Thus massive unrest and political confrontation have been key reasons for the collapse of governments in post-communist Albania.

Administrative characteristics

The Albanian cabinet meets formally every Monday but it also meets occasionally informally. Meetings are chaired by the prime minister or, in his absence, by the deputy prime minister. Attendance at the meetings includes, beyond the ministers, the secretary-general of the government, secretaries of state when the corresponding minister is unable to attend and advisory staff of the prime minister if invited by the prime minister to discuss specific items on the agenda.

The government is primarily composed of the prime minister and ministers, including the deputy prime minister and the ministers of state. There is also generally a number of secretaries of state, the maximum having been eight in the second Meksi cabinet of May 1996; there were four of them in the third Nano cabinet of July 1997. There is no provision for these posts in the Constitution and the practice is wholly informal.

Meetings of the cabinet are prepared by the Office of the Council of Ministers. This body, which is about ten strong, combines the roles of prime minister's office and of cabinet office. It seems that the function of 'preparation' with which the Office is entrusted with is not always implemented as effectively as it might be, however. In particular the agenda of cabinet meetings appears to be sometimes unrealistic. The prime minister also has a 'cabinet' of his own (in the French sense of the expression) as well as five special advisers dealing respectively with foreign affairs, national security, economic policy, legislative matters and general political issues. Except when there is urgency, these advisers communicate with the prime minister through the Minister of State to the prime minister.

Cabinet committees, both permanent and ad hoc, have been in existence from the beginning of the transition period. Since 1995, there have been three permanent 'sectoral' committees, the Committee on Economic Policy, the Committee on Social Policy and the Committee on National Security Policy. These committees are chaired by the prime minister or, at his request, by the deputy prime minister or a minister of state. An anti-corruption committee, chaired by the deputy prime minister, was set up in 1997. It would appear that the committees do not play a major part in policy development. They also seem to meet infrequently, with the exception of the Economic Policy Committee. One committee does stand out, however. Under the provisional arrangements which were in force up to late 1998, the president was described as commander of the armed forces and chairman of the Defence Council. Whether this provision is still applied in practice is not clear, but so long as the new Constitution had not been adopted, that power gave the president a major opportunity to influence defence policy and, indirectly, foreign policy in general.

Decision-making

President and prime minister

The Constitution of 1998 specifies (and so did the 1991 provisional arrangements which were in force up to 1998) that the cabinet directs domestic and foreign policy and supervises the public services. The president and the prime minister do have a special role, however. The president's position of commander of the armed forces together with the formal power of signing treaties, which is specifically mentioned in the Constitution, enables the president to have a say in a variety of aspects of foreign policy. Both President Alia and President Berisha did use these powers to a substantial extent, while President Mejdani has been more restrained in this respect.

As mentioned earlier, President Berisha did exercise considerable influence over all aspects of policy and his prime minister, Meksi, has to be regarded as having been a 'manager' rather than a true political leader. This has not been the case of the previous and subsequent prime ministers and in particular of Nano, whose two terms in office have been marked by a major effort to concentrate executive power in his hands.

The role of the cabinet

However, the cabinet appears to be generally weak. This is in part because of the power exercised by the president (in the case of the governments led by the Democratic Party) or by the prime minister (in the case of at least several of the governments led by the Socialist Party). This is also because the cabinet is not helped as effectively as it might be by the Office of the Council of Ministers or by the committees of the cabinet. It seems that the co-ordination of decisions needs to be markedly strengthened. As we noted, most cabinet committees meet infrequently and there appears also to be limited informal communication between ministers and between ministries before the presentation of proposals to the cabinet.

Rules do exist which stress the need for policy preparation and co-ordination but, to say the least, these rules are far from being carefully implemented, a state of affairs which is perhaps not altogether surprising, given the limited experience and the high turnover of ministers which was described earlier. Thus, although there does not appear to be an 'inner cabinet' in post-communist Albania, this does not suggest that the cabinet as a whole is able to exercise substantial influence on governmental policy-making. What does seem to be the case is that, occasionally at least, some ministers individually have been highly influential – and indeed, especially under Berisha, may have had to resign after having confronted the president. Whether or not, among these ministers, the Minister of Finance plays a truly special part is rather unclear. Two different persons held the post in the Meksi governments; two different persons also held the post in the Socialist governments which have been in office since 1997.

Given that Albania experienced the most rigid and indeed backward communist regime and despite the massive disorders which characterised the country in at least two occasions, in 1991–92 and in 1996–97, political developments in Albania can be regarded as positive. With parties having emerged, however based and geographically circumscribed, some structure has been given to the government and to the opposition in a way which has been basically lacking in many ex-communist countries and in particular in the core of what was the Soviet Union. In the tense socio-economic climate that characterised the politics of the country, it would have been astonishing if the machinery of government had functioned truly efficiently; but a framework exists. What has been detrimental to the political development which followed the collapse of the institutions has been the highly confrontational nature of political life in the country. Yet, although the battles between the two sides have been unruly, in the literal sense, on many occasions, they have not led to the suppression of one side by the other, surely in part thanks to the action of the international community. The rise of new younger political leaders among the different parties should gradually reduce the extreme personalisation of politics in the country around two political figures and open up a new political climate. What is clearly in need of improvement, alongside a political society conceiving of negotiation as the only political option within a democratic system, is a 'ministerial class' which is better prepared for its tasks and whose members remain in office for substantially longer periods. To this extent, the experience of the last years of the 1990s has been rather disappointing, even by comparison with what occurred earlier in the decade. Albania may therefore not have reached the state of 'consolidated' politics but it has surely taken some important steps in the direction of that state.

Notes

1   Ahmeti's government of December 1991 to March 1992 was a caretaker government set up for the sole purpose of ensuring that the first multiparty election was conducted in a fair manner. It was composed of ministers nominated by the parties, and in particular by the two main parties, among persons not directly involved in politics, but four of them, including the prime minister, all from the Socialist Party, had already been members of previous governments.
2   The Republican Party joined the government led by A. Meksi in 1992, alongside the Democratic Party of Albania (DPA), thus giving the government a 'surplus' majority, since the Democratic Party alone had 66 per cent of the seats in parliament at the 1992 election. It had 87 per cent of the seats at the 1996 election.
3   The small parties which joined the governments led by B. Fino, F. Nano and I. Meta, alongside the Socialist Party of Albania (SPA), were the Democratic Party of Albania (DAP), the Social Democratic Party of Albania (SDP), the Democratic Alliance Party (DAP), the Agrarian Party (AP) and the Union for Human Rights Party (UHRP). The DAP had two ministers and the other parties had one minister each. There was also an independent. These parties gave a 'surplus' majority to the government, since the Socialist Party alone had 65 per cent of the seats in parliament at the 1997 election.
4   This average is calculated on the basis of a total of 1905 monthly ministerial positions or approximately 159 yearly positions.

13
Macedonia

J. Blondel

Cabinet setting

Macedonian developments since 1990

In October and November 1998, at the parliamentary elections in Macedonia, the coalition led by the Social Democratic Alliance for Macedonia (SDAM), a party made up of communists and in power since the country became independent, was defeated and was replaced by the opposition led by the Internal Macedonian Revolutionary Organization – Democratic Party for Macedonian National Unity (IMRO-DPMNU). This was the first time that alternance was taking place in a country of the former Yugoslavia.

The first multiparty parliamentary election had taken place in Macedonia in December 1990. At that election, the former communists, renamed Party of Democratic Reform and later Social Democratic Alliance for Macedonia (SDAM), gained 31 seats in the 120-seat parliament (*Sobranje*), the IMRU-DPMNU obtained 37, the Liberal Party 19 and two Albanian parties 25 (Albanians being almost a quarter of the population). The leader of the former communists, Kiro Gligorov, was elected president of Macedonia by the Assembly while the leader of IMRO-DPMNU, Ljupco Georgievski, became vice-president and the leader of the Liberal Party became the speaker of the Assembly. But these parties disagreed over the allocation of ministerial portfolios. A formally 'technical' government was constituted, under the leadership of Nikola Kljusev, himself an expert, but dissensions continued. The Constitution was nonetheless approved by parliament in November 1991, by a majority of 96 deputies out of 120 which also included most of the IMRO-DPMNU deputies, the opposition being mainly drawn from the Albanian representatives on the grounds that the rights of Albanians were not formally recognised.

One key problem of the subsequent six years was to be that of the recognition of the independence of the country, essentially because of the opposition of Greece, on the grounds that the name Macedonia given to the country suggested that a claim was being made on the Macedonian part of

Greece. Only in 1997 was the matter finally resolved, but not before an assassination attempt had been made against the Macedonian president in October 1995, at which Gligorov was seriously injured, because the president was pursuing too moderate a line.

Serious conflicts also occurred with the ethnic Albanian minority. In 1993 a number of arrests had been made on the grounds that there were attempts to establish an independent republic in a part of the country; in 1994, the former leader of one of the ethnic Albanian parties was in turn arrested and sentenced to eight years' imprisonment for 'associating in order to engage in hostile activities', a decision which led to the split of the main ethnic Albanian party, the Party for Democratic Prosperity (PDP), between a moderate wing represented in the government and a radical wing. The intention of the ethnic Albanian community to establish an Albanian language university was to create further difficulties in 1994 and in 1995.

Meanwhile, the political situation had been stabilised. The problems posed by the recognition of Macedonia as an independent state had led to the resignation of Kjlusev and his replacement by the chairman of SDAM, Branko Crvenkowski, who was to remain in office for the following six years, mainly at the head of a coalition including the Liberal Party, while IMRO-DPMNU was to constitute the main opposition party during that period. The presidential and parliamentary elections which took place in October 1994 strengthened the government coalition. Gligorov was easily re-elected president against the leader of IMRO-DPMNU and the SDAM gained almost an absolute majority of seats (58 out of 120) while the Liberal Party obtained 29 seats instead of 19 in 1990. Yet a major conflict occurred in the coalition within little more than one year as a result of which the Liberal Party was excluded from the government in February 1996. In 1997, a major scandal occurred in connection with 'pyramids'. The government survived a vote of confidence, but it was markedly bruised in the process. These difficulties were combined with the consequences of the crisis in Albania and of the repression in Kosovo, IMRO-DPMNU supporting a more 'active' line in defence of the interests of Albanians.

The government was therefore in serious decline when it affronted the presidential and parliamentary elections of October–November 1998 despite the fact that the economic situation had improved markedly in the course of the decade. Inflation, at one point extremely high, had been reduced to less than 5 per cent by 1996. The election campaign was marked by a series of incidents, including the assassination of a prominent member of the moderate party of ethnic Albanians, the PDP. At the polls, the government coalition was defeated, the SDAM retaining only 29 of the 58 seats which it had obtained in 1994. Crvenkowski resigned and was replaced by the leader of the winning party, Ljupco Georgievski, as the prime minister, who formed a cabinet based on what had previously been the core of the opposition. The presidential election followed a year later, in October 1999.

Gligorov was barred by the Constitution from standing again. The candidate of the Socialist Party, Tito Petkovski, was defeated at the second ballot with 47 per cent of the votes by the candidate of the governmental coalition, Boris Trajkovski, who thus became the second president of independent Macedonia.

Cabinets since 1991

Macedonia has had only three prime ministers but six cabinets between March 1991 and 2000. Crvenkowski presided over three cabinets during his prime ministership if the 1994 election is considered as constituting a formal interruption, but the coalition remained the same before and after the election and there was no change in ministerial personnel. The six cabinets were:

- N. Kljusev (1) (Grand coalition), March to October 1991
- N. Kljusev (2) (Small coalition), October 1991 to August 1992
- B. Crvenkovski (1) (Small coalition), SDAM, Liberal Party, Socialist Party, Party for Dem. Prosperity (ethnic-Albanians), August 1992 to October 1994
- B. Crvenkovski (2) (Small coalition), same parties, October 1994 to February 1996
- B. Crvenkovski (3) (Small coalition), SDAM, Socialist party, Party for Dem. Prosperity (ethnic-Albanians), February 1996 to November 1998
- L. Georgievski (Small coalition) from IMRO-PDMNU, Democratic Alternative, November 1998.

There has therefore been considerable prime ministerial stability and even substantial cabinet stability in Macedonia. The Social Democratic Alliance managed to retain its 'hegemony' over the political system much longer than in the other countries of the region, both within and outside of former Yugoslavia. This may have been because the SDAM never attempted to govern alone but studiously attempted to build alliances, including electoral alliances, to a much greater extent than in other countries of the Balkans. Prime Minister Crvenkowski's term of office was indeed a record for the region. Where powerful presidents remained in power throughout the period, such as in Croatia or Serbia, there were nonetheless many changes of prime ministers.

The stability of prime ministerial leadership in Macedonia was coupled with the stability of the ministerial personnel. This was indeed the highest in the whole of the southern part of Eastern Europe. There was naturally a substantial change of personnel with the arrival of the Crvenkowski cabinet in 1992 and with the upset resulting from the defeat of the government at the October–November 1998 elections, but during Crvenkowski's tenure between 1992 and 1998, membership of the cabinet was profoundly altered in two occasions only. The first was the result of the departure of the Liberals, when 13 ministers out of 20 left to be replaced by others. There was again a major reshuffle in May 1997 when eight ministers were replaced by others. However, between August 1992 and February 1996, only one minister was replaced and there was again only one change between May 1997 and October 1998.

Moreover, the size of the cabinet did not vary almost at all during the years of the Crvenkowski administrations. There were 23 ministers under Kljusev; this number was reduced to 20 afterwards when Crevenkowski came to power and it remained the same up to 1998 except for a short while in 1997 when there were 19 ministers. However, the coming to power of the IMRO-DPMNU resulted in a substantial increase of the cabinet in 1998 from 20 to 27.

The ministerial posts in the 1999 Georgievski cabinet were deputy prime minister; deputy prime minister; deputy prime minister and Minister of Labour and Social Security; Internal affairs; Defence; Foreign Affairs; Justice; Finance; Development; Economy; Urban Planning and Construction; Transport and Communications; Agriculture, Forestry and Water Resources Management; Education; Science; Culture; Health; Emigration; Information; Trade; Sports and Youth; Environment; Local Self- Government; without portfolio (three).

The number of deputy prime ministers was reduced from three to two under the socialists; it was to revert to three in the IMRO-DPMNU cabinet. The number of ministers without portfolio also varied. There were four up to 1995, two during 1995–97, four again in 1997–98 and three after 1998. The positions of minister without portfolio and of deputy prime minister seemed to have been to an extent interchangeable – two of the four ministers without portfolio between May 1997 and April 1998 became subsequently deputy prime ministers.

The Constitution of 1991

As was noted earlier, at the end of 1991, parliament adopted a Constitution whose main controversial element within the Macedonian polity was that it did not specifically protect the right of ethnic Albanians. That Constitution was modified in 1993 and 1995 in order to go some way towards meeting the objections of Greece, both in relation to the name of the country and with respect to the flag.

The structure of the executive

The Macedonian Constitution establishes a parliamentary form of government. The president is elected for five years by popular vote but has limited powers; the government is responsible to the single chamber of parliament

(*Sobranje*) which is elected for four years only, hence the situation which occurred at the end of 1998 when president and the majority of the Assembly came to be of different parties. There is an important variation from most parliamentary governments, moreover, because members of the government cannot be members of the parliament. It should be noted that such a rule obtains also in some established parliamentary systems, not just in France, but, for instance, in the Netherlands and Norway.

The president can be re-elected only once. There is provision for two ballots, such as in France, where if no candidate obtains half the valid votes at the first ballot, a second ballot takes place among the top two candidates. There is no vice-president, although there had been one before the Constitution was adopted. If the president dies or is incapacitated, the interim is assured by the speaker of parliament.

The president selects the 'mandator to constitute the Government of the Republic' (Article 84). For all intents and purposes, this means that the president selects the prime minister, but this power is circumscribed. The 'mandator' must be chosen within ten days of the constitution of the assembly; he/she must be drawn 'from the party or parties which has/have a majority in the Assembly' (Article 90 (1)), although this cannot be from among members of the Assembly. The 'mandator' has then a further ten days to present the programme and composition of the government to the Assembly. For the government to be in power, an absolute majority of the Assembly must vote in its favour.

The president does not chair the Council of Ministers. He/she does not really 'form part' of the government, which is described in Article 89 as being composed of the prime minister and the ministers. However, the president chairs the Security Council. Indeed, the president is manifestly expected to exercise a strong influence in that council since, out of its nine members including himself, the president appoints three and needs only to find one supporter among the other five members (prime minister, speaker of parliament, ministers of security, defence and foreign affairs) to have a majority.

The fact that the system is parliamentary is emphasised in two ways. First, the president does not have the power of dissolution of the assembly, which does therefore run its four year course in the normal way. Second, the president does not have the power to interfere in any way with the laws passed by the parliament, having no right of veto, but merely the right to ask for a second deliberation. Laws are not mentioned at all in the list of the powers of the president given in Article 84. The only point made in the subsequent article is that the president addresses the assembly once a year and that the assembly can ask the president to state an opinion 'on issues within his/her sphere of competence' (Article 85 (2)). It is the government, which is composed of the prime minister and ministers, which is in charge of national policy.

Within that government, the prime minister does not have a special position, except that, in view of the procedure described for the appointment of the government by the assembly, the prime minister formally appoints the ministers and clearly must exercise at least some substantial influence on the selection of the cabinet, a selection in which the president is not mentioned by the Constitution as being involved. Once appointed, minister can be dismissed only with the approval of parliament, as the Constitution states that 'the prime minister may propose the dismissal of a member of the government' (Article 94 (2)). While in office, ministers appear to have the same status as that of the prime minister. The Constitution refers to the government only and it does not state for instance that the prime minister 'leads' the government. The only way in which the prime minister may be 'above' his/her colleagues results from the fact that, as 'mandator', he/she presents both the programme and the list of ministers for approval by parliament. It is at least probable that the prime minister will have played a substantial part in elaborating that programme.

Cabinet life

Political characteristics

Formation of cabinets

The formation of Macedonian cabinets has been relatively simple from 1992 with the appointment of Crvenkowski as prime minister in August of that year. There had been major difficulties in 1991, as the grand coalition led by the non-party prime minister Kljusev broke up in October and, in the following summer, the whole government in turn fell as a result of the apparent impossibility to come to an agreement with Greece over the recognition of the new nation. The governmental crisis lasted three months, before the leader of the Socialist Party (SDAM), Crvenkowski, was able to form a cabinet. The same leader was easily able to form another cabinet after the October 1994 election, as socialists and liberals had won under the general label of the Social Democratic Alliance for Macedonia. But the liberals left the government eighteen months later and the parliamentary base of the Crvenkowski cabinet became rather narrow. Yet it was able to continue in office for a further two and a half years. The last change of government was straightforward because the victory of IMRO-DPMNU at the November 1998 election directly resulted in the setting up of the georgievski cabinet.

The role of the president in selecting prime ministers

President Gligorov was actively involved in the choice of the first two prime ministers of independent Macedonia, but the choices he made were based on a close examination of the political situation rather than on the basis of his own personal inclinations. Kljusev was selected because, being non-party, he was expected to be able to lead a grand coalition. This was indeed the case for a few months. Crvenkowski was selected because he was the leader of the Socialist Party and after the other major party, IMRO-DPMNU, had been asked to form the government and was shown not to be in a position to constitute one which would obtain a majority in parliament. The selection of Georgievski in 1998 was straightforward and directly based on the electoral result. The president did not exercise any genuine choice in this respect.

The role of parties in cabinet formation and development

Parties have played a major part in the formation of Macedonian cabinets, a part which the president recognised. All six cabinets were coalitions, although, throughout much of the period at least, two of the parties have been prominent. Yet no party has felt it possible to govern alone, both because no party had an absolute majority, although since 1994 one of these two has been very close to obtaining it, and because the need to have a relatively large majority, typically including at least some representatives of the Albanian community, was continuously recognised. Thus while the two major parties, SDAM and IMRO-DPMNU, were very influential, the latter especially in 1991–92 and in 1998, and the Liberal Party, which became the second party at the 1994 election, was a major player during the 1994–96 period, no party ever governed alone in independent Macedonia.

The position of parties in the government differed appreciably under the first two prime ministers. Kljusev's cabinet was regarded as technical, although it seems that at least the three deputy prime ministers, one of the ministers without portfolio and the Minister of the Interior were party men. These, together with two other ministers, those of Labour and of Education, remained in office in the first Crvenkowski cabinet, while the Minister of Construction and the Environment was a member of IMRO-DPMNU and left the government when his party went into opposition. Thus the Kljusev cabinets were manifestly in part political as well as technical and the first of these cabinets indeed constituted a grand coalition. However, none of the other eleven portfolio ministers and of the other three non-portfolio ministers returned to office subsequently.

The Crvenkowski cabinets were also all coalitions. The first two were four-party coalitions which included members of the three parties which constituted the electoral 'Alliance for Macedonia', the Social Democratic Alliance (former communists), the Liberal Party and the Socialist Party as well as members of the Party for Democratic Prosperity which represented ethnic Albanians; the third was a three-party coalition, as the Liberal Party no longer formed part of the government. The SDAM always had more cabinet seats than the others, but this was more marked, perhaps naturally, in the third coalition. In 1997, out of 20 members of the government, 12 were from the SDAM, six were from the PDP and only two from the SP.

Given its numerical supremacy in the cabinet, the SDAM played a major part in Macedonian decision-making. Yet the more remarkable point is the converse, namely that this supremacy of the reconstructed Communist Party was far from absolute. Other parties have been involved in policy making, even if this has been on a limited basis. In particular, the SDAM has clearly been anxious to associate ethnic Albanians to the life of the government; so has the government elected in 1998. This has made Macedonia markedly more 'consociational' than the two major countries which emerged from former Yugoslavia, Croatia and Serbia.

Turnover of ministers

The rate of turnover of cabinets has been very low in Macedonia after the end of communism. Between March 1991 and the autumn of 1998 (up to the election which led to the resignation of Crvenkowski), there were three cabinets only, as previously mentioned, with the first Crvenkowski cabinet having lasted three and a half years and the second two and a half years. This cabinet stability was coupled with a marked stability of the ministers as well. Only 60 different persons occupied cabinet positions during the period (87 if the Georgievski cabinet of November 1998 is taken into account). As there were 162 yearly cabinet posts between March 1991 and November 1998, the average duration of the ministers who served in these cabinets was 2.70 years. Macedonian ministers stayed in office longer than ministers in any other country of the Balkans during the same period.

Moreover, Macedonia did not know the kind of 'culture of the reshuffle' which prevailed in several other countries of the Balkans. The first prime minister, Kljusev, did not reshuffle his cabinet at all during the 15 months of his tenure. Crvenkowski effectively did so on two occasions only, one of which was prompted by the departure of Liberal Party members from the government. It may be that the fact that the prime minister (or the president) cannot dismiss ministers without the approval of the parliament partly accounts for the stability of the cabinet; but this stability may also be because all three Crvenkowski cabinets were coalitions and, as in the case of most coalitions, the prime minister would have needed the support of the leaders of the other parties to reshuffle the government.

The end of cabinets

Two cabinets out of the five which had ended by the spring of 2000 resigned because of an election. In the first case, in 1994, the Crvenkowski cabinet was effectively continued; in the second case, the Crvenkowski cabinet left office having lost the election. Two of the other three cases of cabinet resignation and reconstruction were due to the departure of a party from the government, IMRO-DPMNU in October 1991 from the Kljusev cabinet and the Liberal Party in February 1996 from the Crvenkowski cabinet. Only in one case, in June–July 1992, did a cabinet truly disintegrate. This occurred when a member of the Kljusev cabinet resigned and the political temperature increased as a result of the failure of the negotiations with Greece over the recognition of the country.

Administrative characteristics

The Macedonian cabinet meets normally once a week on Mondays. Meetings are convened and chaired by the prime minister or, in his absence, by a deputy prime minister. Attendance at the meetings consists of the ministers, including the ministers without portfolio, and, but without a right to vote, the secretary of the government, the head of the secretariat of legislation, the staff ('cabinet') of the prime minister and members of administrative bodies, as invited by the prime minister. Deputy ministers attend when the corresponding minister is unable to be present.

Meetings of the cabinet are prepared by the secretary-general of the cabinet, who draws up the agenda. Matters must be submitted at least a week in advance of the meeting and indeed two weeks in advance if they relate to major issues. The draft agenda is then distributed to members of the government at least five days before the meeting. The preparation of the meetings is entrusted to the secretariat of the government, which includes several organisational units able to give expert advice. The most important part of the secretariat of the government is constituted by what is in effect the 'cabinet office', which is in charge of the preparation of the agenda. Its units are organised on a sectoral basis corresponding to the ministries. It has approximately 90 employees.

There are several permanent committees of the cabinet. In the Crvenkowski cabinet of 1998, there were six committees charged respectively with foreign affairs and defence, economic development, economic policy, the political system, public and social services and personnel and human resource issues. These cabinet committees are chaired either by one of the deputy prime ministers or by a minister. They include the ministers of the relevant departments, a number of high-ranking officials and a representative of the secretariat of the government. The committees have important preparatory functions and all legislative proposals must first go to the relevant committee before being discussed in cabinet; they also have implementation functions as they are charged with reviewing policy developments.

Decision-making

President and prime minister and cabinet

The Constitution of 1991 specifies that 'executive power is vested in the Government of the Republic of Macedonia' (Article 88). Article 91 then details all the many activities for which the cabinet is responsible. The president is thus not formally part of 'the executive'. His role is limited to security matters, since he is president of the Security Council and, in a somewhat indirect, but important manner, to questions of ethnic relations, sine he appoints the members of the Council dealing with these matters. Yet, if the president has a limited role, that of the prime minister is also formally perhaps even smaller. While the prime minister is mentioned in the Constitution, the only power which is specified is that of proposing the dismissal of ministers (Article 94), but, somewhat curiously, not of proposing their appointment. It is not said, for instance, as in many other constitutions of the area, that the prime minister is the leader of the government. The Constitution of Macedonia refers continuously to the government but only to the government. In practice, however, the Macedonian prime ministers, especially after 1992, appear to have played a major part in the policy-making process.

The role of the cabinet

The cabinet appears to play a substantial part in decision-making, although many of these decisions are prepared by committees. However, how large the effective role of ministers is is somewhat unclear, especially in the case of the Georgievski government. The task of the cabinet office is to ensure that matters that come to the cabinet meeting have not been overloaded. One reason may be that not enough matters are delegated to the individual ministers and to the departments.

The Macedonian governmental system did thus develop successfully in the course of the 1990s. It has been based on a party system which was quickly established and remained solid throughout the decade. Cabinets and ministers have been able to stay in office for longer periods than in many of Macedonia's neighbours. This is a clear tribute to the level-headedness of the political elite, and indeed of the political elites of both major ethnic groups, ethnic Macedonian and ethnic Albanian. This is also a tribute to the successive cabinets and to the three prime ministers, as well as perhaps, above all, to President Gligorov who was at the head of the country for most of the period.

14
Croatia

J. Blondel and S. Selo-Sabic

Cabinet setting

Croatian developments since 1990 and the end of the Tudjman era

With the death of president Franjo Tudjman in December 1999, Croatian politics took an entirely new turn. Until then, the first president of independent Croatia had dominated the country. Tudjman, who had been imprisoned for nationalism between 1972 and 1981, formed the Croatian Democratic Union (CDU, but HDZ in Croat). During the campaign for the elections which were to follow in April – May, Tudjman fought a nationalistic campaign, portraying himself as 'father of all the Croats'. The CDU obtained 42 per cent of the votes, but, thanks to the first past the post system, it obtained an absolute majority of seats against the former communists, who had changed their name to that of 'League of Communists of Croatia-Party of Democratic Reform'. The CDU had 205 seats out of 351 while the communists obtained 73. Tudjman was the uncontested leader of the new country and he was elected president of Croatia by the new parliament. As a gesture he offered the vice-presidency to a Serb from Croatia, Jovan Raskovic, the leader of the Social Democratic Party (of Croatia) (SDP) who refused, but the office was accepted by another Serb (from Croatia).

The Republic of Croatia was proclaimed in Zagreb in August 1990, but the Serbs from three parts of the country, Krajina, and Eastern and Western Slavonia were organising themselves against Zagreb. A referendum took place in Krajina in July 1990, despite the attempt made by the Croat authorities to prevent it and it was overwhelmingly in favour of Serb autonomy. Croatian autonomy followed by independence and the autonomy and virtual independence of the Serb area of Croatia occurred in parallel. A new Constitution for Croatia was adopted by parliament in December 1990, and this included a right to secede from Yugoslavia. Ordered by the Yugoslav government to disarm their troops, the new Croat authorities refused to do so. This meant war; it also meant independence, which the Croat government declared in June 1991, after a further referendum boycotted by the

Serbs from Croatia. Tudjman set up a coalition government of almost all the (non-Serb) parties of Croatia in August. Meanwhile, the three areas of the country mainly populated by Serbs moved towards the setting up of a 'Republic of Serbian Krajina' which was declared in December 1991.

The efforts made by the international community to preserve Yugoslav unity were effectively abandoned when Germany and Austria recognised Croatia in December 1991. The war was interrupted by several cease-fires which were periodically broken. In the spring of 1992 Croatia attempted to reconquer Slavonia from the Serbs; this was inconclusive, but a further Croat army offensive took place in January 1993 in Krajina, with the United Nations succeeding eventually in September to stop the hostilities.

Elections had taken place in August 1992 according to the new Constitution. Tudjman was elected president with 56 per cent of the votes while the CDU won 85 of the 138 seats of the lower house of what had become a bicameral legislature. The president chose the former head of his personal staff, Hrvoje Sarinic, to become prime minister, clearly marking that he was to continue to exercise strong control on the government. Yet there were internal difficulties for Tudjman in Croatia, largely due to the the deterioration of the economic situation and to financial scandals. The prime minister resigned and was replaced by a 'non-political' businessman, Nikita Valentic, who set up a single-party CDU government. Difficulties persisted, however. Opposition grew within the CDU, and this was led by the speaker of the upper chamber (known as the Chamber of the Municipalities), Josip Manolic, who held more liberal views than those of the president and favoured an arrangement with the Muslims of Bosnia-Hercegovina. Manolic left the CDU in April 1994 and founded a new party, the Croatian Independent Democrats (CID, HND in Croat), along with Stipe Mesic, who was to become the first president of post-Tudjman Croatia in early 2000.

Yet Tudjman was also under pressure from nationalists in the CDU pressing for the re-conquest of the Serb parts of Croatia which had *de facto* become independent. This led to the army attack in Western Slavonia in May 1995. A ceasefire was rapidly ordered under UN pressure, but in late July the Croatian government started military operations again. The whole of Croatia rapidly fell under Zagreb rule with a massive exodus of Serb refugees. A degree of 'normalisation' did occur later in the year, however, when an agreement was signed between the Croatian government and the East Slavonian Serbs in November 1995.

The general election of October 1995 took place in the wake of the Croatian army victory in Serb-held parts of the country, after an election campaign which was said to have been heavily biased against the opposition, especially on television. The CDU secured 45 per cent of the votes but obtained only 42 of the 80 seats of the lower house (elections to the upper house were to be held later) as the first-past-the-post system had been replaced in 1993 by proportional representation. A change of government followed, the former Minister of the Economy, Zlatko Matesa, becoming prime minister. After the electoral victory, the Croatian government and president displayed a marked authoritarian behaviour, both in relation to the press and in relation to local authorities. The opposition Zagreb municipal council was dissolved in May 1996 on the grounds that it was refusing to endorse the nominee for mayor which the government had proposed. Efforts were also made in November to close an independent radio station.

Meanwhile, Tudjman was normalising relations with the new Yugoslavia (in effect essentially Serbia) and full diplomatic links between the two countries were established in November 1996. The president also endeavoured to help stabilise the situation in Bosnia-Hercegovina. Within Croatia itself, efforts were made to repair relations with the Serbs, in particular in the context of the municipal elections and of the election to the upper house which was to be held in April 1997. The Serb minority was allocated two seats in the upper house, but this was two out of 63!. The CDU did win a majority in the upper house, obtaining 37 of the 63 seats while Tudjman was re-elected with 61 per cent of the votes after a campaign which was described as having been unfair. In the wake of the election, pressure against the opposition continued and plans were afoot in October 1997 to prosecute journalists for publishing 'false information' while a constitutional amendment was passed by parliament prohibiting the reconstitution of Yugoslavia.

With Tudjman's fatal illness in 1999, the political outlook of the country changed dramatically. At the general election of January 2000, Tudjman's party was routed by the social democrats (former communists) which became the first party in the country. Their leader, Ivica Racan, was appointed prime minister by the interim president and he built a cabinet coalition of six parties. Less than two months later, at the presidential election of February 2000, Stipe Mesic was elected president at the second ballot with 56 per cent of the votes against the candidate of the Liberal Party, Drazen Budisa. Mesic had been the last president of the old Yugoslavia in 1991 and, after leaving the ruling HDZ in 1994, had become one of the leaders of the opposition Croatian Independent Democrats which at a later stage joined the Croatian People's Party, the HNS.

Cabinets since 1990

Despite the fact that Croatia had the same president between 1990 and late 1999, the country had had four prime ministers and five cabinets during the same period, a sixth having come to office after the electoral upset of January 2000. Three of the changes of prime ministers occurred after general elections (in 1992, 1995 and 2000), but, the changes which occurred before 2000 were not primarily due to the result of the elections as such. Thus the 1995 change occurred, as was also pointed out, because the prime minister, a close associate of the president, had been unable to prevent economic decline while a number of financial scandals had become public. The government also ceased to be a coalition, not because of a general election result, but it came about when the president decided to replace his prime minister in March 1993. The most important alteration in the character of the government occurred therefore between elections and manifestly because the president decided that this should be the case. The six cabinets were:

- F. Greguric (1) (Seven-party coalition – CDU, CCDP, CPP, CSLP, SP, SDPC, SDP-PDR, plus independents) September 1990 to December 1991
- F. Greguric (2) (Six-party coalition, as above except CCDP), December 1991 to August 1992
- H. Sarinic (coalition, same as above), August 1992 to March 1993
- N. Valentic (single-party, CDU), March 1993 to November 1995
- Z. Matesa (single-party, CDU), November 1995 to January 2000
- I. Racan (Five-party coalition – SDP, CSLP, CPP, IDP, LP), from January 2000

There have therefore been periodic prime ministerial changes in Croatia but these have taken place in the context of a substantial degree of stability based on the fact that the Croatian Democratic Union of President Tudjman exercised its 'hegemony' over the political system throughout the 1990s. The very serious internal and external problems which the country had to face also contributed to what might be regarded as a degree of ministerial and prime ministerial fatigue. There was probably a desire on the part of the president to ensure that the government, rather than himself, be blamed within public opinion for any shortcomings of public policy. International pressure as well as divisions within the CDU itself over the line to take with respect to Croatian Serbs, to Croats and to Muslims in Bosnia, and to the new Yugoslavia must have also accounted for the changes in governmental leadership.

Changes of prime ministers in Croatia were coupled with a degree of ministerial instability. The Sarinic government of 1992 was almost entirely different from the Greguric government of 1990. The Valentic government of 1993 was of course appreciably different from its predecessor since it was composed of members of the CDU only but that government was appreciably modified during the two and a half years of its existence. The Matesa government of 1995 was not markedly different from the one which it followed but it was also appreciably reshuffled in 1997 after little more than a year. Over the period, the size of the cabinet also varied appreciably in size. The Greguric government had 29 members; its successor was much smaller, with 21 members. The membership of the cabinet seemed to be stabilised from 1993 at 24 or 23 members.

The ministerial posts in the 2000 Racan cabinet were First deputy prime minister; Deputy prime minister; Deputy prime minister; Defence; Foreign

Affairs; Finance; Education and Sports; European Integration; Economy; Tourism; Science and Technology; Interior; Agriculture and Forestry; Culture; Public Works, Reconstruction and Construction; Labour and Social Welfare; Trade, Small and Medium-sized Businesses; Maritime Affairs, Transportation and Communications; Health; Environmental Protection and Zoning; Homeland War Veterans; Justice, Administration and Local Self-Government.

Under Tudjman, the number of deputy prime ministers was always relatively large, varying from three in the first cabinet to five in the fourth. However, the deputy prime ministers also had a post and were even expected to co-ordinate an area of government in the Matesa cabinet at least. This is why, in that government, there were in effect two ministers of the interior and three ministers concerned with finance and/or the economy. The number of ministers without portfolio varied even more. There were six of them in the Greguric government, thus explaining in part the large size of that government; there were three only in the next cabinet and four in the third cabinet, as well as in the early period of the Matesa cabinet. By 1996, however, there was only one non-portfolio minister.

The Constitution of 1990

As was noted earlier, the Croatian parliament adopted a new Constitution at the end of 1990 as a prelude to independence. The Constitution proclaims the rights characterising a liberal democratic polity, for instance the freedom of establishment of political parties, as well as all the basic rights, including some rights for minorities (but Bosniaks and Slovenes were no longer designated as minorities by a constitutional amendment which was passed in 1998). In particular, while the Croat language is declared to be the official language of the country, the right to use Cyrillic, that is, the form which the Serbs use, is mentioned. There is also a long section relating to economic, social and cultural rights.

The structure of the executive

In 1990, the Croatian constitution established a semi-presidential system. The president, elected by popular vote, has substantial powers, and the government was said to be responsible to both the president and to the lower house of parliament. The upper house of parliament, the House of Municipalities, has restricted powers. Much of the architecture of the executive is modelled on the French constitution, although executive-legislative relations were organised in a simpler manner than that of the French system.

The president is elected for five years and can be re-elected only once. There is provision for two ballots. As in France, if no candidate obtains half of the valid votes at the first ballot, a second ballot takes place among the top two candidates. There is no vice-president, although there had been one, before the constitution was adopted. If the president dies or is incapacitated, the interim is assured by the speaker of parliament. This was to be the case at the end of 1999 and beginning of 2000.

The powers of the president are substantial. He/she can call referendums, passes decrees having force of law and takes emergency measures in case of war or of 'immediate danger to the independence and unity of the Republic' (Article 101 (1)), may obtain from parliament for one year the right to issue decrees to regulate issues which are normally regulated by Act of Parliament and can dissolve parliament with the countersignature of the prime minister. He/she appoints and dismisses the prime minister and appoints and dismisses ministers on the proposal of the prime minister. He/she also appoints the members of the National Defence Council and the members of a 'presidential council'. He/she chairs the Council of Ministers when present. In this indirect manner, the president forms part of the government.

The powers of the president have been curtailed by an amendment to the constitution adopted by parliament in the autumn of 2000. Although still to be elected by universal suffrage, the president has lost control over the government, with the political system becoming tilted towards the parliamentary model. The president remains the supreme commander of the armed forces, represents Croatia abroad and keeps the right to appoint ambassadors on the proposal of the prime minister. The president is also the arbiter in conflicts between government and parliament, with the right to dissolve parliament and give voters the last word.

Strictly speaking, however, the government is composed of 'the prime minister, deputy prime ministers, ministers and other members' (Article 108). Within the government, the prime minister is not given a special position, except that he/she does have to present the government to the house of representatives and ask for a vote of confidence. Yet, together with the president, who formally appoints the ministers, the prime minister must clearly exercise at least some substantial influence on the selection of the cabinet. Once appointed, however, and so long as they are not dismissed, ministers appear to have the same status as that of the prime minister. The constitution refers to the government only and it does not state for instance that the prime minister 'leads' the government. The only way in which the prime minister may be 'above' his/her colleagues results from the fact that he/she presents both the programmes to the lower house to obtain the vote of confidence. It is at least probable that the prime minister will have played a substantial part in elaborating that programme.

Votes of confidence and no-confidence are regulated only in so far as the Constitution states that, to be adopted, they must obtain the absolute majority of the members of the lower house (Article 113). A vote of no-confidence can also be passed against individual members of the government (Article 113 (7)). In such cases the prime minister can choose either to resign or to request the president to dismiss the minister against whom the vote of no-confidence was directed.

Cabinet life

Political characteristics

Formation of cabinets

The process of formation of cabinets under Tudjman's presidency was rapid and so was, perhaps more surprisingly, the formation of the Racan cabinet in January 2000. In a sense, Racan's was the first fully political cabinet, as the predecessors had had, with perhaps the exception of those of Greguric in the early phase, a somewhat technical character in that they were the governments of the president.

The role of the president in selecting prime ministers

During Tudjman's regime, prime ministers were selected by the president and by him alone. This was already the case with Greguric, even though the aim was then to establish the legitimacy of the new political system. The second prime minister, Sarinic, had been at the head of his staff and it was as if he appointed his 'chef de cabinet' as his prime minister. The experience proved quickly a failure and Tudjman then appointed a 'non-party' businessman, Valentic, to set up the first wholly CDU government. As economic difficulties piled up and scandals occurred, Matesa, an economist, was chosen to lead the government. Thus the appointment of Racan was the first instance in the history of post-communist Croatia of a prime minister being selected because he had been at the head of a victorious coalition at the polls.

The role of parties in cabinet formation and development

The contrast between Tudjman's governments and the Racan government also provides evidence of the different part played by the parties in the two periods. Racan's government was set up by those parties which had opposed the previous regime and agreed to form a coalition to run the country 'differently'. Parties as such played little part, and indeed a decreasing part, in the composition and characteristics of the previous cabinets.

Admittedly, the first Greguric cabinet, which was set up in September 1990 was a large seven-party coalition, which included even the former communists: although Tudjman's party had won the election of 1990, the president obviously wanted to show that he had a very broad support during the period of transition leading to independence. There were indeed only nine CDU ministers in the first government out of a total of 29, many of whom were independents. Power was shared, ostensibly at least, among all the political forces (at least all the political forces representing the Croatian, although not the Serb part of the population). This was already no longer the case with the second government and the appointment of the former chief of staff of the president as the second prime minister signalled the fact that the head of state was feeling more assured and could rely on a more narrowly based government.

That move was even more marked after the second election victory, in 1993, as the victory indicated to the president that he had by then acquired a solid authority and that he could steer the country in the direction he wished. This meant going towards a form of dominant single-party rule in which other parties were authorised but marginalised. With the departure in 1994 of the more liberal elements of the party, the monolithic character of the CDU became more marked and its dependence on the president more pronounced.

The strong influence of the president over the government raises the question as to whether the single-party CDU governments of prime ministers Valentic and Matesa were in reality truly CDU governments and were not simply governments of the president. What occurred in Croatia was thus the opposite to the one which occurred in most countries of Eastern Europe and indeed in the rest of former Yugoslavia except Serbia. While parties and party systems became more open and pluralistic, allowing indeed in the majority of cases for alternance, the evolution which characterised Croatia was one of 'closure of the ranks' around President Tudjman. What had begun as the president's successful operation of party-building which could ensure that politics in Croatia would be stable in the future became gradually an arrangement of political control and even of dominance. Only with the final illness and death of Tudjman were parties as such restored to a position of power in the political system.

Turnover of ministers

As noted previously, the rate of turnover of cabinets has been neither very high nor very low in Croatia in the 1990s. The first two cabinets had a relatively short life, in particular the second, which lasted under one year, from August 1992 to March 1993. The last two cabinets of the Tudjman regime lasted longer. By the end of 1999 the Matesa cabinet had already outlasted the other three as it had been in office for over four years. As also noted previously, these changes of prime ministers were accompanied with a relative instability of ministers. Eighty-three different persons occupied cabinet positions during the period. As there were 214 yearly cabinet posts between the end of 1990 and December 1999, the average duration of the ministers who served in these cabinets was 2.6 years. Croat ministers under Tudjman lasted in office appreciably longer than their colleagues in Albania, Bulgaria and Romania, but their duration was about the same as that of ministers in Serbia and in Macedonia.

Tujdman's Croatia has been characterised by the kind of 'culture of the reshuffle' which has prevailed in several other countries of the Balkans. The only prime ministers who did not reshuffle their cabinet at all were the first two, Greguric and Sarinic, but Sarinic remained in office nine months only and Greguric a year and a half. Moreover, as was noted earlier, practically the whole cabinet was replaced when the prime ministership passed from Greguric to Sarinic. However, the last two prime ministers reshuffled their cabinet regularly, in effect every year. There were thus six new ministers in 1994 and eight new ministers in 1995 under Valentic; there were six new ministers in 1997 under Matesa. Valentic appointed ten new ministers when he took office in 1993 and Matesa appointed five new ministers when he took office in 1995. Only in 1998 was there scarcely any reshuffle, as one minister was appointed during that year. There was also a tendency for changes of posts to take place within the government. This occurred to a limited extent under Valentic but more under Matesa, as three ministers changed posts when he became prime minister in 1995 and there were three further changes of posts in 1997.

The end of cabinets

Three cabinets out of the five ended as a result of an election having taken place, but, as noted earlier, only the end of the Matesa cabinet was the direct result of the election. While the second Greguric cabinet and the Valentic cabinet ended formally as a general election occurred, Tudjman simply used that opportunity to change the head of the government, the aim being to enable the president to protect his own image in the population by placing the blame on the prime minister. Thus there is no real difference between the end of these two cabinets and the end of the Sarinic cabinet. They all ended because the president decided that this should be the case. Indeed, the watershed in the Tudjman regime was the end of the Sarinic cabinet, as this marked the end of the coalition (and thus somewhat more consensual) period of that regime, the change between the first and second Greguric governments being perhaps a sign of the first crack in that consensus as one of the seven parties of the coalition decided to leave the government.

Administrative characteristics

Under Tudjman, the cabinet met once a week on Thursdays. Some sessions were open, but not all. The sessions which took place in the last month of Tudjman's life, in November 1999, were closed. The secretary of the cabinet attends the meetings. The prime minister is normally in the chair and in his absence, meetings have been chaired in the Matesa government by the Minister of Finance or, more rarely, by the Minister of Foreign Affairs. Tudjman chaired the meeting when he decided to attend. He did so especially at the end of each year and would on such occasions receive the state-of-the-country report of cabinet. There never were representatives of minorities in the post-independence cabinets under Tudjman – the representation of the

Serb minority in Parliament was derisory (three members in the lower house and two in the upper house).

Meetings of the cabinet are prepared by the secretary-general of the cabinet who draws up the agenda.

There were eight standing cabinet committees in the Matesa government, the last under Tudjman. Only one of these, the Committee for State Property Management, was chaired by the prime minister. The others were chaired by the ministers most closely connected with the area covered by the committee.

The Racan government of January 2000 is proposing to amend the Law on Government and the Law on the Organisation and Jurisdiction of Ministries and Organisations of the State Administration. As a matter of fact, the new position of First Deputy Prime Minister has already been created; so have new ministries, in particular the Ministry of European Integration. It is also proposed to abolish the positions of state secretaries.

Decision-making

President and prime minister

The Constitution of 1990 does not specify, as in many other countries of the region, that the government is in charge of policy: it merely states that 'the Government of the Republic of Croatia exercises executive powers in conformity with the Constitution and law' (Article 107). Thus the government seems presented by the Constitution as having an 'administrative' rather than a 'political' role. This is presumably designed to enhance the position of the president, although it is not said either that the president does lead the nation; indeed, the president is not listed by Article 108 as being part of the government. However, the government, as was noted earlier, is responsible to both the president and to the lower house of parliament.

Meanwhile, the president can obviously play a large legal part in decision making as he/she is commander of the armed forces and heads the National Security Council. This gives the president a crucial part in a variety of aspects of foreign policy. The role of the president in home affairs is not based in the same way on any constitutional provision, except when there is an emergency (a provision which appears to come straight from the French 1958 constitution) as well as from the fact that the president can present items to meetings of the government if he so wishes. In practice Tudjman did of course play a key part in decision making. His successor appears to have a more 'normal' view of the role of the president and the fact that his party is not the same as that of the prime minister suggests that it would be difficult for him to act otherwise. Thus the prime minister may, for the first time in the history of post-communist Croatia, be the true leader of the government, although the Constitution says nothing about his role.

The role of the cabinet

Meanwhile, the role of the cabinet may also change and it may play a larger part in decision making, a role which it did not play under Tudjman, at least since the end of the coalition in 1993 and perhaps even before. The character of the Croatian executive is likely to change markedly as a result of the more 'parliamentary' character which the regime has acquired after the death of Tudjman. Yet it is still not clear whether the country will move towards some form of two-party or two-party dominated system or whether multiparty coalitions will become the rule, as has been the case in neighbouring Slovenia. From this would follow striking differences in the character of the executive and of the role of prime minister and ministers.

15
Bosnia-Hercegovina

J. Blondel and S. Selo-Sabic

Cabinet setting

Bosnia-Hercegovina since 1990

One can distinguish three phases in the difficult emergence of Bosnia-Hercegovina as a polity. The first phase started with the election of September 1990, when three main parties emerged, representing respectively the Bosniaks, the Serbs and the Croats. The Bosniak party, the Party for Democratic Action (PDA), was the largest and obtained 86 of the 240 seats of the Assembly; the Serb Democratic Party (SDP) was second with 72 seats; the Croat Democratic Union of Bosnia and Hercegovina (CDU-BH) was third with 44 seats. These three parties took also all the seats in what was still the 'collective presidency' of the country on the communist Yugoslav model. An agreement was struck among these three parties on the basis of which the Bosniak Alija Izetbegović became president, the Croat Jure Pelivan prime minister and the Serb Momilo Krajisnik the speaker of the Assembly. However, less than one year later, in October 1991, the agreement was effectively ended, with the Serb speaker of the Assembly declaring the session closed. The Serb representatives withdrew from the chamber and set up an 'Assembly of the Serb Nation'. Despite some negotiations which had little impact on events, a referendum took place in November 1991 in the Serbian parts of the country and this supported overwhelmingly the existence of a Serb state. Another referendum took place in February 1992 in the whole of Bosnia-Hercegovina but was boycotted by the Serbs and resulted in almost unanimous support for independence which was declared a month later in March 1992. The country was by then entirely split and war was about to start.

The second phase of post-communist Bosnia-Hercegovina was characterised by alternating periods of war and ceasefire, one of the worst episodes being the bombing of the Sarajevo market in February 1994, when 68 civilians were killed in the attack. President Izetbegovic and his government were exercising very little control and the country seemed to be moving towards a three-way partition or to a complete takeover by Serbs and Croats.

Gradually, however, in part as a result of the NATO air strikes on Serb positions, the situation improved on the ground for the 'regular' government.[1] The last Serb attacks occurred in the spring of 1995 and then peace negotiations began in earnest.

Meanwhile, ideas about the restructuration of the country had led to the creation of two component units, defined as 'entities', a 'Federation of Bosnia and Hercegovina', comprising the Bosniak and Croat parts, and a 'Serb Republic of Bosnia and Hercegovina'.[2] The institutional shape of the country came to be agreed upon at Dayton, Ohio, under the auspices of President Clinton, between the presidents of Bosnia, Croatia and Serbia in the summer of 1995. The accord, including a Constitution, was then signed in Paris on 14 December 1995. Ethnic tension did continue for a period, and the president of the Serb part of the country, Radovan Karajdzić, refused to implement the agreement. But he resigned in June 1996 and his successor, Biljana Plavsić, was markedly more amenable to the peace process. Elections were thus able to take place in September 1996 throughout the whole of the country.

At the election, which was monitored by large numbers of international supervisors, President Izetbegović obtained 80 per cent of the Bosniak vote, the president of the Federation, Kresimir Zubak, 88 per cent of the Croat vote and the 1991 speaker of the Assembly, Momcilo Krajisnik, 67 per cent of the Serb vote. At the Assembly election, the Bosniak PDA obtained 56 per cent of the votes in the Federation part of the country, but it also obtained nearly 18 per cent of the votes in the Serb Republic section. Complaints of fraud were very limited.

The third phase of the life of Bosnia-Hercegovina began. President Izetbegović remained at the head of the collective presidency of Bosnia-Hercegovina until the next parliamentary election which took place in September 1998. He again obtained the largest number of votes for the presidency among the candidates from the three ethnic groups. However, on the basis of a provision stipulating that an elected nominee for the presidency could not hold the office for two consecutive terms, Živko Radišić (Serb) became the president for eight months, followed by Ante Jelavić (Croat) and, by Alija Izetbegović again for a few months from February 2000 until his final resignation later in the year.

In early 2000, the president of the federation was Ejup Ganić (Bosniak) and the vice-president was Ivo Andrić Luzanski (Croat). Andric Plavsić was subsequently replaced by Nikola Poplasen as president of the Serb Republic, but Poplasen was removed from the office in the spring of 1999 by the EU High Representative on the grounds that he was undermining the implementation of the Dayton Agreement. Up to the Summer of 2000 the Serb Republic effectively remained without a president. Yet political life seemed gradually to become more normal. After having been postponed for a year, municipal elections took place in September 1997, with the three main parties continuing to receive the most votes on a turnout of 60 per cent. The same trend was repeated at the 2000 local elections, although at that contest a non-ethnic party did make a breakthrough among Bosniaks.

Cabinets since 1990 in Bosnia-Hercegovina

The structure of the government of Bosnia-Hercegovina was sharply modified in the course of the 1990s. At first, and for a short while, the government operated on the basis of the arrangements inherited from Yugoslavia. Amendments to the Constitution were adopted in 1991 to replace that of 1974 under what was still the rule of the League of Communists. However, the new Constitution was not implemented. In late 1991, Serb representatives left the government while the area controlled by the Bosnian government shrank markedly. The first step towards a more effective form of government was taken in 1994 when the 'Federation of Bosnia and Hercegovina' was set up between Bosniaks and Croats.[3] The government of the overall country did continue to exist under the presidency of Izetbegović, however.

As a result of the agreement of December 1995, many, if not most, of the powers of the Bosnia-Hercegovina government were transferred to the two 'entities'; but the size of the government of all of Bosnia-Hercegovina remained large for a while, with ministers of the three constituent peoples being appointed, mostly as deputy ministers, in each department. The ministries have had to rely on the 'entity' institutions to enforce their decisions. In August 1999, however, Bosnia's Constitutional Court declared the composition of the Council of Ministers unconstitutional; it decided that the Bosnia-Hercegovina Constitution allows only for one chairperson of the Council and not for the two co-chairs, plus a deputy chair, which existed at the time. As a result, in April 2000, parliament approved a bill on the Council of Ministers setting up an eight-month rotating chair for the Council of Ministers, on the same principle as the one applied to the presidency. Three new ministries, the Ministry for European Integration, the Ministry for Human Rights and Refugees and the Ministry of the Treasury were added to the Council of Ministers.

Four different persons became prime ministers of Bosnia-Hercegovina between 1991 and 2000. There were seven cabinets during the period, as the Serb representatives left the first cabinet soon after its constitution in late 1991 and as one of the prime ministers returned to office for a second time in 1997 and for a third time in 1999. These seven cabinets were:

- J. Pelivan (1), three-party coalition (PDA, CDU, SPD), September to November 1991
- J. Pelivan (2), two-party coalition (PDA, CDU), November 1991 to December 92
- M. Akhmadzić, two-party coalition, December 1992 to August 93

- H. Silajdžić (1), four-party coalition[4] (PDA, CDU, Socialist Democratic Party (ex-communist), Croatian Peasant Party) August 1993 to February 1996
- H. Muratović, three-party coalition, February to September 1996
- H. Silajdžić (2), three-party coalition, January 1997 to September 98
- H. Silajdžić (3), three-party coalition, February to December 1999

During 1996–98, the 'Federation' had three cabinets, headed successively by I. Kapetanović, E. Bikakcić and E. Ganić; the 'Serb Republic' had three cabinets headed successively by R. Kasagić, G. Klicković, M. Dodik to September 1998 when the newly elected president of the Serb Republic, N. Poplasen, became engaged in a long series of unsuccessful efforts to replace Dodik. It was in this context that the EU High Representative decided to remove Poplasen. From March 1999, Dodik was to be a caretaker prime minister.

There was therefore a substantial amount of governmental instability in Bosnia-Hercegovina throughout the period, not altogether surprisingly, although the president remained the same. Instability was as pronounced before and after the Dayton agreement. It was marked at both levels, but the government of the 'Serb Republic' was the most unstable of the three.

The turnover of ministers from one cabinet to the next was substantial in Bosnia-Hercegovina; there was little change within each cabinet, in part because none of them lasted much. Although Serb ministers effectively left the Pelivan cabinet, the fiction that they were still members was maintained and they were not replaced. Given that the Bosnia-Hercegovina government did not control large sections of the territory, the cabinet had little impact on the life of the country between 1992 and 1995, however.

It is therefore practically impossible to calculate precisely the size of the pre-1996 Bosnia-Hercegovina cabinet. The Pelivan government was set up in 1991 with 19 ministers. Akmadzić's cabinet of 1992–93 is reported as having had 24 ministers, but five of these were members of the Serb Democratic Party who had in effect left the government. The first Silajdžić cabinet, which took office in the middle of 1993 was said to have had at first 20 members, but four Serb Democratic Party ministers were still listed as members; by 1995, their names disappeared but they were not replaced immediately and the posts were officially designated as being vacant. The gradual decrease in the size of the cabinet from 1993 was due essentially to these 'vacancies'. There were three such vacancies, including that of the Minister of Finance, in 1993; the posts were filled subsequently but six further vacancies occurred in 1995.

As mentioned earlier, the nature and size of the Bosnia-Hercegovina cabinet was radically altered in 1996. The first Silajdzic cabinet ended in February 1996 with sixteen ministers, not including the vacant posts. The Muratović cabinet which succeeded it had only seven ministers, including the prime minister and a minister without portfolio. The second Silajdzic cabinet which succeeded that of Muratović had three departmental ministers only, although there were altogether twelve different members of that cabinet, including the two co-prime ministers.[5] Meanwhile, the government of the 'Federation' had 12 departments and 14 to 15 ministers, including the prime minister, and the Serb Republic government had between 19 and 23 departments and between 20 and 24 ministers, including the prime minister.

The ministerial posts at the end of the first Silajdzić government, in February 1996, were Defence; Interior; Foreign Affairs; Finance; Economy (vacant); Trade; Agriculture (vacant); Environment; Transport; Energy and Communications; Information (vacant); Justice; Health and Labour; Education, Culture and Science; Veterans (vacant); Social Welfare and Refugees; Religion (vacant); Reconstruction and Refugees; Construction; Supply (vacant).

The ministerial posts in the Muratović (1996) and the second Silajdzić cabinets (from 1997) were

Muratović	*Silajdzić*
Foreign Affairs	Foreign Affairs
Finance	Foreign Trade and
Foreign Trade	Economic Relations
Justice	Civil Affairs and Communications
	Refugees

Most of the departments which were part of the pre-1996 Bosnia-Hercegovina government were thus transferred to the Federation and the Serb Republic, indeed including defence in both cases and including foreign affairs up to 1998 and foreign economic relations from 1997 in the 'Serb Republic'. It should be noted that the Constitution of Bosnia-Hercegovina gives the central state one source of revenue only – consular fees. The central state is therefore dependent on transfers from the 'entities' to run institutions and to service the external debt, while foreign finance covers almost 40 per cent of the expenditure of that state.

There were five ministers without portfolio at the Bosnia-Hercegovina level before 1996, but only one in 1996–97 and none at all from 1997 onwards. There were two deputy prime ministers in the Akmadzić government of 1993 and one in first Silajdzić government which succeeded it. Since 1997, they have been replaced by a 'co-prime minister' from the Serb Republic area and a deputy prime minister from the Croat part of the country, thus ensuring that the three 'constituent peoples' were represented in the prime ministerial group. Since 1997, there have also been two deputy ministers in each of the three departments of the Bosnia-Hercegovina government and these deputy ministers are listed as forming part of the cabinet. Each department is thus run by a committee of three persons, one from each party. Similarly, the whole cabinet is led by a three-person committee. This practice emphasises the desired 'consociational' character of the government of Bosnia-Hercegovina, a character which is indeed to some extent in keeping with the traditions of former Yugoslavia. There was a collective presidency composed of seven members, including its chairman, in 1990–91 and of six members subsequently. The members of that collective presidency were drawn from the different parties which formed part of the coalition. With the reconstruction of the Bosnia-Hercegovina governmental structure as a result of the Dayton agreement of late 1995, the collective presidency was reduced to three members representing the three 'constituent peoples' of the country, although these members happened at the same time to be drawn from and therefore to represent also the three main parties of Bosnia-Hercegovina.

The constitutional amendments of 1992 and the Constitution of 1995

Up to 1995, the Bosnia-Hercegovina government was organised on the basis of the socialist constitution of 1974, as amended in 1992 when the country declared its independence. The system was based on a collective presidency, a bicameral legislature and a cabinet responsible to both the presidency and the legislature. These arrangements came quickly to be merely formal, however, as a result of the secession of the Serb areas, except for the fact that the Constitution legitimised the continuation of President Izetbegović and his government in office.

As the years passed and alongside the secession of the Serb areas, an accord was gradually taking shape between Bosniaks and Croats, and it became increasingly clear that Bosnia-Hercegovina could be maintained as a country only if a sharp distinction was drawn between two levels of government, an 'upper level' which would have residual powers and would have a fully 'consociational' structure and a 'lower level', composed of two units, which would exercise most of the state functions. This was to be the basis on which the Dayton agreement was negotiated in November 1995 and the Constitution was adopted in Paris in the following December. The arrangement bears some similarities with both the former Yugoslav and the Swiss systems, in that every branch of the Bosnia-Hercegovina structure, presidential, governmental, legislative and indeed judiciary is based on collegiality, a collegiality which is built on the three 'constituent peoples' sections of the country, although there are only two formal 'pillars', the 'entities', since two of these three 'constituent peoples', Bosniak and Croat, had agreed to form a Federation.

The structure of the Bosnia-Hercegovina executive

Given that the 1995 arrangements formalise the entrenched position of the three 'constituent peoples', the governmental system cannot be parliamentary, semi-presidential or presidential. It has to be based on the permanent representation of all three of these 'peoples' in the executive. Thus the executive is collegial in character; thus, too, it cannot be removed easily and any removal which takes place has to be done within the context of each of (or all of) the 'constituent peoples'.

That executive is composed of two elements, the presidency and the cabinet. The presidency is in effect a presidential college of three members, as mentioned in the previous section. The Bosniak and Croat members are elected according to the rules of the Federation, while the Serb member is elected according to the rules of the Serb Republic. The members of the presidency are elected for four years; the chairman of the presidency is to be selected according to a procedure adopted by the legislature, but, it was decided that in the first occasion the chairman would be the member of the college who had obtained most votes, in this case the Bosniak member. The presidency is responsible collectively for the foreign policy of Bosnia-Hercegovina. There is no provision for its removal before the end of its term.

The cabinet or council of ministers is composed of a collective prime ministerial group, of ministers and of deputy ministers. It is specified that the deputy ministers must be drawn from a different 'constituent people' from that from which the minister is drawn. The presidency nominates the 'chair' of the Council of Ministers, that is to say the three-person prime ministerial group, but these appointments have to be confirmed by the lower house, known as the House of Representatives, two-thirds of whose members are drawn from the Federation and one-third from the Serb Republic. As in parliamentary governments, the ministers are nominated by the prime ministerial group and the appointments have to be ratified by the House of Representatives. There is no provision for votes of censure, however. In practice, after the first and apparently transitional government appointed in early 1996, the Council of Ministers has remained in office unchanged.

Cabinet life

Political characteristics

Formation of cabinets

One key element of political life in Bosnia-Hercegovina is the role of the international community, which has become increasingly interventionist and has contributed to a degree of irresponsibility on the part of the country's leaders.

The role of the president in selecting prime ministers

As there is no single president of the country, the structure of the cabinet has first to be agreed among the three members of the presidency to meet the ethnic criteria. Once that is resolved, the selection of particular individuals is discussed.

The role of parties in cabinet formation and development

Bosnia-Hercegovina cabinets have always been coalitions; but these coalitions changed, because the Serb representatives first went out of the government and later rejoined it. Thus, after having been a coalition of the three main parties of the constituent peoples in 1991, the coalition included, between 1992 and 1996, the Bosniak PDA, the Croat CDU and two small 'all-Bosnia' parties, the Socialist Democratic Party (former communist) and the Croatian Peasant Party. From 1996 onwards, the government returned to being composed of a coalition of the three main parties representing the three constituent peoples.

Yet it is questionable as to whether these three parties are truly decision-making organisations, as power is markedly personalised in Bosnia-Hercegovina. The country cannot be dominated by a single leader, as Serbia or Croatia have been, but it may be dominated by a small group drawn from the constituent peoples. A degree of consociationalism has to exist in the government if the country is to survive, but whether this consociationalism is sufficiently widespread to constitute genuine pluralism is less clear. What is clear, meanwhile, is that the consociational system precludes alternance at the top level, even if, as has partly taken place in the Serb entity, alternance may occur at the level of the component units.

Turnover of ministers

Given the precarious conditions under which the government of Bosnia-Hercegovina operated between 1992 and 1996 and given the subsequent radical overhaul of the constitutional arrangements which drastically reduced the powers of the top level of government, it is manifestly wrong to calculate the rate of ministerial turnover for the whole of the 1990–98 period. What must be done is to calculate this turnover separately before and after 1995. Moreover, before 1995, although ministers from the Serb area had ceased to participate early on, they were nonetheless listed as belonging to the government, as previously mentioned, at least up to 1994. Yet, even if these defections are taken into account at the date at which they were formally recognised, the rate of turnover has been high in pre-1996 Bosnia-Hercegovina – 48 different ministers occupied 79 yearly posts during the period, an average duration of 1.64 years.

The reconstruction of the Bosnia-Hercegovina government from 1996 on the basis of a much smaller cabinet was still too recent in 2000 for firm conclusions to be drawn about the turnover of ministers. All that can be noted is that Alija Izetbegović remained a member of the presidency, while the two other members changed after the 1998 election: Ante Jelavić replaced Kreaimir Zubak as Croat representative and Živko Radišić replaced Momilo Krajianik as Serb presentative. There was hardly continuity in the cabinet. Only three of the seven members of the Muratović 1996 government had previously been ministers; only three of the twelve members of the 1997 Silajdzić government had participated in the Muratović administration, the prime minister being one of them, and all three of these ministers occupied posts different from those which they had earlier occupied.

There has also been a substantial turnover of ministers in the two 'entities', although more in the Serb Republic than in the Federation, possibly because of the political upheavals resulting from the departure of the former Serb president, Karajdzić, and of Plavsić and Poplasen subsequently. Twenty-two different persons occupied one of the fourteen or fifteen ministerial posts in the Federation over the three years of its existence; over the same period, fifty-one persons occupied one of the twenty to twenty-four departments of the government of the Serb Republic. The average of duration of Federation ministers was exactly two years and that of Serb Republic ministers was 1.27 years, a very marked difference, even if over a few years only.

Administrative characteristics

It was only in late November 1997 that a first bill on the Council of Ministers was adopted by the cabinet and forwarded to parliament for approval, which occurred soon afterwards. One of the issues at stake was the location of the cabinet meetings and of the ministries. After a period during which the cabinet moved between two locations (Sarajevo and Lukavica – in Serb territory), it was agreed in 1998 that meetings would take place in Sarajevo. Meetings are usually held on Thursdays. The co-chairmen take the chair on the basis of weekly rotation. A second bill on the Council of Ministers was forwarded to the parliament by the presidency of Bosnia-Hercegovina in February 2000 with a request to adopt it speedily. This bill was the result of a decision of the Constitutional Court, which had declared unconstitutional the institution of the two co-prime ministers. The new bill proposes that the Council of Ministers should be reorganised; there would be one prime minister and two deputy prime ministers who would also lead two new ministries. The rotating prime ministership would be occupied for a period of eight months by a representative of each constituent people. As was noted earlier, the bill was adopted by parliament in April 2000.

Meetings of the cabinet are prepared by the secretary-general of the cabinet who draws up the agenda. Given the small size of the cabinet, there are no standing committees in the Bosnia-Hercegovina government.

Decision-making

As a result of the highly polarised politics among the three ethnic groups as well as because of the strong interventionist role of the international community, decision-making in the Council of Ministers tends to be rather formal as there are in effect previously agreed settlements. Up to the formation of the new Council of Ministers in 2000, the Council was almost entirely a fiction. With the July 1999 ruling of the Constitutional Court which stated that the three ethnic groups have constituent powers within the entire territory of the country and not only in their respective 'entities', as was the case previously, and with the enlargement of the Council of Ministers from three to six ministries, the Council may take new powers and come to represent a somewhat more centralised and integrated country.

President and prime minister

The Croat and Bosniak members of the presidency have had a marked influence on the functioning of the Croat and Bosniak sections of the executive, that is to say the Federation, while the role of the Serb member of the presidency appears to have been less marked in the Serb Republic.

The role of the cabinet

As pointed out earlier, the central government of Bosnia-Hercegovina – the Council of Ministers – has had a limited impact in the post-Dayton period, as a result of internal turmoil and of external intervention. Meetings of the Peace Implementation Council in 1997 and 1998 increased the powers of the EU High Representative to impose decisions and the threat of intervention is also used to push the authorities into reaching decisions. As a matter of fact, the Council of Ministers is hardly able to reach a common agreement without outside intervention while, at the same time, the decision-making process within the cabinet is markedly circumscribed.

Notes

1   In July 1995, Serb forces attacked Srebrenica, which was the UN-designated safe area in Eastern Bosnia, killed thousands of civilians and expelled tens of thousands. A shell in August 1995 killed many civilians in the centre of Sarajevo. It provoked an international outrage and led to NATO air strikes against Bosnian Serb positions.
2   In September 1993, the term 'Bosniak' was introduced to replace the term Bosnian Muslim. In this text, the term Bosniak is used to refer to Bosnian Muslims, unless otherwise specifically required by the context. The local name for the Serb Republic is Republika Srpska, the term also commonly used in foreign texts to refer to the Serb Republic.
3   The US initiative of late 1993 had led to the cessation of hostilities between Bosniaks and Croats in Central Bosnia and resulted in the creation of the Federation of Bosnia and Hercegovina, comprising 51 per cent of the territory, on the basis of the Washington agreement of 1 March 1994.

4 Haris Silajdzić was a member of the SDA, but he left in early 1996 and formed a new party, the Party for Bosnia and Hercegovina. However, that party, along with two others, entered a four-party Coalition for United and Democratic Bosnia and Hercegovina together with the main party, the SDA.

5 It was a 12-member cabinet for three ministries, Foreign Affairs, Foreign Trade and Economic Affairs and Civil Affairs and Communications. Each minister was a member of one of the three ethnic groups and each had two deputies who were members of the two ethnic groups to which the particular minister did not belong.

16
Serbia and the new Yugoslavia

J. Blondel and F. Privitera

Cabinet setting

Serbia and the new Yugoslavia since 1990: the rise and fall of Milošević

The dramatic fall of Slobodan Milošević, at first president of Serbia between 1989 and 1997 and, from 1997 to October 2000, president of the new Yugoslavia which includes only Serbia and Montenegro, closed a ten-year period during which Serbia isolated itself from the rest of Europe and, alone with Croatia, was ruled in an authoritarian manner apparently irrespective of the consequences for the country.

The domination of Milošević over Serbia, which began in the last years of the communist regime, was confirmed at the first multiparty presidential and parliamentary elections of December 1990. At the presidential election, Milošević was popularly elected as a moderate former communist against Vuk Drasković, whose platform was anti-communist but also was then virulently nationalistic. At the parliamentary election, Milošević's Socialist Party of Serbia (SPS) obtained 194 out of 250 seats, the Serbian Renaissance Movement (SRM) of Drasković was second with 19 seats.

Milošević had already entrenched his power earlier in the year when a new Serbian Constitution was adopted by the parliament of Serbia in June 1990 subsequently approved in September by the people in a referendum (which was boycotted by ethnic Albanians) and when he ensured in the following month that what was once the League of Communists remained in power under the new name of Socialist Party of Serbia. The dominance of that party was in part assured by the nationalistic twist which Milošević gave to the organisation. The new Constitution had abolished the autonomous status granted by the communist constitution of Serbia of 1974 to Voivodina in the north – largely populated by ethnic Hungarians – and to Kosovo in the south, where ethnic Albanians were the immense majority. This development was held to be a patriotic necessity given that the region was considered sacred in Serbian mythology for having been the 'cradle' of the country. Thus Milošević could exercise effective control of the government both in

Serbia through the three prime ministers who headed the government between 1991 and 1998 and in the new Yugoslavia which was constituted in 1992 in which the small Montenegro (600,000 inhabitants as against the nearly 10 million of Serbia) was bound to play only a limited part.

Milošević's power came to be challenged in the course of the following two years, both as a result of the war which Yugoslavia (in effect Serbia) was conducting, directly or indirectly, in Croatia and Bosnia and of the serious consequences of the war for the economy of the country. Despite some successes, the army was unable to prevent the break up of the old Yugoslav federation and by 1992 Yugoslavia was effectively reduced to Serbia and Montenegro. The challenger of Milošević at the election of 1990, Drasković, by then no longer taking a nationalistic line, demanded that Serbia followed a peaceful policy. He led a campaign of civil disobedience against the president whom he attacked for causing the war with the rest of Yugoslavia and for destroying the economy of the country. These moves played a part in forcing Milošević to soften his line in particular in relation to Bosnia.

A new federal Constitution was adopted in April 1992 for what remained of Yugoslavia to take account of the new situation and to introduce the changes in the structure of government corresponding to the end of communism. Elections for the federal assembly took place in May. Although the Socialist Party of Serbia came first, it obtained 47 seats only out of 138 and Milošević had to agree to the appointment, as first federal prime minister, of Milan Panić, a Serb who had returned from the United States after having been a successful businessman there. Panić adopted a moderate line and condemned the policy of 'ethnic cleansing' in September 1992. But he was not to remain in office long. Presidential and parliamentary elections at both the federal and the state level took place in December of that year, at which Milošević was re-elected with 58 per cent of the votes against Panić who obtained 35 per cent (but alleged that there had been extensive fraud). Strengthened by the election result, Milošević ensured Panić's defeat in a vote of no-confidence in the Yugoslav assembly. He was replaced by a prime minister favourable to the president of Serbia. A few months later, in June 1993, the federal assembly also passed a vote of no-confidence against the president of Yugoslavia, the Montenegrin Cosić, although he had been elected a little a year earlier with 85 per cent of the votes and despite demonstrations in his support led by Drasković. Cosić had to resign and was replaced by the Serbian Zoran Lilić, a supporter of Milošević. The whole of the Yugoslav structure thus became dominated by the Serb president.

At the December 1992 elections, Milošević's party, the SPS, had obtained 101 seats, out of 250, however. The president had to rely on the support of an ultra-nationalist party, the Serbian Radical Party (SRP) which had obtained 73 seats and on its leader, Vojislav Seselj. The alliance did not last and by the end of 1993, prominent members of the Radical Party, including its leader, were arrested. As the SPS no longer had a majority, Milošević dissolved parliament once more. The SPS obtained only 37 per cent of the votes but, thanks to the electoral system, the party obtained nearly an absolute majority (123 seats out of 250); a small party with six deputies was detached from the main opposition coalition, DEPOS, led by Drasković. The government no longer needed to rely on the ultra-nationalists. Milošević then pursued a somewhat more moderate line with respect to Croatia and Bosnia, imposed a blockade on the Bosnian Serbs in 1994 and, in 1995, took part in the Dayton negotiations which led to the Bosnian settlement. Yet the Serb president continued with his nationalistic economic policy. The head of the National Bank, who criticised the government for not making a deal with the IMF, was quickly dismissed.

New federal and local elections took place in November 1996. The government coalition failed to win an absolute majority at the federal level (64 out of 138 seats). It lost control of a number of cities and in particular of Belgrade to the opposition coalition, known as Zajedno. But the government refused to recognise the results of these elections and obtained the annulment of the results by courts and electoral commissions. This led to a long period of mass demonstrations, bans of demonstrations and further illegal demonstrations. Under international and indeed a certain amount of Orthodox Church pressure, the government did eventually give way. The Serb parliament agreed in February 1997 to accept the validity of the annulled results in Belgrade and thirteen other cities. Yet the government continued to harass the opposition in relation to the media. A law was introduced in parliament, also in February 1997, to that effect, but, under pressure from the Zajedno opposition, the most illiberal clause of the proposed legislation was removed in April.

At that point, the Serb president came under attack from the hitherto loyal prime minister of Montenegro. A series of problems had arisen over the years, in particular over economic policy, but the specific question at stake was that of the candidature of Milošević to the federal presidency, since the Serb Constitution did not allow for the president to stand more than twice. Milošević was duly elected by the federal parliament in November, admittedly, but this took place after a number of hurdles were overcome. The power of Milošević was thus beginning to be seriously challenged. As the Montenegrin president had helped the Serb president, he was rewarded by receiving the prime ministership of the federal government, while a supporter of Milošević, Milan Milutonović, previously foreign minister of the Yugoslav federation, was elected Serb president. Once elected, the new president maintained the same Serb prime minister in office, but the cabinet came to be based on a coalition including both the Radical Party of Seselj and the Yugoslav United Left, the party of the wife of Milošević, Mirjana Marković. The presence of this small party was presumably designed to help Milošević to continue to exercise strong influence on the policies of the Serb government.

Milošević was thus confronted with strong challenges. He remained in control on the basis of a mixture of authoritarianism and of concessions made grudgingly and after a long time had elapsed. The nationalism (latent or overt) of a substantial proportion of the population was also unquestionably an important element in Milošević's enduring political strength. The war in Kosovo in the spring of 1999 seemed at first not to change the situation appreciably. However, over the subsequent months, the position of Milošević became increasingly shaky, in part because Montenegro had ceased to be a 'loyal' supporter. This was also because of internal developments in Serbia. The prestige of the leader was markedly diminished as he had successively lost control of the Croat Serbs and of the Bosnian Serbs and was forced to abandon Kosovo as a result of the war. The cards at his disposal had become rather weak. Moreover, the death of Tudjman in late 1999 had left the strong man of Yugoslavia in an awkward solitary position.

Milošević tried to recover support by what turned out to be a massive mistake, namely by allowing his popularity to be tested at a presidential election on 24 September 2000. This move was to prove fatal as the opposition united behind Vojislav Kostunica, a moderate nationalist who had not been associated either with the old communist system or with Milošević's regime. Kostunica obtained 54 per cent of the votes. At first, Milošević did not recognise the result and insisted that a second ballot should take place. But demonstrations demanding his departure, including large contingents from the provinces, took place on such a scale (with the army, largely drawn from conscripts, and even the police remaining neutral) that Milošević had to give in and to allow Kostunica to take over power.

Cabinets since 1990 in Serbia and in the new Yugoslavia

Although Milošević remained president of Serbia from the break up of the old Yugoslavia to 1997, that country had three prime ministers and four cabinets between 1991 and 1998. The changes of prime ministers occurred after the general elections which had followed the two dissolutions of parliament decided by Milošević, in late 1992 in connection with the problems arising from the presence of prime minister Panić at the federal level and in late 1993 as a result of the desire of Milošević to reject the support hitherto given by Seselj's Radical Party. The third prime minister was appointed in February 1994 and lasted throughout the rest of Milošević's presidency and was maintained in office by his successor, although the cabinet was almost entirely modified in March 1998. Meanwhile, there were also three federal cabinets between 1992 and 1998; the short cabinet of Panić was succeeded by the long period of rule of Radoje Kontić, who was only replaced as prime minister in 1998 by Momir Bulatović, the former president of Montenegro, when Milošević became president of the federation.

The four Serb cabinets were:

- R. Bozović (SPS), December 1990 to January 1993
- N. Sainović (SPS), minority, with Radical Party support, January 1993 to February 1994
- M. Marjanović (1) (SPS), minority with New Democracy support, February 1994 to March 1998
- M. Marjanović (2) (SPS, SRP, YUL), three-party coalition, from March 1998.

The three cabinets of the new Yugoslavia were:

- M. Panić, April 1992 to February 1993
- R. Kontić, February 1993 to May 1998
- M. Bulatović, May 1998 to October 2000.

There was therefore a degree of instability in both Serbia and the new Yugoslavia in the early period; this was followed by marked stability once Milošević was able to establish his dominance at both levels, directly in Serbia up to 1997 and indirectly up to 1997 in the new Yugoslavia.

While the turnover of ministers in Serbia was extensive from one cabinet to the next, their tenure was relatively stable in each cabinet and in particular in the four-year long first Marjanović cabinet. There was only one reshuffle at mid-point in 1996, which concerned six ministers. Cabinet stability was not as marked in the federal government. Not only was only one of the members of the Panić cabinet appointed by his successor, Kontić, but that second prime minister proceeded to reshuffle his cabinet every year of his five-year tenure, while the third cabinet, that of Bulatović, was almost entirely new.

Over the period, the size of the cabinet increased appreciably and regularly in Serbia. The Bozović government had 23 members; the Sainović government had 25. The first Marjanović cabinet started with 27 members in 1994 and ended with 29 members in 1998, while the second had a record 36 members. Yugoslav cabinets have tended to be smaller, although they have oscillated in size around 20 members. The Panić cabinet had 20 members, the same number as the Kontić cabinet during its first phase; that cabinet then increased to 23 members only to decrease to 16 in 1995 and to increase subsequently to 19. The 1998 Bulatović cabinet had 21 members.

The ministerial posts in the 1998 second Marjanović Serb cabinet were Finance; Energy; Interior; Local Administration; Economic Development; Tourism; Justice; Agriculture; Public Works; Transport; Trade; Industry; Labour and Social Welfare; Health; Science; Culture; Education; Family; Religion; Information; Environmental Protection; Youth; Serbs Abroad.

The ministerial posts in the 1998 Kontić Yugoslav cabinet were Foreign Affairs; Defence; Interior; Finance; Economy; Trade; Industry and Transport; Agriculture; Health and Labour; Justice; Environment.

There were many deputy prime ministers and ministers without portfolio at both levels. In Serbia, there were three deputy prime ministers at the beginning and at the end of the period, but there had been four at some point; at the federal level, there had been two at the beginning and there were three and even four at some point in the Kontić government. There was indeed a degree of interchange at that level between the two governments. The former prime minister of Serbia, Sainović, became deputy prime minister in the federal government; a former deputy prime minister of Serbia, J. Zebić, also became deputy prime minister in the federal government. The peak was reached in the Bulatović Federal government of 1998, which had five deputy prime ministers. The inflation of ministers without portfolio was particularly noticeable in the second Marjanović cabinet, possibly because the needs of the new coalition had to be fulfilled. Seven of them were appointed while there had been three or four only during the first cabinet of that prime minister. The number of ministers without portfolio also increased in the federal cabinet, from two in the Panić cabinet to four in the latest version of the Kontić government. In this case the ministers without portfolio were all former ministers with portfolio whose department appeared to have been abolished.

The Serb Constitution of 1990 and the new Yugoslav Constitution of 1992

As was noted earlier, the Serb electorate adopted by referendum in July 1990 amendments to the constitution of the Republic of Serbia, mainly in order to abolish the autonomy of the two provinces of Voivodina and Kosovo. Two years later, in April 1992, a new constitution was adopted for the Federal Republic of Yugoslavia, which explicitly stated in the same sentence that given 'the historical ties and shared interests of the state of Serbia and the state of Montenegro' and 'arising from the unbroken continuity of Yugoslavia' the Constitution of the Federal Republic of Yugoslavia was promulgated. It is also stated in Article 2 that the Republic 'may be joined by other member republics'. A long series of articles follow which specify the rights of Yugoslav citizens and in particular give minorities 'the right to education in their own language, in conformity with the law' (Article 46 (1)) as well as other rights, proclaimed in subsequent articles. Article 77 then gives a long list of matters which are within the competence of the Federal Republic of Yugoslavia, including, alongside international relations, the defence of individual rights, a single market, health and environmental protection and technical and technological systems.

Structure of the Serb and Yugoslav executives

Both the Serb Constitution and the Yugoslav Constitution establish semi-presidential systems, although the method of election of the president differs. He/she is elected by popular vote in Serbia and by the federal assembly in Yugoslavia. In both cases, however, he/she has substantial powers, but the governments are also said to be responsible to the respective parliaments, despite the fact that, in the Yugoslav case, the federal government is said to be 'formed for a four-year term' (Article 100 (2)). In the federal assembly, the upper house, The Chamber of Republics, has somewhat restricted powers compared to those of the Chamber of Citizens.

In both cases the president is elected for four years and can be re-elected only once. There is provision for two ballots in the Serb case. If no candidate obtains half the valid votes at the first ballot, a second ballot takes place among the top two candidates. In the Yugoslav case, the federal assembly is said to have the right to both appoint and dismiss the president (Article 78 (7) and Article 92 (2)). There is no vice-president. If the president dies or is incapacitated, the interim is assured by the speaker of the lower house in the Serb case and of the upper house in the Yugoslav case.

The powers of the president are relatively important at both levels, but more so in Serbia, where he/she can in particular call referendums. Both presidents can dissolve their respective parliaments and appoint and dismiss their respective prime ministers. Curiously, however, the powers of the president stop there; in the Yugoslav case, it is not even said whether he/she formally appoints the ministers. It must be assumed that he/she does not.

In both cases the government is composed of the prime minister, deputy prime ministers and ministers (Article 100 of the federal Constitution, for instance). Within the government, the federal Yugoslav prime minister is given a special position. He/she 'appears before the federal assembly to present his programme' (Article 101 (2)) as well as to announce the composition of the government. Article 102 states, unlike the other constitutions of the area, that the prime minister directs the work of the federal government, appoints and dismisses ministers and asks for a vote of confidence. The government is clearly the prime minister's government. Votes of confidence and no-confidence are only regulated in so far as the constitution states that they are adopted if they obtain the absolute majority of the members of the lower house in the Serb case and of both chambers in the Yugoslav case.

Cabinet life

Turnover of ministers

Overall, the rate of turnover of cabinets has been neither very high nor very low in Serbia and in the new Yugoslavia in the 1990s. However, as previously mentioned, this is because, in Serbia, the first two cabinets and, in Yugoslavia, the first cabinet were relatively short-lived and coincided with a period in which the power of President Milošević did not appear to have been fully established. The subsequent cabinets, both in Serbia and in Yugoslavia, lasted for a full parliamentary term. As also mentioned, there was a degree of instability of ministers – and thus a certain 'culture of the reshuffle' – in the Yugoslav case, even in the Kontić cabinet which lasted five years, while the stability of ministers in their posts was appreciably greater in the long-lasting Marjanović first cabinet of 1994–98. Thus 96 different persons occupied cabinet positions between 1992 and 1998 in Serbia and 71 in the federal government. As during that period there were 196 yearly cabinet posts in the first case and 141 in the second, the average duration of the ministers who served in these cabinets was respectively 2.04 and 1.98 years. This is about the same rate as that which has been found in Croatia and Bosnia, lower than that found for Macedonia but appreciably higher than that found for Albania, Bulgaria and Romania.

Parties in government

As was noted earlier, the first three Serb cabinets were single party, but only the first was single-party majority. The Sainović government was truly a minority government as it was far short of a majority and needed to rely on the votes of the right-wing Radical Party. It lasted one year only because Milošević decided that his government should not depend on the support of such a party. The first Marjanović cabinet was a near-majority cabinet which needed only to be supported by the six deputies of the New Democracy Party, who did not create particular problems for the government. Only the fourth cabinet, that which Marjanović reconstructed when Milošević became president of Yugoslavia, was a coalition. The Socialist Party was not even in a majority in the cabinet, having only 13 ministers, including the prime minister, while the Radical Party, which returned to power and whose leader, V. Seselj, became one of the deputy prime ministers, had 15 ministers and the Yugoslav United Left of M. Marković, the wife of Milošević, had four.

The Yugoslav cabinet is necessarily a coalition in the sense that it includes both Serb and Montenegrin representatives and therefore its ministers are drawn from among two different parties at least. This is enshrined in the Constitution, which specifies that president and prime minister should come from a different republic.

The strong influence, not to say more, which President Milošević has exercised over the Serb government raises the question as to whether the single-party socialist cabinets have been in reality truly SPS governments and not simply governments of the president. What occurred in Yugoslavia up to 1998 and what occurred in Serbia during 1998–2000 was a little more complex, since the influence of the president has had to be more indirect.

The end of the Milošević era poses many questions about the future of Serbia and of the federation. Despite Vojislav Kostunica's great personal and political success, prospects remain unclear both on the domestic and the international fronts. The new president is confronted with formidable tasks.

He has to preserve the unity of the federation, to depoliticise the media, the military, the police and the judiciary as well as to implement profound political and economic reforms.

The renegotiation of the constitutional relationship between Serbia and Montenegro poses major problems. Both republics now have democratic governments, but the relations between them are rather tense. The leadership of Montenegro has manifested a strong desire to distance itself from Serbia and perhaps even to go it alone, although there would unquestionably have to be a reaction on the Serbian side if a formal declaration of independence was made. Montenegro is so small that remaining tottering on the brink may be more realistic than making a clean break.

The most important set of external issues involves the other former Yugoslav republics as well as Kosovo. Kostunica will be hard pressed to square the circle between his desire to keep Kosovo as part of Serbia and the determination of the Albanians to become independent. The new government will also have to address the Slovenian, Croat, Bosnian and Macedonian demands for a fair division of the assets of former Yugoslavia. Kostunica will have in particular to deal with suspicious leaders in Zagreb and in Sarajevo who regard him as a diehard nationalist and remember his opposition to the 1995 Dayton agreement. If the new Belgrade government want to develop good relations with the former Yugoslav republics and with the international community, it will also sooner or later have to address the question of co-operation with the Hague-based War Crimes Tribunal.

The international community appears eager to welcome a democratic Serbia with open arms. The end of the embargo was the first clear sign of this policy. Kostunica's government has to take advantage of this massive goodwill and quickly show that Serbia has indeed entered a new era.

17

Cabinets in post-communist East-Central Europe and the Balkans: Empirical findings and research agenda

Ferdinand Müller-Rommel

The aim of this volume is to start to providing a picture of cabinets in post-communist East-Central Europe and the Balkans. The sixteen country chapters give details of the development and the functioning of these cabinets under different political and institutional settings, coalition structures, administrative rules and leadership styles of prime ministers and presidents. What this study did show, first and foremost, was that there was a mass of available information regarding most Eastern European executives. Admittedly, we know more about the formal composition of cabinets than about their working practices. We may have some image of the leadership style of prime ministers and presidents, but little is known of the impact of this leadership style on cabinet decision-making. Yet, despite these limitations, enough information is available on the governments of the region since 1989–90 to allow for overall conclusions to be drawn, for instance on the form which cabinet government takes, on the duration in office of ministers and prime ministers, on the social background of these ministers and prime ministers or on the institutional setting under which cabinets operate. Despite the availability of this information, however, there are nonetheless hardly any comprehensive single-country studies, let alone comparative analyses on these cabinets.

The purpose of this chapter is, first, to summarise the main empirical findings from the single country studies. This will allow for conclusions to be drawn about similarities and differences between cabinets in Eastern and Western Europe. Second, it will be possible to elaborate an agenda for further comparative research on cabinets in Eastern Europe, while bearing in mind the cabinet studies which have been conducted in Western Europe.

Empirical findings

Numbers of cabinets

It is generally agreed that cabinets should be defined by means of three criteria, the same prime minister continuously in office, the same party or parties in government and the same legislative period. On this basis, from the early 1990s to the end of 1999, there were exactly ninety-eight cabinets in the sixteen Eastern European countries analysed here (see Table 1).

The number of cabinets did naturally vary appreciably from one country to another during the period: Albania had nine, Romania and Bulgaria eight, while the Czech Republic, Hungary and Slovenia had four. There are also differences across the two sub-regions of Eastern Europe. In the eight countries of East-Central Europe, there were forty-five cabinets, while there were fifty-three in the eight Balkan states. Part of the difference may be because the first post-communist cabinets were formed in 1990 or 1991 in the Balkan states, while in East-Central Europe, with the exception of Hungary (1990) and Poland (1991), the first post-communist cabinets were formed in 1992 or 1993 only.

Types of cabinet governments

The literature on types of cabinets in Western Europe and on the impact of these cabinets on policy making is large. It is generally agreed that the form which cabinet government takes is based on the number of parties in cabinet (from single party to coalitions of many parties) and on whether or not these cabinets are of a majority or minority character. Single party cabinets and majority cabinets are more stable than coalitions and minority cabinets respectively. In addition, empirical findings for Western Europe suggest a link between the effectiveness of governmental problem solving and the number of parties in cabinet. The larger the number of parties in cabinet, the more cabinet decision-making is conflictual.

The number of parties in Eastern European cabinets did vary markedly. In eight countries (Latvia, Poland, Slovakia, Slovenia, Romania, Albania, Macedonia, and Croatia) the number of parties in cabinet was between three and four; in the remaining eight it ranged between 1.5 and 2.7. These averages do not differ appreciably from those of Western Europe and any problems experienced by Eastern European cabinets in decision-making cannot therefore be primarily due to the presence of many parties in the executive.

Of these ninety-eight cabinets, sixty were majority coalitions, twenty-one single-party cabinets and seventeen were minority coalitions. Data were missing for seven (see Appendix 2). Majority cabinets figure most prominently in Albania, Macedonia and Bosnia-Hercegovina; minority cabinets were formed especially in Estonia, Poland and the Czech Republic. Single-party cabinets are, with the exception of Lithuania, a characteristic feature of the Balkan states. Romania, Moldova, Bulgaria and Serbia formed

Table 1 Types of cabinet governments in Eastern Europe

	Year of first cabinet after independence	Numbers of cabinets (until 1999)	Average numbers of parties in cabinet	Number of majority coalition cabinets	Number of minority coalition cabinets	Number of one-party cabinets
East-Central Europe						
Estonia	1992	7	2.3	4	3	0
Latvia	1993	8	3.4	5	2	1
Lithuania	1992	6	2.0	3	0	3
Poland	1991	7	3.3	4	3	0
Czech Republic	1993	4	2.7	1	3	0
Slovakia	1993	5	3.2	3	2	0
Hungary	1990	4	2.7	4	0	0
Slovenia	1993	4	3.2	3	1	0
The Balkans						
Romania	1991	8	3.2	4	1	3
Moldova	1991	6	1.8	3	0	3
Bulgaria	1990	8	1.5	3	2	3
Albania	1991	9	3.7	7	0	2
Macedonia	1991	6	3.5	6	0	0
Croatia	1990	5	3.2	3	0	2
Bosnia-Hcg.	1991	7	2.7	7	0	0
Serbia-new Yugoslavia	1990	4	1.8	0	0	4

three single-party cabinets respectively over a period of about ten years (see Table 1).

Cabinet stability

Stable cabinets are those in which the prime ministers and the ministers remain in office for substantial periods. Thus, the longer the duration of the cabinet itself and of the prime ministers and of the ministers in office, the greater the probability that the cabinet system will be stable. Three tests can be applied on this basis to assess the extent of stability of Eastern European cabinets (see Table 2).

Duration of cabinets

In the literature, the duration of cabinets has been linked to the concept of cabinet effectiveness. Short-lived cabinets are regarded as being ineffective in terms of policy making, while long-lasting cabinets are more effective.[1]

Western European cabinets lasted on average 1.9 years between 1965 and 1983, that duration being calculated from the day the government is formed to the day it is dissolved or new elections are held, whichever comes first.[2] If one bears in mind that the democratic system was new in Eastern Europe, the cabinets of the region performed surprisingly well – on average these cabinets lasted 1.4 years. There are appreciable variations, however. In six countries out of sixteen, cabinets lasted on average less than one year (Estonia, Latvia, Poland, Romania, Bulgaria, and Albania); however, the duration of Hungarian and Moldovan cabinets has been as long as that of German and in Irish cabinets (2.3 years). The duration of cabinets was identical in Croatia and in Sweden (1.8 years) and cabinets of Slovenia score better (1.7 years) than those of the Netherlands and Norway (1.6 years). It thus seems that the majority of Eastern European cabinets might be able to function as efficiently as their Western European counterparts.

Duration of Prime Ministers

Prime ministers are typically the most powerful members of cabinets. Empirical research suggests that a minimum of three years duration in office is needed for a prime minister to become an effective decision maker, however. This means that duration can provide some indication of the potential impact of the head of government on cabinet and national policy-making.

Up to the end of 1999, 78 persons served as prime ministers in the sixteen Eastern European countries. They lasted on average 2.3 years in office. In contrast, Western European prime ministers lasted in office on average 3.8 years since 1945.[3] Variations around this average are large, however; 77 per cent of all prime ministers served during one term only – some of them only for a few months. Nine heads of government stayed in office two terms and seven three terms but even among these sixteen prime ministers, only eight were in office for 3.8 years and more. They were Klaus (Czech Republic, 4.9 years), Sangeli (Moldova, 4.6 years), Meciar (Slovakia 4.8 years), Vacaroiu (Romania 4.0 years), Meksi (Albania 4.9 years), and Crvenrovski (Macedonia 6.2 years). The record was held by Dronovsek of Slovenia, who stayed in office for 7.2 years, followed by Marjanović of Serbia in office for 5.8 years, both up to the end of 1999. Thus over 90 per cent of the prime ministers of post-communist Eastern Europe seem not to have stayed in office long enough to exercise a major policy impact and only a very small group of (eight) prime ministers (nine per cent of the total) can be assumed to have had enough time to develop and implement effective policies.

Duration of Ministers

Ministerial duration is closely linked to prime ministerial duration and tends to be higher in countries where prime ministers last longer. Cabinets with long-standing ministers also tend to have a more pronounced hierarchical or oligarchical character while cabinets in which ministers last less tend to be more collective. Moreover, research on Western European ministers suggests that expertise in cabinet decision-making is likely to become greater as ministers acquire more experience in office. Variations in ministerial duration are thus likely to play an important part in the working of cabinet government.

In the sixteen Eastern European countries under consideration here, 1292 men and women have been cabinet members, an average of 80 ministers per country in less than ten years. This means that the turnover of ministers was very high in most countries during the phase of democratic consolidation. Among the countries with the highest number of ministerial posts are Albania (131), Bulgaria (126), Romania (116) and Poland (106). There was a small number of ministerial positions in Bosnia (48), Slovenia (47), Macedonia (60), and the Czech Republic (60).

First, the average duration of ministers in Eastern Europe was 1.8 years, markedly less than the average duration of prime ministers which, as mentioned above, was 2.3 years. Thus there seems to be no overall direct association between the duration of the prime ministers and that of ministers. However, if one analyses the duration of ministers and prime ministers on a country-by-country basis, a relationship emerges. Ministers lasted longest in such countries as Slovakia, Hungary, Croatia, Serbia and Macedonia, where prime ministers have been long lasting.

Table 2   Cabinet stability in Eastern Europe

	Average duration of cabinets (years)	Average duration of prime ministers (years)	Average duration of ministers (years)
East-Central Europe			
Estonia	0.9	1.6	1.5
Latvia	0.9	1.3	1.6
Lithuania	1.4	1.4	1.9
Poland	0.9	1.2	1.6
Czech Republic	1.5	2.2	1.5
Slovakia	1.4	2.8	2.8
Hungary	2.3	2.3	2.0
Slovenia	1.7	6.7	1.6
The Balkans			
Romania	1.0	1.7	2.1
Moldova	2.3	3.8	1.3
Bulgaria	0.9	0.9	1.3
Albania	0.9	1.5	1.2
Macedonia	1.5	3.7	2.7
Croatia	1.8	2.3	2.6
Bosnia-Hcg.	1.2	1.5	2.1
Serbia-new Yugoslavia	1.4	2.8	2.0

Second, the duration of ministers has been significantly lower in Eastern Europe than in Western Europe. Between 1945 and 1984, Western European ministers were on average 4.5 years in office.[4] This seems to indicate that cabinet decision-making may be more collective in character in Eastern Europe, but this also indicates that ministerial experience and ministerial expertise did not have time to develop sufficiently in most Eastern European cabinets.

The end of cabinets

The analysis of the end of cabinets is closely linked to the analysis of duration and indeed of the formation of successor cabinets. Depending on the reasons which account for the end of cabinets, the parties' election campaigns might be affected, the continuation of coalitions might be in question or even the policy performance of governments might be jeopardised. The literature on Western European cabinets distinguishes, among the reasons accounting for the end of cabinets, between elections, the resignation of the prime minister and such political problems as dissension in cabinet, loss of parliamentary support and the intervention by the head of state.

The reasons leading to the end of cabinets are markedly different in Eastern Europe from what they are in Western Europe. In Western Europe, between 1950 and 1983, 46 per cent of cabinets ended for political reasons, 43 per cent because of an election and only 10 per cent as a result of the resignation of the prime minister.[5] In Eastern Europe new elections have been the reason for the end of 41 per cent of the cabinets, political reasons for the end of 34 per cent and the resignation of the prime minister for the end of 21 per cent (see Table 3). In eleven Eastern European countries at least one prime minister resigned. Indeed, in Lithuania, three out of the six prime ministers resigned. Dissension in cabinet led to the end of thirteen cabinets in the Balkans but of only five in East-Central Europe. Intervention by the head of state did occur in seven countries, but this was mostly during the first years following the end of communism.

Future research agenda

The essays in this volume describe the main features of post-communist cabinets in Eastern Europe on the basis of a common framework. These cabinets have been assessed in the context of the general political setting within which they have operated. On this basis, their current structure, the main aspects of their life and their decision-making procedures have been examined. While it would be painstakingly long to summarise even the main findings with respect to all aspects of cabinet government in the sixteen countries, there is evidence from these findings that a common approach to analyse cabinets is needed. On this basis, it would become possible to incorporate and interrelate the various characteristics of cabinet

Table 3 Cabinet terminations in Eastern Europe

	Elections	Resignation of prime minister	Death of prime minister	Dissension in cabinet	Lack of parliamentary support	Intervention by head of state
East-Central Europe						
Estonia	2	3	0	1	0	0
Latvia	2	2	0	2	0	0
Lithuania	1	3	0	0	0	1
Poland	2	1	0	1	1	1
Czech Republic	2	1	0	0	0	0
Slovakia	3	0	0	0	2	0
Hungary	2	0	1	0	0	0
Slovenia	2	0	0	2	0	0
The Balkans						
Romania	2	2	0	3	0	1
Moldova	2	1	0	0	0	2
Bulgaria	2	2	0	1	1	1
Albania	4	1	0	3	0	0
Macedonia	2	1	0	2	0	0
Croatia	3	1	0	1	0	0
Bosnia-Hcg.	2	1	0	1	0	1
Serbia-new Yugoslavia	3	0	0	2	0	1

structure, of cabinet life and of cabinet decision-making. Such an approach has to be conceptualised in terms of a combined structural and functional framework which would make it possible to determine the conditions under-which cabinets develop and to discover the main characteristics of the behaviour of cabinet ministers, of prime ministers and of officials belonging to the core executive. This means embarking in a systematic examination of what cabinets are, of what they do, of how they do it and of how they can do better.

Let us attempt to list the key factors likely to account for the functioning of cabinets in Eastern Europe. First, the *structural characteristics of the political system* affect the functioning of cabinets. Since most of these characteristics are determined by the constitutions, future research needs to analyse systematically the constitutional powers of presidents, prime ministers and ministers in parliamentary and semi-presidential systems in Eastern Europe.

Second, *political parties* have a strong impact on the functioning of cabinets. That impact depends on the overall number of parties in the cabinet (single-party against multiparty government) and the type of cabinet coalition (with or without a dominant party, minority against majority). In

Western Europe, parties play a major part in single party cabinets and in minimum winning coalitions, while their role is less pronounced in surplus coalitions and multiparty minority coalitions. However, these conclusions are based on the assumption that political parties are highly developed institutions operating as strong political players within advanced political systems. In most Eastern European countries, however, political parties are still rather weak. This may explain to an extent why the duration of cabinets during the first phase of democratic transition and consolidation has tended to be low. Eastern European parties are likely to become gradually stronger; as in Western Europe, they will become office seekers as well as policy seekers. Factionalism is also a danger, since factions within governing parties are likely to affect patterns of cabinet behaviour and indeed affect the composition of cabinets. However, once ministers have been in office for a substantial period, the probability that policies will be carefully elaborated and subsequently implemented will strengthen party coalitions. Thus future research on cabinets in Eastern Europe has to study the organisation of parties in cabinet and in particular the impact of factions and of conflicts within coalition parties on the overall process of cabinet decision-making.

Third, the political experience and the *role of individual ministers* determine the functioning of cabinets. Studies on Western European governments have shown that ministers with greater political experience or greater expert knowledge can be expected to exercise more influence on cabinet decision-making than other cabinet members. Research on Eastern European cabinets has therefore to collect information on the social background and the careers of ministers. Furthermore, in order to understand ministerial behaviour, one must know what ministers think about their own work, about the work of their colleagues and about the part played by the cabinet meeting itself. If cabinet decisions matter, cabinet members also matter. It is therefore essential to find out how ministers view their role in cabinet government. This means interviewing (former) ministers in Eastern Europe – an enterprise which may be long and complex but surely rewarding.

Fourth, the functioning of cabinet government is strongly dependent upon *the behaviour of prime ministers* as heads of cabinets. Prime ministers are 'arbitrators' or 'activists' with respect to the implementation of cabinet policy goals. If they are arbitrators, prime ministers may not be involved personally in policy proposals and be content to move the cabinet towards an acceptable solution. If they are activists, they are likely to be deeply interested in particular proposals and to attempt to push these proposals through cabinet. The arbitrator role may lead to a reduction of collective decision making if many arrangements are made behind the scenes; an active posture, however, will tend more often to result in tension within the cabinet. A comparative investigation of cabinets in Eastern Europe has therefore to develop a typology of prime ministerial leadership style and to relate this typology to the different phases and aspects of cabinet decision-making.

Fifth, the administrative characteristics of the *prime ministers' offices* affect markedly the functioning of cabinets. Studies conducted in Western Europe have shown that the impact of prime ministerial staffs on cabinet government can be excessive. The functions of these staffs range between an administrative and a political pole. These officials act administratively when organising meetings of the cabinet and the flow of business between prime minister and ministers. They also play a part in the development of long-term ideas about cabinet activities and on the improvement of cabinet decision-making. But these last forms of activities are never wholly administrative. In most cases, they affect the political operation of the cabinet. Thus, the administrative and political roles of prime ministerial staffs need to be examined systematically. Research must consider, in a comparative manner, not just personnel and budget, but also the actual tasks of the prime ministers' offices in Eastern Europe. Those likely to know to what extent and in what ways prime ministerial staffs affect the character of cabinet decision-making need to be interviewed.

Thus systematic research on the functioning of Eastern European cabinets has first to focus on these five aspects in succession in order to obtain reliable and comparable information. Meanwhile, hypotheses linking these five aspects need to be formulated and tested. This is a vast undertaking, especially since the principles of classification still have to be elaborated in a number of ways: if such an approach is adopted, however, it will become possible to discover and assess the explanations which account for the operation of cabinets in Eastern Europe and to do so at various points is time.

References

1   Arend Lijphart, *Democracies* (New Haven CT: Yale University Press 1984) p. 165.
2   Ian Budge and Hans Keman, *Parties and Democracy* (Oxford: Oxford University Press 1990) p. 161.
3   Wolfgang Müller and Wilfried Philipp, 'Prime Ministers and other Government Heads', in Jean Blondel and Jean-Louis Thiebault (eds), *The Profession of Ministers* (London: Macmillan 1991) p. 137.
4   Wilma E. Bakema, 'The Ministerial Career', in Jean Blondel and Jean-Louis Thiebault (eds), *The Profession of Ministers* (London: Macmillan 1991) p. 74.
5   Ian Budge and Hans Keman, *Parties and Democracy* (Oxford: Oxford University Press 1990) p. 161.

Appendices

Appendix 1   Political parties in Eastern European Cabinets

Albania

Agrarian Party (AP)
Albanian Republican Party (ARP) (Partia Republikane Shqiptare – PRS)
Democratic Alliance Party (DAP)
Democratic Party of Albania (DPA) (Partia Demokratike e Shqipërísë – PDSH)
Social Democratic Party of Albania (SDP) (Partia Social Demokratike e Shqipërise – PSDS)
Socialist Party of Albania (SPA) (Partia Socialiste e Shqipërisë – PSS)
Union for Human Rights Party (UHRP) (Partia për Mbrojtjen e te Dreijtave te Njeriut – PBDNj)
Union of Social Democrats (USD)

Bosnia-Hercegovina

Party for Democratic Action (PDA) (Strančka Demokratske Akcije – SDA)
Serb Democratic Party of Bosnia and Hercegovina (SDP) (Srpska Demokratska Strančka Bosne i Hercegovine – SDS BiH)
Social Democratic Party (Socijaldemokratska Partija – BiH)

Bulgaria

Aleksandur Stamboliyski Bulgarian Agrarian People's Union (Bulgarski Zemedelski Naroden Sayuz Aleksandur Stamboliyski)
Bulgarian Socialist Party – BSP (Bulgarska Sotsialisticheska Partiya)
Ecoglasnost National Movement
Movement for Rights and Freedom – MRF (Dvizhenie za Prava i Svobodi – DPS)
Union of Democratic Forces – UDF (Sayuz na Demokratichni Sili – SDS)
Bulgarian Agrarian People's Union (BAPU) (Bulgarski Zemedelski Naroden Sayuz – BZNS)

Croatia

Christian People's Party (CPP) (Kršćanska Narodna Strančka – KNS)
Croatian Christian Democratic Union (CCDU) (Hrvatska Kršćanska Demokratska Unija – HKDU)
Croatian Democratic Party (CDP) (Hrvatska Demokratska Strančka – HDS)
Croatian Democratic Union (CDU) (Hrvatska Demokratska Zajednica – HDZ)
Croatian People's Party (CPP) (Hrvatska Narodna Strančka – HNS)
Croatian Social-Liberal Party (CSLP) (Hrvatska Socijalno-Liberalna Strančka – HSLS)
Social Democratic Party of Croatia (SDP) (Socijaldemokratska Parti Hvratske – SPH)
Social Democratic Union of Croatia (SDUC) (Socijalno Demokratska Unija Hvratske – SDUH)

Czech Republic

Christian Democratic Union – Czechoslovak People's Party (Křestanská a demokra-
tická unie-KDU – Československá srana lidova – CSL)
Civic Democratic Alliance (CDA) (Občanská demokratická aliance – ODA)
Civic Democratic Party (CDP) (Občanská demokratická strana – ODS)
Czech Social Democratic Party (CSDP) (Česká strana sociálne demokratická – CSSD)
Freedom Union (Unie Svobody – US)

Estonia

Coalition Party and Rural Union (Koonderakond ja Maarahua Ühendus – KMÜ)
Estonia National Independence Party (ENIP) (Eesti Rahvuhsliku Soltumatuse Partei –
ERSP)
Estonian Reform Party (ERP) (Eesti Reformierakond – ER)
People's Party Moderates (Moodukad – MOD)
Progressive Party (Arengupartei – KPP)
Pro Patria (Fatherland) Alliance (Isamaaliit – NFP)

Hungary

Alliance of Free Democrats (Szabad Demokraták Szövetsége – SzDSz)
Christian Democratic People's Party (Kereszténydemokrata Néppárt – KDNP)
Federation of Young Democrats – Hungarian Civic Party (FIDESz – Magyar Polgári Párt
– MPP)
Hungarian Democratic Forum (Magyar Demokrata Fórum – MDF)
Hungarian Social Democratic Party (Magyarországi Szocialdemokrata Párt – MSzDP)
Hungarian Socialist Party (Magyar Szocialista Párt – MSzP)
Independent Smallholders' and Civic Party (Független Kisgazda-, Földmunkás- és
Polgári Párt – FKgP)

Latvia

Christian Democratic Union of Latvia (Latvijas Kristīgo Demokātu savienība)
Conservative Union for Fatherland and Freedom/LNNK (Aprienība Tēvzemei un
brīvībai – LNNK)
Democratic Party Saimnieks (The Master) (Demokrātiskāpartija Saimnieks – DPS)
Latvian Farmers' Union (Latvijas Zemnieku savienība – LZS)
Latvian Unity Party (Latvijas Vienibas partija – LVP)
Latvian Way (Latvijas celš – LC)
New Party (Jauna partija)

Lithuania

Christian Democratic Party of Lithuania (CDP)
Conservative Party of Lithuania (CPL)
Lithuanian Centre Union (LCU)
Lithuanian Democratic Labour Party (LDLP)

Macedonia

Democratic Alternative (DA)
Democratic Party of Albanians (DPA)
Internal Macedonian Revolutionary Organization – Democratic Party for Macedonian National Unity (IMRO – DPMNU)
Liberal-Democratic Party (LP)
Party for Democratic Prosperity (PDP) (Partija za Demokratski Prosperitet)
Social Democratic Alliance of Macedonia (SDAM) (Socijaldemokratski Sojuz na Makedonije – SDSM)
Socialist Party of Macedonia (SPM)

Moldova

Agrarian Democratic Party (ADP) (Partidul Democrat Agrar din Moldova)
Democratic Convention of Moldova (DCM)
Christian Democratic Popular Front (CDPF) (Frontul Popular Creştin şi Democrat)
Party of Revival and Accord of Moldova (PRAM) (Partidul Renasterii şi Concilierii din Moldova)
Moldovan Party of Democratic Forces (Partidul Fortelor Democrate)
Movement for a Democratic and Prosperous Moldova (MDPM)
Reform Party
Social Democratic Party of Moldova

Poland

Centre Alliance (Porozumienie Centrum – PC)
Christian National Union (Zjednoczenie Chrześcijańsko Narodowy – ZChN)
Democratic Left Alliance (Sojusz Lewicy Demokratycznej – SLD)
Democratic Union (Unia Demokratyczna – UD)
Freedom Union (Unia Wolności – UW)
Liberal-Democratic Congress (Kongres Liberalno-Demokratyczny – KLD)
Party of Christian Democrats (Partia Chrześcijańs Kich Domocrtów – PCHD)
Polish Convention (Konwencja Polska – KP)
Polish Economic Programme (Polski Program Gospodarczy – PPG)
Polish Liberal Programme (Polski Program Liberalny – PPL)
Polish Peasant Party (Polskie Stronnictwo Ludowe – PSL)
Solidarity Election Action (Akcja Wyborcza Solidarność – AWS)

Romania

Christian Democratic National Peasants' Party of Romania (CDNPP) (Partidul Naţional Ţărănesc Creştin-Democrat din România – PNŢCD)
Hungarian Democratic Union of Romania (HDUR) (Uniunea Democrată Maghiară din România)
National Liberal Party (NLP) (Partidul Naţional Liberal)
Party of Social Democracy of Romania (PSDR) (Partidul Democraţiei sociale din România)
Romania's Alternative Party (RAP)

Romanian Ecological Movement (Mişcarea Ecologistă din România)
Romanian National Unity Party (RNUP) (Partidul Unității Naționale Române)
Democratic Party (DP)

Slovakia

Alliance of Democrats (Alianca Demokratov – AD)
Alternative of Political Realism (Alternativa politickeho realizmu – APR)
Association of Workers of Slovakia (Združenie robotníkov Slovenska – ZRS)
Movement for a Democratic Slovakia (Hnutie za demokratické Slovensko – HZDS)
National Democratic Club (Narodno-demokraticky club – NDK)
Party of Civic Understanding (SOP)
Party of the Democratic Left (Strana demokratickej l'avice – SDL)
Party of the Hungarian Coalition (Strana madarskej koalicie – SMK)
Slovak Democratic Coalition (Slovenská demokratická Koalicia – SDK)
Christian Democratic Movement (Krest'ansko-demokratické hnutie – KDH)
Slovak National Party (Slovenská národná strana – SNS)

Slovenia

Christian Democratic Party (SKD)
Democratic Party of Pensioners of Slovenia (DESUS)
Greens of Slovenia (Zeleni Slovenije – ZS)
Liberal Democracy of Slovenia (LDS) (Liberalna demokracija Slovenije – LDS)
Slovenian Christian Democrats (SCD) (Slovenski krščanski demokrati – SKD)
Slovenian People's Party (Slovenska ljudska strančka – SLS)
Social Democratic Party of Slovenia (SDPS) (Socialdemokratska strančka Slovenije – SDSS)
United List of Social Democrats (ULSD) (Združena lista socialnih demokratov – ZLSD)

Yugoslavia

Democratic Party of Montenegrin Socialists (DPMS) (Demokratska Partija Socijalista – DPS)
New Democracy Party
Serbian Radical Party (SRP) (Srpska Radikalna Stranka – SRS)
Socialist Party of Serbia (SPS) (Socijalistička partija Srbije)
(SAWP) of Serbia
Yugoslav United Left

Appendix 2   Cabinet compositions in Eastern Europe

In these charts of cabinet compositions, the following codings are used:
Types of government (coalition)
1   Single-party majority
2   Coalition majority
3   Single-party near majority (40–50 per cent of seats in parliament)
4   Coalition near majority
5   Single-party minority (below 40 per cent of seats in parliament)
6   Coalition minority
7   None party/none caretaker (technical government)
8   Caretaker

Modes for termination of cabinet
1   Elections
2   Resignation of prime minister
3   Death of prime minister
4   Dissension within cabinet (coalition breaks up)
5   Lack of parliamentary support
6   Intervention by head of state

Albania

Cabinet	Date In	Date Out	Name of prime minister	PM's party	Type of government	Number of ministries	Modes for termination
1	02/91	04/91	Nano (1)	PLA/PSS	1	19	1
2	04/91	06/91	Nano (2)	PLA/PSS	1	23	4
3	06/91	12/91	Bufi	PLA/PSS	3	21	4
4	12/91	04/92	Ahmeti	Independent	3	18	1
5	04/92	07/96	Meksi (1)	PDS	1	18	1
6	07/96	03/97	Meksi (2)	PDS	1	17	Civil war
7	03/97	07/97	Fino	PSS	3	16	1
8	07/97	09/98	Nano (3)	PSS	2	18	2
9	09/98	10/99	Masko	PSS	2	17	4

	Parties in government — Percentage of government strength									Strength of government — Parties in parliament (%)								
Cabinet	P1	P2	P3	P4	P5	P6	P7	P8	P9	P1	P2	P3	P4	P5	P6	P7	P8	P9
1	PLA/PSS 100									PLA/PSS 100								
2	PLA/PSS 100									PLA/PSS 68								
3	SP 52	PDS 33	PRS 14							SP 68	PDS 30							
4	SP 50	PDS 39	PRS 6	PSDS 6						SP 68	PDS 30							
5		PDS 89	PRS 11								PDS 66	PRS 11						
6		PDS 94	SDP 6								PDS 87		SDP 2					
7	PSS 25	PDS 25	PRS 12	SDS 6	SOV 6	HRP 6	MLP 6	PAP 6	BK 6	PSS 7	PDS 87	PRS 2		HRP 4				
8	PSS 61	PSDS 11	AP 6	DAP 6	PAD 6	HRP 6	IND 6			PSS 65	PSDS 5	DAP 3	PAP 1	HRP 1				
9	PSS 66	PSDS 6	AP 6	DAP 6		HRP 6	IND 12			PSS 65	PSDS 5	DAP 3	PAP 1	HRP 1				

Bosnia-Hercegovina

Cabinet	Date In	Date Out	Name of prime minister (PM)	PM's party	Type of government	No. of ministries	Modes for termination
1	09/91	06/92	Pelivan (1)	Croat. DU (CDU)	2	19	4
2	06/92	11/92	Pelivan (2)	Croat. DU (CDU)	2	19	2
3	11/92	10/93	Akhmadzk	Croat. DU (CDU)	2	19	6
4	10/93	02/96	Silajdzić	SDA	2	21	new government after Dayton
5	02/96	01/97	Muratović	SDA	2	7	1
6	01/97	02/99	Silajdzić	SDA	2	12	1
			Tomić	CDU			
			Bosić	SDS			
7	02/99	10/00	Silajdzić	SDA	2	12	
			Mihailović	SDS			
			Tomić	CDU			

Cabinet	Parties in government Percent government strength					Strength of government parties in parliament (%)				
	P1	P2	P3	P4	P5	P1	P2	P3	P4	P5
1	SDA 42	CDU 21	SDS 32		IND 5	SDA 36	CDU 18	SDS 30		
2	SDA missing	CDU data				SDA 36	CDU 18			
3	SDA missing	CDU data				SDA 36	CDU 18			
4	SDA missing	CDU data		BiH		SDA 36	CDU 18		BiH 8	
5	SDA 33	CDU 33	SDS 33			SDA 45	CDU 17	SDS 21		
6	SDA 33	CDU 33	SDS 33			SDA 45	CDU 17	SDS 21		
7	SDA 33	CDU 33	SDS 33			SDA 40	CDU 14	SDS 10		

Cabinet	Date In	Date Out	Name of prime minister (PM)	PM's party	Type of government	No. of ministries	Modes for termination
1	09/90	12/90	Lukanov	BSP	1	18	2
2	12/90	11/91	Popov	Non-party	2	18	2
3	11/91	12/92	Dimitrov	SDS	5	14	5
4	12/92	10/94	Berov	Indendent	7	14	6
5	10/94	12/94	Indzhova	Indendent	8	17	1
6	01/95	02/97	Videnov	BSP	2	18	4
7	02/97	05/97	Sofiyanski	Indendent	8	17	1
8	05/97		Kostov	SDS	1	17	

Parties in government
Percentage of government strength

Cabinet	P1	P2	P3	P4	P5	P6
1	BSP 89					
2	BSP 39	SDS 17	DPS 11			
3	BSP 100					
4			missing	data		
5			missing	data		
6	BSP 39	BZNS 11	ECONA 6			
7			missing	data		
8		SDS 100				

Strength of government
parties in parliament (%)

Cabinet	P1	P2	P3	P4	P5	P6
1	BSP 53					IND 11
2	BSP 53	SDS 36	DPS 6			IND 33
3	BSP 46					
4	missing	data				
5	missing	data				
6	BSP/BZNS 52					IND 44
7	missing					
8		SDS 57				

Croatia

Cabinet	Date		Name of prime minister (PM)	PM's party	Type of government	No. of ministries	Modes for termination
	In	Out					
1	09/90	12/91	Gregorić (1)	HDZ	2	29	4
2	12/91	08/92	Gregorić (2)	HDZ	2	28	1
3	08/92	03/93	Sarinić	HDZ	2	21	2
4	03/93	10/95	Valentić	Independent	1	24	1
5	10/95	01/00	Matesa	HDZ	1	23	1

Cabinet	Parties in government Percentage of government strength				Strength of government parties in parliament (%)			
	P1	P2	P3	P4	P1	P2	P3	P4
1	HDZ	SPH/SP	HNS/HSLS/ SDUH/HKDU	HDS	HDZ	SPH/SP	HNS/HSLS/ SDUH/HKDU	HDS
	56	17	29	6	60	28	3	3
2	HDZ	SPH/SP	HNS/HKDU/ SDUH		HDZ	SPH/SP	HNS/HKDU/ SDUH	
	59	18	24		60	28	3	
3	HDZ		SDUH		HDZ		SDUH	
	87		7		87		missing data	
4	HDZ				HDZ			
	100				62			
5	HDZ				HDZ			
	100				53			

Czech Republic

Cabinet	Date In	Date Out	Name of prime minister (PM)	PM's party	Type of government	No. of ministries	Modes for termination
1	01/93	07/96	Klaus (1)	ODS	2	18	1
2	07/96	12/97	Klaus (2)	ODS	4	15	2
3	01/98	07/98	Tosovsky	Independent	8	15	1
4	08/98		Zeman	CSSD	5	18	

Cabinet	Parties in government Percentage of government strength					Strength of government parties in parliament (%)				
	P1	P2	P3	P4	P5	P1	P2	P3	P4	P5
1	ODS 52	KDU/CSL 21	ODA 15	KDS 10		ODS/KDS 38	KDU/CSL 7	ODA 7		
2	ODS 50	KDU/CSL 25	ODA 25			ODS 34	KDU/CSL 9	ODA 6		
3		KDU/CSL 18	ODA 17	US 24	IND 41		KDU/CSL 9	ODA 6	US 15	IND 1
4	CSSD 94				IND 6	CSSD 37				

Estonia

Cabinet	Date		Name of prime minister (PM)	PM's party	Type of government	No. of ministries	Modes for termination
	In	Out					
1	10/92	10/94	Laar (1)	NFP	2	11	2
2	10/94	04/95	Tarand	Mod/Ind	2	11	1
3	04/95	10/95	Vähi (1)	KMÜ	2	11	2
4	11/95	11/96	Vähi (2)	KMÜ	2	12	4
5	12/96	02/97	Vähi (3)	KMÜ	3	12	2
6	03/97	03/99	Siimann	KMÜ	3	12	1
7	03/99		Laar (2)	NFP	2	12	1

Cabinet	Parties in government percentage of government strength				Strength of government parties in parliament (%)		
	P1	P2	P3	P4	P1	P2	P3
1	NFP	ERSP	MOD	IND	NFP	ERSP	MOD
	38	25	25	13	29	10	12
2	NFP	ERSP	MOD	IND	NFP	ERSP	MOD
	20	20	25	26	13	10	10
3	KMÜ	ER	K	IND	KMÜ	ER	K
	53	7	33	7	41	19	16
4	KMÜ	ER	(RPP)	IND	KMÜ	ER	
	40	40	13	7	40	19	
5	KMÜ		(RPP)	IND	KMÜ		
	53		13	34	40		
6	KMÜ		(RPP)	IND	KMÜ		
	60		13	27	40		
7	NSF	ER	MOD		NSF	ER	MOD

Hungary

215

Cabinet	Date In	Date Out	Name of prime minister (PM)	PM's party	Type of government	Number of ministries	Modes for termination
1	05/90	12/93	Antall	MDF	2	18	3
2	12/93	07/94	Boross	MDF	8	17	1
3	07/94	07/98	Horn	MSzP	2	14	1
4	07/98		Orbán	FIDESz-MPP	2	16	

Cabinet	Parties in government Percentage of government strength P1	P2	P3	P4
1	MDF 52	FKgP 19	KDNP 5	IND 24
2	MDF 50	FKgP 17	KDNP 17	IND 16
3	MSzP 79	SzDSz 21		
4	FIDESz-MPP 71	FKgP 23	MDF 6	

Cabinet	Strength of government parties in parliament (%) P1	P2	P3	P4
1	MDF 43	FKgP 11	KDNP 5	IND
2	MDF 35	FKgP 10	KDNP 6	
3	MSzP 54	SzDSz 18		
4	FIDESz-MPP 38	FKgP 12	MDF 4	

Latvia

Cabinet	Date In	Date Out	Name of prime minister (PM)	PM's party	Type of government	No. of ministries	Modes for termination
1	08/93	09/94	Birkavs	LC	4	13	4
2	09/94	12/95	Gailis	LC	5	13	1
3	12/95	02/97	Skele (1)	DPS	2	17	2
4	02/97	08/97	Skele (2)	DPS	2	14	2
5	08/97	04/98	Karsts (1)	LNNK	2	13	1
6	04/98	11/98	Karsts (2)	LNNK	2	12	4
7	11/98	06/99	Kristopans	LC	4	14	2
8	07/99	04/00	Skele (3)	DPS	2		

Parties in government / Percentage of government strength

Cabinet	P1	P2	P3	P4	P5	P6
1	LC 85	LZS 15				
2	LC 77	TPA/IND 23				
3	DPS 27	TB 27	LC 20	LNNK 13	LVP 6	LZS 6
4	DPS 21	TB 21	LC 28	LNNK 15		LZS 15
5	DPS 31	TB/LNNK 31	LC 31			LZS 7
6		TB/LNNK 44	LC 44	NP 14		LZS 12
7		TB/LNNK 35	LC 44			
8	DPS	TB/LNNK	LC			

Strength of government / Parties in parliament (%)

Cabinet	P1	P2	P3	P4	P5	P6
1	LC 36	LZS 12				
2	LC 36					
3	DPS 18	TB 14	LC 8	LNNK 8	LVP 17	LZS 8
4	DPS 18	TB 14	LC 17	LNNK 8		LZS 8
5	DPS 18	TB/LNNK 22	LC 17			LZS 18
6		TB/LNNK 22	LC 17	NP 8		LZS 18
7		TB/LNNK 17	LC 21			LZS 18
8	DPS 18	TB/LNNK 17	LC 21			

Lithuania

Cabinet	Date In	Date Out	Name of prime minister (PM)	PM's party	Type of government	No. of ministries	Modes for termination
1	12/92	03/93	Lupy	LDLP	1	16	6
2	03/93	02/96	Slezevicius	LDLP	1	17	2
3	02/96	12/96	Stankevicius	LDLP	1	19	1
4	12/96	04/99	Vagnorius	CPL	2	17	2
5	04/99	10/99	Pakas	CPL	2	14	2
6	10/99	10/00	Kubilius	CPL	2	14	2

Cabinet	Parties in government Percentage of government strength					Strength of Government Parties in parliament (%)					
	P1	P2	P3	P4	P5	P1	P2	P3	P4	P5	P6
1	LDLP 100					LDLP 52					
2	LDLP 100					LDLP 52					
3	LDLP 100					LDLP 52					
4	CPL 65	CDP 18	LCU 12		IND 5	CPL 49	CDP 11	LCU 9		IND 5	
5	CPL	CDP	LCU		IND	CPL 49	CDP 11	LCU 9		IND	
6	CPL	CDP	LCU			CPL 49	CDP 11	LCU 9			

Macedonia

Cabinet	Date In	Date Out	Name of prime minister (PM)	PM's party	Type of government	No. of ministries	Modes for termination
1	03/91	10/91	Kljusen (1)	Independent	2	23	4
2	10/91	08/92	Kljusen (2)	Independent	2	23	2
3	08/92	10/94	Crvenrovski (1)	SDSM	2	20	1
4	10/94	02/96	Crvenrovski (2)	SDSM	2	20	4
5	02/96	10/98	Crvenrovski (3)	SDSM	2	20	1
6	10/98		Georgievski	VMRO-DPMNE	2	27	

Parties in government / Percentage of government strength

Cabinet	P1	P2	P3	P4	P5	P6
1	SDSM / missing	PDP	SPM	VMRO/DPMNE		
2	SDSM / 61	PDP / 22	SPM / 17			
3	SDSM / 42	PDP	SPM / 53	LP		IND / 5
4	missing data	PDP	SPM			
5	SDSM / 60	PDP / 30	SPM / 10	LP		
6	VMRO/DPMNE / 52	DPA / 19	DA / 26	LP / 4		

Strength of government / Parties in parliament (%)

Cabinet	P1	P2	P3	P4	P5	P6
1	SDSM	PDP	SPM	VMRO/DPMNE / 31		
2	SDSM / 26	PDP / 21	SPM / 3			
3	SDSM / 26	PDP / 21	SPM / 3		LP	
4	SDSM / 48	PDP / 8	SPM / 7		5	
5	SDSM / 48	PDP / 8	SPM / 7			
6	VMRO/DPMNE/IDA / 49	DPA / 20			LP / 3	

Moldova

Cabinet	Date In	Date Out	Name of prime minister (PM)	PM's party	Type of government	No. of ministries	Modes for termination
1	05/91	06/92	Muravshi	CDPF	5	19	2
2	06/92	04/94	Sangeli (1)	ADP	1	26	1
3	04/94	01/97	Sangeli (2)	ADP	1	25	6
4	01/97	03/98	Ciubuc (1)	Independent	7	21	1
5	04/94	02/99	Ciubuc (2)	Independent	2	19	6
6	02/99		Sturza	MDPM	2	20	6

Cabinet	Parties in government Percentage of government strength P1	P2	P3	Strength of government parties in parliament (%) P1	P2	P3
1	CDPF 100			CDPF 33		
2	ADP 100			ADP 55		
3	ADP 100			ADP 55		
4	missing data			missing data		
5	PRCM	MDMP	PFD	PRCM 25	MDMP 23	PFD 11
6	PRCM	MDMP	PFD	PRCM 25	MDMP 23	PFD 11

Poland

Cabinet	Date		Name of prime minister (PM)	PM's party	Type of government	No. of ministries	Modes for termination
	In	Out					
1	11/91	07/92	Olszewski	PC	6	17	6
2	07/92	04/93	Suchocka (1)	UD	6	23	4
3	04/93	10/93	Suchocka (2)	UD	6	22	1
4	10/93	03/95	Pawlek	PSL	2	20	5
5	03/95	02/96	Olesky	SLD	2	20	2
6	02/96	10/97	Cimoszewich	SLD	2	20	1
7	10/97		Buzek	AWS	2	23	

Parties in government
Percentage of government strength

Cabinet	P1	P2	P3	P4	P5	P6	P7	P8
1	PC 23	ZCHN 18	PSL 12	IND 47				
2	UD 20	ZCHN 20	KLD 16	PSL 16	PCHD 4	SL-CH 4	PPG 4	IND 16
3	UD 20	ZCHN 20	PSL 16	PPL 20	PK 8	IND 16		
4	SLD 30	PSL 40	IND 30					
5	SLD 38	PSL 24	IND 33					
6	SLD 33	PSL 33	IND 33					
7	AWS 74	UW 22	IND 4					

Strength of government
Parties in parliament (%)

Cabinet	P1	P2	P3	P4	P5	P6	P7	P8
1	PC 10	ZCHN 11	PSL 6	IND 0				
2	UD 13	ZCHN 11	KLD 8	PSL 4	PCHD 1	SL-CH 2	PPG 3	
3	UD 13	ZCHN 10	PSL 4	PPL 11	PK 6	IND 0		
4	SLD 37	PSL 24	IND 0					
5	SLD 37	PSL 29						
6	SLD 37	PSL 29						
7	AWS 44	UW 13						

Romania

Cabinet	Date In	Date Out	Name of prime minister (PM)	PM's party	Type of government	No. of ministries	Modes for termination
1	04/91	09/91	Roman	PDSR	1	21	6
2	09/91	11/92	Stolojan	PDSR	2	20	1
3	11/92	08/94	Vacaroiv (1)	PDSR	5	18	4
4	08/94	09/96	Vacaroiv (2)	PDSR	2	22	4
5	09/96	11/96	Vacaroiv (3)	PDSR	5	21	1
6	11/96	03/98	Ciorbea	PNTCD	2	23	2
7	03/98	11/98	Vasile (1)	PNTCD	2	24	4
8	11/98	12/99	Vasile (2)	PNTCD	2	18	2

Parties in government / Percentage of government strength

Cabinet	P1	P2	P3	P4	P5	P6	P7
1	PDSR 100						
2	PDSR 85	PNL 5	AUR 1	MER 1			
3	PDSR 63						
4	PDSR 35	RSDP 5	PUNR 15	MER 5			
5	PDSR 100						
6	PNTCD 50	PNL 17	DP 25	UDMR 8			
7	PNTCD 42	PNL 13	DP 21	UDMR 8	RSDP 4	RAP 4	
8	PNCTD 44	PNL 17	DP 17	UDMR 11	RSDP 6		

Strength of government / Parties in parliament (%)

Cabinet	P1	P2	P3	P4	P5	P6	P7
1	PDSR 66						
2	PDSR 66	PNL 11	AUR 3	MER 5			IND 8
3	PDSR 36						IND 37
4	PDSR 36	RSDP n.a.	PUNR 9				IND 40
5	PDSR 36						
6	PNCTD 27	PNL 8	DP 13	UDMR 8			IND 8
7	PNCTD 27	PNL 8	DP 13	UDMR 8	RSDP 3	RAP 1	IND 8
8	PNCTD 27	PNL 8	DP 13	UDMR 8	RSDP 3		IND 8

Serbia

Cabinet	Date		Name of prime minister (PM)	PM's party	Type of government	Number of ministries	Modes for termination
	In	Out					
1	12/90	01/93	Bozović	SPS	1	23	1
2	01/93	02/94	Sainovil	SPS	5	25	1
3	02/94	09/97	Marjanović (1)	SPS	5	29	1
4	09/97	03/98	Marjanović (2)	SPS	4	missing data	6
5	03/98	06/99	Marjanović (3)	SPS	2	36	4
6	06/99	08/99	Marjanović (4)	SPS	2	34	4
7	08/99		Marjanović (5)	SPS	2	missing data	4

Cabinet	Parties in government Percentage government strength			Strength of government Parties in parliament (%)					
	P1	P2	P3	P1	P2	P3	P4	P5	P6
1	SPS			SPS					
	100			78					
2	SPS			SPS					
	100			34					
3	SPS			SPS					
	100			49					
4	SPS	SRS	YUL	SPS	SRS	YUL			
5	SPS	SRS	YUL	SPS	SRS	YUL			
	44	42	14						
6	missing data			missing data					
7	missing data			missing data					

Slovakia

Cabinet	Date		Name of prime minister (PM)	PM's party	Type of government	No. of ministries	Modes for termination
	In	Out					
1	01/93	11/93	Mečiar (1)	HZDS	2	18	5
2	11/93	03/94	Mečiar (2)	HZDS	4	18	5
3	03/94	12/94	Moravčík	APR	4	18	1
4	12/94	10/98	Mečiar (3)	HZDS	2	18	1
5	10/98		Dzurinda	SDK	2	20	1

	Parties in government Percentage of government strength				
Cabinet	P1	P2	P3	P4	P5
1	HZDS 86	SNS 6	IND 13		
2	HZDS 67	SNS 17	IND 17		
3	SDL 39	KDH 28	APR 22	AD 6	NDK 6
4	HZDS 67	SNS 11	ZRS 22		
5	SDK 45	SDL 30	SMK 15	SOP 10	

	Strength of government Parties in parliament (%)				
Cabinet	P1	P2	P3	P4	P5
1	HZDS 49	SNS 10			
2	HZDS 44	SNS 5			
3	SDL 19	KDH 12	APR 7	AD 5	NDK 3
4	HZDS 41	SNS 6	ZRS 9		
5	SDK 28	SDL 15	SMK 10	SOP 9	

Slovenia

Cabinet	Date		Name of prime minister (PM)	PM's party	Type of government	No. of ministries	Modes for termination
	In	Out					
1	01/93	04/94	Drnovšek (1)	LDS	2	15	4
2	04/94	01/96	Drnovšek (1)	LDS	2	16	4
3	01/96	02/97	Drnovšek (1)	LDS	4	15	1
4	02/97	04/00	Drnovšek (1)	LDS	2	16	1

Parties in government
Percentage of government strength

Cabinet	P1	P2	P3	P4	P5
1	LDS 32	SKD 27	ZL 27	SDSS 7	(ZS) (7)
2	LDS 50	SKD 25	ZL 25		
3	LDS 73	SKD 27			
4	LDS 50	SLS 44	DeSus 6		

Strength of government
Parties in parliament (%)

Cabinet	P1	P2	P3	P4	P5
1	LDS 24	SKD 17	ZL 15	SDSS 4	(ZS) (5)
2	LDS 37	SKD 17	ZL 15		
3	LDS 28	SKD 17			
4	LDS 28	SLS 23	DeSus 3		

Yugoslavia (Fed.)

Cabinet	Date In	Date Out	Name of prime minister (PM)	PM's party	Type of government	No. of ministries	Modes for termination
1	04/92	02/93	Panić	Independent	2	22	5
2	03/93	11/96	Kontić (1)	SPPM	2	21	1
3	11/96	05/98	Kontić (2)	SPPM	2	19	6
4	05/98		Bulatović	SPPM	2	30	

| Cabinet | Parties in government Percentage of government strength | | | | | | Strength of government Parties in parliament (%) | | | | | |
	P1	P2	P3	P4	P5	P6	P1	P2	P3	P4	P5	P6
1												
2			missing data						missing data			
3												
4												

Bibliography

General

Agh, A., *The europeanization of Central European polities: the search for a viable perspective* (Budapest papers on democratic transition; no. 23) (Budapest: Hungarian Center for Democracy Studies Foundation 1992).

Agh, A., *The emerging party system in East Central Europe* (Budapest papers on democratic transition; no. 13) (Budapest: Hungarian Center for Democracy Studies Foundation 1992).

Agh, A., (ed.), *The Emergence of East Central European parliaments: the first steps* (Budapest: Hungarian Centre of Democracy Studies 1994).

Agh, A., *Emerging Democracies in East Central Europe and the Balkans* (Studies of Communism in Transition). (Northampton, MA: Edward Elgar 1998).

Batt, J., *East Central Europe from Reform to Transformation: A Comparison of Poland, Hungary and Czechoslovakia* (London: Pinter Publishers 1991).

Berglund, S. and F. H. Aarebrot, *The Political History of Eastern Europe in the Twentieth Century: The struggle between Democracy and Dictatorship* (Aldershot: Edward Elgar 1997).

Berglund, S., T. Hellén and F. H. Aarebrot (eds), *Handbook of Political Change in Eastern Europe* (Cheltenham: Edward Elgar 1998).

Bucar, B. and S. Kuhnle (eds), *Small states compared: politics of Norway and Slovenia* (Bergen: Alma Mater 1994).

Burger, R. H. and H. F. Sullivan, *Eastern Europe: A Bibliographic Guide to English Language Publications 1986–1993* (Englewood, CO: Libraries Unlimited 1995).

Cipkowski, P., *Revolution in Eastern Europe: Understanding the Collapse of Communism in Poland, Hungary, East Germany, Czechoslovakia* (New York, Chichester: Wiley 1991).

Courbis, R. and W. Welfe (eds), *Central and Eastern Europe on its way to European Union* (Frankfurt: Lang Verlag 1999).

Crampton, R. and B. Crampton, *Atlas of Eastern Europe in the Twentieth Century* (London, New York: Routledge 1996).

Dawisha, K. and B. Parrott (eds), *The Consolidation of Democracy in East-Central Europe* (New York: Cambridge University Press 1997).

Dellenbrant, J., 'The Re-Emergence of Multi-Partyism in the Baltic States', in S. Berglund and J. Dellenbrant (eds), *The New Democracies in Eastern Europe: Party Systems and Political Cleavages* (Aldershot: Edward Elgar 1994), 74–116.

Elster, J., C. Offe and U. K. Preuss, *Institutional Design in Post-Communist Societies: Rebuilding the Ship at Sea* (New York: Cambridge University Press 1998).

Enyedi, Z, 'Organizing a subcultural party in Eastern Europe', *Party Politics*, vol. 2, (1996), 377–97.

Evans, G. and S. Whitefield, 'Identifying the basis of party competition in Eastern Europe', *British Journal of Political Science*, vol. 23, no. 4, (1993) 521–48.

Fitzmaurice, J., *Politics and Government in the Visegrad Countries; Poland, Hungary, the Czech Republic and Slovakia* (New York: St. Martin's Press 1998).

Flint, D. C., *The Baltic States: Estonia – Latvia – Lithuania (The Former Soviet States)* (London: Franklin Watts 1992).

Gaber, S., J. Celmin and V. Petrescu, 'Ministers from Hungary, Latvia, Slovenia and Romania respond to questions on the process of vocational education and training reform in their countries', *Vocational Training – Berlin – CEDEFOP*, 11, (1997), 43 ff.

Garber, L. and E. Bjornlund (eds), *The new democratic frontier: a country by country report on elections in Central and Eastern Europe* (Washington, DC: National Democratic Institute for International Affairs 1992).

Gerner, K. and S. Hedlund, *The Baltic States and the End of the Soviet Empire* (London, New York: Routledge 1993).

Goralczyk, B., Kostecki, W. and K. Zukrowska (eds), *In pursuit of Europe: transformations of post-communist states, 1989–1994* (English editor: D. V. Powers, lead editor: E. Wosik) (Warsaw: Institute of Political Studies, Polish Academy of Sciences 1995).

Henderson, K. (ed.), *Back to Europe: Central and Eastern Europe and the European Union* (London; Philadelphia: UCL Press 1999).

Henderson, K. and N. Robinson, *Postcommunist Politics* (New York: Prentice Hall 1998).

Hiden, J., *The Baltic nations and Europe: Estonia, Latvia and Lithuania in the twentieth century* (London: Longman 1991).

Hofferbert, R. (ed.), *Parties and Democracy: Party Structure and Party Performance in Old and New Democracies*, (Oxford: Blackwell 1998).

Ishiyama, J. T., *Electoral rules, ethnic politics, and political party development in new democracies: the cases of Estonia, Latvia, and Czechoslovakia* (PhD thesis: Michigan State University, Dept. of Political Science) (Ann Arbor, MI: UMI 1992).

Iwaskiw, W. R., *Estonia, Latvia and Lithuania – Country Studies* (Lanham, MD: Bernan 1996).

Kirchner, E. J., *Decentralization and Transition in the Visegrad: Poland, Hungary, the Czech Republic and Slovakia* (New York: St Martin's Press 1999).

Kitschelt, H., 'The Formation of Party Systems in East Central Europe', *Politics & Society*, vol. 20, no.1, (1992).

Kitschelt, H., 'Formation of Party Cleavages in Post-Communist Democracies', *Party Politics*, vol. 1, no. 4, (1995), 447–72.

Lawson, K., A. Rommele and G. Karasimeonov (eds), *Cleavages, Parties, and Voters: Studies from Bulgaria, the Czech Republic, Hungary, Poland, and Romania* (Westport: Praeger 1999).

Leff, C. S., *The Czech and Slovak republics: nation versus state* (Boulder, CO, Oxford: Westview Press 1997).

Lieven, A., *The Baltic Revolution – Estonia, Latvia, Lithuania and the Path to Independence*, 2nd edn (New Haven CT: Yale University Press 1997).

Loeber, D. A., 'Regaining Independence – Constitutional Aspects: Estonia, Latvia, Lithuania', *Review of Central and East European Law*, vol. 24, no. 1, (1998), 1 ff.

Longworth, Ph., *The Making of Eastern Europe* (London: Macmillan 1992).

Nørgaard, O., *The Baltic States after Independence* (Cheltenham: Edward Elgar 1996).

Olson, D., 'Party Formation and Party System Consolidation in the New Democracies of Central Europe', in R. Hofferbert (ed.), *Parties and Democracy* (Oxford: Blackwell 1998) 10–42.

Papp, T., *Who is in, who is out ? Citizenship, nationhood, democracy, and European integration in the Czech Republic and Slovakia* (EUI working papers, RSC; no. 99/13) (Florence: European University Institute 1999).

Pfaff, D., 'On the State of the Political and Economic Preconditions for the Economic Development in Albania, Bulgaria and Romania', *Südosteuropa. Zeitschrift für Gegenwartsforschung*, vol. 45, no. 2, (1996), 115 ff.

Seroka, J. and V. Pavlovic (eds), *The tragedy of Yugoslavia: the failure of democratic transformation* (Armonk, NY: M. E. Sharpe 1992).

Sitter, N., *The East Central European party systems: the development of competitive politics in a comparative politics perspective* (PhD thesis 1999; London School of Economics and Political Sience 1999).

Smith, G., *The Baltic States – The National Self-Determination of Estonia, Latvia and Lithuana* (New York: St Martin's Press 1994).

Sorensen, L. B. and L. C. Eliason (eds), *Forward to the Past: Continuity & Change in Political Development in Hungary, Austria, & the Czech & Slovak Republics* (Oakville, CT: Aarhus University Press 1997).

Steen, A., *Between Past and Future: Elites, Democracy and the State in Post-communist Countries – Comparison on Estonia, Latvia and Lithuania* (Aldershot: Ashgate 1997).

Taras, R., *Postcommunist Presidents* (New York: Cambridge University Press 1997).

Todorova, M., *Imagining the Balkans* (Oxford: Oxford University Press 1997).

Tóka, G., 'Being Represented-Being Satisfied? Political Support in East-Central Europe', in H.-D. Klingemann and D. Fuchs (eds), *Citizens and the State* (Oxford: Oxford University Press 1995), 354–82.

Tóka, G., 'Parties and Electoral Choices in East Central Europe', in P. Lewis and G. Pridham (eds), *Stabilising Fragile Democracies* (London: Routledge 1996) 100–125.

Tóka, G., 'Political Parties in East Central Europe', in L. Diamond *et al.* (eds), *Consolidating the Third Wave Democracies, Themes and Perspectives* (Baltimore: Johns Hopkins University Press 1997) pp. 93–134.

Verheijen, T., *Constitutional pillars for new democracies: the cases of Bulgaria and Romania* (Leiden, Netherlands: DSWO Press 1995).

Vienna Institute for Comparative Economic Studies (Wiener Institut für Internationale Wirtschaftsvergleiche) (ed.) (1995 ff.) *Countries in transition: Bulgaria, Croatia, Czech Republic, Hungary, Poland, Romania, Russia, Slovak Republic, Slovenia, Ukraine* (WIIW Handbook of Statistics, 1995 ff.)

Whightman, G., (ed.), *Party formation in East Central Europe* (Aldershot: Edward Elgar 1995).

White, S., J. Batt and P. G. Lewis, *Developments in Central & East European Politics* (Durham: Duke University Press 1998).

Wollmann, H., 'Institution building and decentralization in formerly socialist countries: the cases of Poland, Hungary, and East Germany', *Environment and Planning*, vol. 5, no. 4, (1997), 463 ff.

World Congress for Soviet and East European Studies, *The Czech and Slovak experience: selected papers from the Fourth World Congress for Soviet and East European Studies, Harrogate, 1990* (John Morison ed.) (New York: St Martin's Press 1992).

Zifcak, S., 'Dealing With the Past: The Constitutional Treatment of Political Laws in Hungary and the Czech Republic', *East European Human Rights Review*, vol. 4, no. 2, (1998), 153 ff.

Albania

Biberaj, E., *Albania in transition: the rocky road to democracy* (Nations of the modern world. Europe) (Boulder, CO: Westview Press 1998).

Economist Intelligence Unit, *Albania. Country Profile* (1990–99).

Economist Intelligence Unit, *Albania. Country Report* (1990–99).

Hamilton, B., *Albania: who cares?* (Grantham: Autumn House 1992).

Schmidt-Neke, M., 'Albania Before a New Turning-Point? The Referendum for the New Constitution and its Consequences', *Südosteuropa. Zeitschrift für Gegenwartsforschung*, vol. 44, no. 1/2, (1995), 63 ff.

Schmidt-Neke, M., 'Change of Government in Albania: The Crisis Reappears', *Südosteuropa. Zeitschrift für Gegenwartsforschung*, vol. 47, no. 10/11, (1998), 516 ff.

Tarifa, F., 'Albania's Road from Communism: Political and Social Change, 1990–1993', *Development and Change*, vol. 26, no. 1, (1995), 133 ff.

Vickers, M. and J. Pettifer, *Albania: From Anarchy to Balkan Identity* (London: C. Hurst 1997).

Zickel, R. and W. Iwaskiw, *Albania: A Country Study* (Washington, DC: The Division 1994).

Bosnia-Hercegovina

Badley, J., 'Elements of Legal Harmonisation Between Bosnia and Herzegovina and the European Union: The Customs Policy Law and the Customs Tariff Law', *Revue des Affaires Européennes*, no. 4, (1997), 431 ff.

Barroso, J. D. (ed.), *Beyond the 96–elections: a two year window of opportunity for democracy: proposals for the transition towards peace and democracy in Bosnia and Herzegovina* (Stockholm: International institute for Democracy and Electoral Assistance 1996).

Cavoski, K., *The Bosnian elections* (Belgrade: Center for Serbian Studies 1997).

Chandler, D., *Bosnia: faking democracy after Dayton* (London: Pluto Press 1999).

Eicher, J., 'The Future Perspectives of Bosnia-Hercegowina', *Südosteuropa. Zeitschrift für Gegenwartsforschung*, vol. 46, no. 1/2, (1997), 1 ff.

Eicher, J., 'The Elections in Bosnia-Hercegowina and their Performance', *Südosteuropa. Zeitschrift für Gegenwartsforschung*, vol. 46, no. 3/4, (1997), 146 ff.

Mueller, S., 'Political and Social Conditions for a Return to Bosnia-Hercegovina', *Südosteuropa. Zeitschrift für Gegenwartsforschung*, vol. 44, no. 9/10, (1995), 593 ff.

Nystuen, G., 'The Constitution of Bosnia and Herzegovina. State Versus Entities', *Revue des Affaires Européennes*, no. 4, (1997), 394 ff.

Reuter, J., 'The Political Development in Bosnia-Hercegovina. Growing Together of the Entities or National Barring?', *Südosteuropa. Zeitschrift für Gegenwartsforschung*, vol. 47, no. 3/4, (1998), 97 ff.

Schmeets, H. *The 1997 municipal elections in Bosnia and Herzegovina: an analysis of the observations* (Dordrecht, London: Kluwer Academic 1998).

Schmeets, H. and J. Exel, *The 1996 Bosnia-Herzegovina elections: an analysis of the observations* (Dordrecht, London: Kluwer Academic 1997).

Szasz, P. C., 'The Quest for a Bosnian Constitution: Legal Aspects of Constitutional Proposals Relating to Bosnia', *Fordham International Law Journal*, vol. 19, no. 2, (1995), 363 ff.

Yee, S., 'The New Constitution of Bosnia and Herzegovina', *European Journal of International Law*, vol. 7, no. 2, (1996), 176–93.

Bulgaria

Atanasow, B., J. Thirkelll and G. Gradev, 'Trade Unions, Political Parties and Governments in Bulgaria, 1982–92', *Journal of Communist Studies*, vol. 9, no. 4, (1993) 98 ff.

Bell, J. D. (ed.), *Bulgaria in Transition: Politics, Economics, Society and Culture After Communism* (Eastern Europe After Communism Series) (Oxford: Westview Press 1998).

Caparini, M., *A Bulgarian political snapshot* (Surrey, England: Royal Military Academy Sandhurst 1995).

Coenen-Huther, J. (ed.), *Bulgaria at the crossroads* (Commack, NY: Nova Science Publishers 1996).

Dainov, E. and V. Garnizov, *Politics, reform and daily life: evolution of popular attitudes to key issues in the reform process in Bulgaria (1993–1994)* (Sofia: New Bulgarian University 1995).

Dainov, E., V. Garnizov and S. Zanev, *The government and the people: conflicts in Bulgarian society in the middle of the 1990s* (Sofia: Centre for Social Practices, New Bulgarian University 1998).

Giuzelev, B., *Electoral attitudes and electoral behaviour of minority groups in Bulgaria* (January 1990–September 1992) (Sofia: Center for the Study of Democracy 1993).

Karasimeonov, G., 'Differentiation Postponed: Party Pluralism in Bulgaria', in G. Whightman (ed.), *Party Formation in East-Central Europe* (Newbury Park: Frank Cass 1995).

Karasimeonov, G. (ed.), *The 1990 election to the Bulgarian Grand National Assembly and the 1991 election to the Bulgarian National Assembly: analyses, documents and* (Berlin: Sigma 1997).

Karasimeonov, G., 'Bulgaria', in S. Berglund, T. Hellén and F. H. Aarebrot (eds), *The Handbook of Political Change in Eastern Europe* (Cheltenham: Edward Elgar 1998) 335 ff.

Meissner, T., 'Bulgaria After the Change of Government of Jan. 1995 – Perils for the Beginning Recovery?', *Südosteuropa. Zeitschrift für Gegenwartsforschung*, vol. 44, no. 8, (1995), 490 ff.

Melone, A. P., *Creating parliamentary government: the transition to democracy in Bulgaria* (Columbus: Ohio State University Press 1998).

Paskaleva, K. *et al.* (eds), *Bulgaria in transition* (Aldershot: Ashgate 1998).

Riedel, S., 'The New Socialist Government of Zhan Videnov – Political Opinions From Bulgaria', *Südosteuropa. Zeitschrift für Gegenwartsforschung*, vol. 44, no. 3/4, (1995), 213 ff.

Riedel, S., 'Bulgaria: The Resignation of the Videnov Government. The Opposition Forces Premature Elections', *Südosteuropa. Zeitschrift für Gegenwartsforschung*, vol. 46, no. 3/4, (1997), 213 ff.

Siegan, B. H., *Drafting a constitution for a nation or republic emerging into freedom*, 2nd edn (Fairfax, VA: George Mason University Press 1994).

Tchakarov, K., *The second floor: an expose of backstage politics in Bulgaria* (London: Macdonald 1991).

Thirkell, J. *et al.*, 'Trade unions, political parties and governments in Bulgaria, 1982–92', *Journal of Communist Studies*, vol. 9, no. 4, (1993), 98–115.

Zloch-christy, I. (ed.), *Bulgaria in a time of change: economic and political dimensions* (Aldershot: Avebury 1996).

Zotova, K., 'Political power and periodicals (Bulgaria)', *The Serials Librarian*, vol. 26, no. 2, (1995), 87–94.

Croatia

Markovich, S. C., 'Democracy in Croatia: Views from the Opposition', *East European Quarterly*, vol. 32, no. 1, (1998), 83 ff.

Pusic, V., 'Constitutional Politics in Croatia', *Praxis International*, vol. 13, no. 4, (1994), 389 ff.

Sabol, Z. (ed.), *Croatian Parliament*, 2nd revised edn (Zagreb: Parliament of the Republic of Croatia: Nakladni zavod Globus: Skolska knjiga 1995).

Sekulic, D. and Z. Sporer, 'Toward Democracy or to the New Authoritarianism? The Case of Croatia', *Humboldt Journal of Social Relations*, vol. 24, no. 1/2, (1998), 129 ff.

Siber, I. (ed.), *The 1990 and 1992/93 Sabor elections in Croatia: analyses, documents and data* (Berlin: Sigma 1997).

Tudman, F., *Croatia at the crossroads: in search of a democratic confederacy* (London: Centre for Policy Studies 1991).

Czech Republic

Blahoz, J., L. Brokl and Z. Mansfeldová, 'Czech political Parties and Cleavages after 1989', in K. Lawson *et al.* (eds), *Cleavages, Parties, and Voters* (Westport: Praeger 1999) 123–40.

Bradley, J. F. N., *Post-Communist Czechoslovakia* (Boulder, CO: East European Monographs 2000).

Brokl, L. and Z. Mansfeldová, 'Czecholslovakia', *European Journal of Political Research*, vol. 24, (1993), 397–410.

Brokl, L. and Z. Mansfeldová, 'Czech Republic', *European Journal of Political Research*, vol. 26, (1994), 269–77; vol. 28, (1995) 305–12; vol. 30, (1996) 307–14; vol. 32, (1997) 339–50; vol. 34, (1998) 373–84; vol. 37, forthcoming.

Brokl, L. and Z. Mansfeldová, 'How the voters respond in the Czech Republic', in I. Gabel (ed.), *The 1990 Election to the Czechoslovak Federal Assembly* (Berlin: Sigma 1996) 51–69.

Broklová, E., 'Historical Roots for the Restorian of Democracy in Czechoslovakia', in I. Gabel (ed.), *The 1990 Election of the Czechoslovak Federal Assembly* (Berlin: Sigma 1996), 25–50.

Bugajski, J., 'Czech Mate: the resignation of Vaclav Klaus', *Analysis of Current Events*, vol. 10, (1998), 2–3.

Fawn, R., 'Symbolism in the Diplomacy of Czech President Vaclav Havel', *East European Quaterly*, vol. 33, no. 1, (1999), 1 ff.

Fitzmaurice, J., 'The 1996 Elections', *Electoral Studies*, vol. 15, (1996), 575–80.

Fuele, E., 'Changes on the Czech Political Scene', *Electoral Studies*, vol. 16, no. 3, (1997), 341 ff.

Glos, G. E., 'The constitution of the czech republic of 1992', *Hastings Constitutional Law Quarterly*, vol. 21, no. 4, S. (1994), 1049–70.

Holy, L., *The little Czech and the Great Czech Nation: national identity and the post-communist transformation of society* (Cambridge: Cambridge University Press 1996).

Hudecek, J., Z. Mansfeldová and L. Brokl, 'Czechoslovakia', *European Journal of Political Research*, vol. 22, (1992), 379–86.

Innes, A., 'Political Developments in the New Czech Republic', *Policy Studies*, vol. 14, no. 4, (1993), 22 ff.

Klima, M., 'Consolidation and Stabilization of the Party System in the Czech Republic', in R. Hofferbert (ed.), *Parties and Democracy* (Oxford: Blackwell 1998) pp. 70–88.

Kopecky, P. and C. Mudde, 'The 1998 parliamentary and senate elections in the Czech Republic', *Electoral Studies*, vol. 18, (1999), 415–24.

Krejci, O., *History of elections in Bohemia and Moravia* (Boulder, CO: East European Monographs 1995).

Magstadt, T. and J. Van Doren, 'Czech Constitutional Democracy: Focus on the Czech Dual Executive and the Future Senate', *Fordham International Law Journal*, vol. 20, no. 2, (1996), 347 ff.

Mansfeldová, Z., 'Czech and Slovak Political and Parliamentary Elites', in J. Higley, J. Pakulski and W. Weselowski (eds), *Postcommunist Elites and Democracy in Eastern Europe* (London: Macmillan 1997).

Myant, M. R., *Czech history and Czech politics* (Paisley: Department of Accounting, Economics and Languages, University of Paisley 1997).

Narwa, D., *An analysis of electoral changes: the case of the Czech Republic* (Essex papers in politics and government; no. 118) (Colchester: Department of Government, University of Essex 1997).

Olson, D., 'Democratization and political participation: the experience of Czech Republic', in K. Dawisha and B. Parrott (eds), *The consolidation of democracy in East-Central Europe* (Cambridge: Cambridge University Press 1997), 150–196.

Reschova, J. and J. Syllova, 'The Legislature of Czech Republic', in A. Agh and G. Ilonski (eds), *Parliaments and Organized Interests: The Second Steps* (Budapest: HCDS 1996).

Estonia

Arter, D., 'Estonia after the March 1995 Riigikogu Election: still an anti-party system', *The Journal of Communist Studies in Transition*, vol. 11, no. 3, (1995), 15 ff.

Arter, D., *Parties and Democracy in the Post-Soviet Republics – The Case of Estonia* (Aldershot: Dartmouth 1996).

Avi, A., K. Hell and H. Pisuke, *Estonia's way to independence: a short overview of the legal developments in Estonian state status from November 1988 to January 1991* (Tartu: Tartu University Laboratory of Legal Aspects of International Relations 1991).

Fitzmaurice, J., 'The Estonian Elections of 1992', *Electoral Studies*, (1993), 168–73.

Kask, P., 'Institutional Development of the Parliament of Estonia', in D. M. Olson and P. Norton (eds), *The New Parliaments of Central and Eastern Europe* (London: Frank Cass 1996).

Kirch, M., A. Kirch, I. Rimm and T. Tuisk, 'Integration Processes in Estonia 1993–1996', in A. Kirch (ed.), *The Integration of Non-Estonians into Estonian Society: History, Problems and Trends* (Tallinn: Estonian Academy Publishers 1997).

Lagerspetz, M. and H. Vogt, 'Estonia', in S. Berglund *et al.* (eds), *The Handbook of Political Change in Eastern Europe* (Cheltenham: Edward Elgar 1997) pp. 55–8.

Lauristin, M. *et al.* (eds), *Return to the Western world: cultural and political perspectives on the Estonian post-Communist transition* (Tartu, Estonia: Tartu University Press 1997).

Park, A. (ed.), *Visions and policies: Estonia's path to independence and beyond; 1987–1993* (New York: Carfax 1995).

Pettai, V., 'Estonia: Old Maps and New Roads', *Journal of Democracy*, vol. 4, (1993), 81–90.

Raun, T. U., *Estonia and the Estonians* (Stanford: University Press 1991).

Raun, T. U., 'Democratization and political development in Estonia', in K. Dawisha and B. Parrott (eds), *The consolidation of democracy in East-Central Europe* (Cambridge: Cambridge University Press 1997) pp. 334–74.

Suksi, M., *On the constitutional features of Estonia* (Turku, Finland: Åbo Akademi University 1999).

Taagepera, R., *Estonia: Return to Independence* (Boulder, CO., San Francisco, London: Westview Press 1993).

Taagepera, R., 'Estonia's Constitutional Assembly, 1991–1992', *Journal of Baltic Studies*, vol. 25, (1994), 211–32.

Taagepera, R., 'Estonian Parliamentary Elections, March 1995', *Electoral Studies*, vol. 14, (1995), 328–31.

Vihalemn, P., M. Lauristin and I. Tallo, 'Development of political culture in Estonia', in M. Lauristin and P. Vihalemn (eds), *Return to the Western World: Cultural and Political Perspectives on the Estonian Post-Communist Transition* (Tartu: Tartu University Press 1997).

Hungary

Agh, A., *Political culture as a dimension of system change* (Budapest: Hungarian Center for Democracy Studies Foundation 1991).

Agh, A., *The parliamentary way to democracy: the case of Hungary* (Budapest: Hungarian Center for Democracy Studies Foundation 1991).

Agh, A., *The permanent 'constitutional crisis' in the demperatic transition: the case of Hungary* (Budapest: Hungarian Center for Democracy Studies Foundation 1992).

Agh, A., *The Hungarian 'law factory': the first two years of the new parliament (1990–1992)* (Budapest: Hungarian Center for Democracy Studies Foundation 1992).

Agh, A., *The Hungarian party system*) (Budapest: Hungarian Center for Democracy Studies Foundation 1993).

Agh, A. and G. Ilonszki, (eds) *Parliament and organized interests: the second steps* (Budapest: Hungarian Centre of Democracy Studies 1996).

Agh, A. and S. Kurtan, *Democratization and Europeanization in Hungary: the first parliament (1990–1994)* (Budapest: Hungarian Centre for Democracy Studies 1995).

Arato, A., 'Election, coalition and constitution in hungary', *The Hungarian Quarterly*, vol. 35, no. 135, (1994), 3–40.

Arato, A., 'Election, Coalition, and Constitution in Hungary', *East European Monographs*, no. 465, (1995) 117 ff.

Braun, A. and Z. Barany (eds), *Dilemmas of transition: the Hungarian* (Lanham, MD, Oxford: Rowman & Littlefield 1999).

Cox, T. *et al.*, 'Political transition in hungary: an overview', *Journal of Communist Studies and Transition Politics*, vol. 10, no. 3, (1994), 1–14.

Cox, T. and A. Furlong (eds), *Hungary: the politics of transition* (London: Frank Cass 1995).

Csanadi, M., *Party-states and their legacies in post-communist* (Cheltenham: Edward Elgar 1997).

Csorba, L., J. Sisa and Z. Szalay, *The Hungarian Parliament* (Budapest: Katalin Asbothne Alvinczy 1993).

Ehrlich, E. and G. Revesz, *Hungary and its prospects, 1985–2005* (Budapest: Akademiai Kiado 1995).

Gombar, C. *et al.* (eds), *Balance: the Hungarian government, 1990–1994* (Budapest: Korridor, Centre for Political Research 1996).

Hajdu, Z. (ed.), *Hungary: society, state, economy and regional structure in transition* (Pecs: Centre for Regional Studies 1993).

Ilonszki, G., *An introduction to the new Hungarian parliament* (Budapest: Hungarian Center for Democracy Studies Foundation 1991).

Ilonszki, G., *An inside view on Parliament: some research results* (Budapest: Hungarian Center for Democracy Studies Foundation 1992).

Ilonski, G. and S. Kurtan, 'Hungary', *European Journal of Political Research*, (1992) 421–7; (1993) 445–50; (1994) 319–25; (1995) 359–68; (1996) 359–65; (1997) 383–90; (1998) 413–22.

Kilenyi, G. and V. Lamm (eds), *Parliamentarism and government in a one-party* (Budapest: Akademiai Kiado 1988).

Koroseny, A., *Government and politics in Hungary* (Budapest: Central European University Press 1999).

Oltay, E., 'Government and parties in Hungary (1990–1994)', *Südosteuropa. Zeitschrift für Gegenwartsforschung*, vol. 45, no. 11–12, (1995), 746–61.

Racz, B., *The Hungarian parliament in transition: procedure and* (Pittsburgh, PA: University of Pittsburgh Center for Russian and East European studies 1989).

Sunley, J., *Hungary: the triumph of compromise* (London: Alliance Publishers for the Institute for European Defence and Strategic Studies 1993).

Szarvas, L., *The Hungarian parliamentary party system from a European perspective* (Budapest: Hungarian Center for Democracy Studies Foundation 1993).

Szoboszlai, G. (ed.), *Politics and political science in Hungary* (Budapest: Institute for Social Sciences 1982)

Szoboszlai, G. (ed.), *Politics and public administration in Hungary* (Budapest: Akademiai Kiado 1985).

Szoboszlai, G. (ed.), *Democracy and political transformation: theories and East-Central European realities* (Budapest: Hungarian Political Science Association 1991).

Szoboszlai, G., 'Parliamentarism in the Making: Crisis and Political Transformation in Hungary', in A. Lijphart and C. H. Waisman (eds), *Institutional Design in New Democracies* (Boulder: Westview Press 1996) pp. 117–36.

Tóka, G., 'Changing Dimensions of Party Competition, Hungary 1990–1991', in G. Meyer (ed.), *The Political Cultures of Eastern Central Europe in Transition* (Tübingen, Basel: Francke Verlag 1992), pp. 165–228.

Tóka, G. (ed.), *The 1990 election to the Hungarian National Assembly: analyses, documents and data* (Berlin: Sigma 1995).

Tóka, G., 'Parties and Elections in Hungary in 1990 and 1994', in B. J. Király and A. Bozóki (eds), *Lawful Revolution in Hungary, 1989–1994* (Highland Lakes: Atlantic Research and Publications 1995), pp. 131–58.

Tóka, G., 'The Working and Political Background of the Hungarian Election Law', in G. Tóka (ed.), *The 1990 Hungarian Elections to the National Assembly* (Berlin: Sigma 1995) pp. 41–66.

Tóka, G., 'Hungary', in S. Berglund, T. Hellén and F. H. Aarebrot (eds), *Handbook of Political Change in Eastern Europe* (Cheltenham: Edward Elgar 1998), pp. 231 ff.

Tóka, G. and Z. Enyedi (eds), *The election to the Hungarian National Assembly 1994: analyses, documents and data* (Berlin: Sigma 1999).

Tökés, R., 'Party politics and poitical participation in postcommunist Hungary', in K. Dawisha and B. Parrott (eds), *The consolidation of democracy in East-Central Europe* (Cambridge: Cambridge University Press 1997) pp. 109–49.

Vass, L., *Changes in Hungary's governmental system* (Budapest: Hungarian Center for Democracy Studies Foundation 1993).

Latvia

Cerps, U., 'The Leftist Parties in Latvia and Their Performance in the 1993 Parliamentary Elections', in J. Å. Dellenbrant and O. Nørgaard (eds), *The Politics of Transition in the Baltic States* (Umeå: Umeå Universitet 1994).

Davies, P. J. and A. V. Ozolins, The Latvian Parliamentary Elections of 1993, *Electoral Studies*, vol. 13, (1994), 83–6.

Davies, P. J. and A. V. Ozolins, 'The Latvian Parliamentary Elections of 1995', *Electoral Studies*, vol. 15, (1996), 124–8.

Dreifelds, J., *Latvia in Transition* (Cambridge: Cambridge University Press 1996).

Freimanis, A. and E. Semanis, 'The Transition of the Political Regime in Latvia', in J. Å. Dellenbrant and O. Nørgaard (eds), *The Politics of Transition in the Baltic States* (Umeå: Umeå Universitet 1994).

Kolstø, P. and B. Tsilevich, 'Patterns of nation building and political integration in a bifurcated postcommunist state: ethnic aspects of parliamentary elections in Latvia', *East European Politics and Societies*, vol. 11, no. 2 (1997).

Plakans, A., *The Latvians: A Short History* (Stanford: Hoover Institution Press 1995).

Plakans, A., 'Democratization and political participation in postcommunist societies: the case of Latvia', in K. Dawisha and B. Parrott (eds), *The consolidation of democracy in East-Central Europe* (Cambridge: Cambridge University Press 1997) pp. 245–89.

Smith-Sivertsen, H., 'Latvia', in S. Berglund, T. Hellén and F. H. Aarebrot (eds), *Handbook of Political Change in Eastern Europe* (Cheltenham: Edward Elgar 1998) pp. 89 ff.

Lithuania

Krickus, R., 'Democratization in Lithuania', in K. Dawisha and B. Parrott (eds), *The consolidation of democracy in East-Central Europe* (Cambridge: Cambridge University Press 1997), pp. 290–333.

Krupavicius, A., 'The Post Communist Transition and Institutionalization of Lithuania's Parties', in R. Hofferbert (ed.), *Parties and Democracy* (Oxford: Blackwell 1998) pp. 43–69.

Palidauskaite, J., *The development of Lithuanian political culture during the re-establishment and strengthening of independence* (Kaunas: Kaunas University of Technology 1996).

Žeruolis, D., 'Lithuania', in S. Berglund, T. Hellén and F. H. Aarebrot (eds), *Handbook of Political Change in Eastern Europe* (Cheltenham: Edward Elgar 1998) pp. 121 ff.

Macedonia

Coutarelli, M.-L., *Nationalism and democracy: a case study of the former Yugoslav Republic of Macedonia* (University of Oxford 1999).

Koursi, M. (ed.), MPhil thesis *Macedonia: history and politics* (Athens: Ekdotike Athenon 1991).

Pettifer, J. (ed.), *The New Macedonia question* (New York: St Martin's Press 1999).

Moldova

Crowther, W, 'Nationalism and Political Transformation in Moldova', *East European Monographs*, no. 454, (1996), 31 ff.

Dawisha, K. and B. Parrott, *Democratic changes and authoritarian reactions in Russia, Ukraine, Belarus and Moldova* (Cambridge: Cambridge University Press 1997).

Hamm, M. F., (1998) *Moldova: the forgotten republic* (Abingdon: Carfax 1998).

King, C., *Post-Soviet Moldova: a borderland in transition* (London: Russian and CIS Programme of the Royal Institute of International Affairs 1995).

Poland

Brzezinski, M., *The struggle for constitutionalism in Poland* (Basingstoke: Macmillan 1998).

Coenen-huther, J. and B. Synak (eds), *Post-communist Poland: from totalitarianism to democracy?* (New York: Nova Science Publishers 1993).

Drag, Z. and J. Indraszkiewicz, *Employee consciousness and reforms of government systems in Poland* (Warsaw: Friedrich Ebert Foundation Poland 1993).

Grzybowski, M., 'Poland', in S. Berglund, T. Hellén and F. H. Aarebrot (eds), *Handbook of Political Change in Eastern Europe* (Cheltenham: Edward Elgar 1998), pp. 157 ff.

Jasiewicz, K., 'Poland', *European Journal of Political Research*, (1992) 489–504; (1994) 397–408; (1995) 449–57; (1996) 433–44; (1997) 469–75.

Jedruch, J., *Constitutions, Elections and Legislatures of Poland, 1473–1993. A Guide to their History* (New York: Hippocrene Books 1998).

Kaminski, B., *The collapse of state socialism: the case of Poland* (Princeton, Oxford: Princeton University Press 1991).

Michta, A., 'Democratic consolidation in Poland after 1989', in K. Dawisha and B. Parrott (eds), *The consolidation of democracy in East-Central Europe* (Cambridge: Cambridge University Press 1997) pp. 66–108.

Millard, F., *The anatomy of the new Poland: post-Communist politics in its first phase* (Aldershot: Edward Elgar 1994).

Millard, F., *Polish politics and society* (New York: Routledge 1999).

Prizel, I., *National Identity and Foreign Policy; Nationalism and Leadership in Poland, Russia and Ukraine* (Cambridge, New York: Cambridge University Press 1998).

Sarnecki, P., A. Szmyt and W. Witkowski (eds), *The principles of basic institutions of the system of government in Poland* (Warsaw: Sejm Pub. Office 1999).

Shleifer, A., *Government in transition* (Cambridge, MA: Harvard Institute for International Development, Harvard University 1997).

Staar, R. F. (ed.), *Transition to democracy in Poland*, 2nd edn (Basingstoke: Macmillan 1998).

Staniszkis, J., *The dynamics of the breakthrough in Eastern Europe: the Polish experience* (Berkeley: University of California Press 1991).

Thompson, K. W. (ed.), *Poland in a World in Change: Constituions, Presidents and Politics* (Lanham: University Press of America 1997).

Thompson, K. W. (ed.), *The Presidency & Governance in Poland: Yesterday and Today* (Lanham: University Press of America 1997).

Tittenbrun, J., *The collapse of 'real socialism' in Poland* (London: Janus 1993).

Tworzecki, H., *Parties and politics in post-1989 Poland* (Boulder, CO: Westview 1996).

Van Der Meer Krok-Poszkowska, A. 'Poland', in R. Elgie (ed.), *Semi-Presidentialism in Europe* (Oxford: Oxford University Press 1999) pp. 170–192.

Wojtaszczyk, K. A. (ed.), *Poland – government and politics* (Warsaw: Dom Wydawniczy 'Elipsa', 1997).

Wyrzykowski, M. (ed.), *Constitution-making process* (Warsaw: Institute of Public Affairs, Center for Constitutionalism and Legal Culture 1998).

Romania

Carothers, T., *Assessing democracy assistance: the case of Romania* (Washington, DC: Carnegie Endowment Book 1996).
Crowther, W., 'Romania', in S. Berglund, T. Hellén and F. H. Aarebrot (eds), *Handbook of Political Change in Eastern Europe* (Cheltenham: Edward Elgar 1998) pp. 295 ff.
Crowther, W., *The Political Economy of Romanian Socialism* (New York: Praeger 1998).
Gabanyi, A. U., 'Systemic Change in Romania: The Constitution and New Institutions', *Südosteuropa. Zeitschrift für Gegenwartsforschung*, vol. 44, no. 9/10, (1995), 533 ff.
Gallagher, T., *Romania after Ceausescu: the politics of intolerance* (Edinburgh: Edinburgh University Press 1995).
Grozea, D., *Romania* (Vienna: Institut für Höhere Studien 1994).
Roper, S. D., 'From Opposition to Government Coalition: Unity and Fragmentation with the Democratic Convention in Romania', *East European Quarterly*, vol. 31, no. 4, (1997) 519 ff.
Shafir, M., *Romania: politics, economics and society* (London: Pinter 1985).
Shafir, M., 'Romania's road to normalcy', *Journal of Democracy*, vol. 8, (1997), 144–58.
Stan, L. (ed.), *Romania in transition* (Aldershot: Dartmouth 1997).

Serbia-Yugoslavia

Goati, V. (ed.), *Elections to the Federal and Republican Parliaments of Yugoslavia (Serbia and Montenegro) 1990–1996: analyses, documents and data* (Berlin: Sigma 1998).

Slovakia

Butora, M. *et al.* (eds) *The 1998 parliamentary elections and democratic rebirth in Slovakia* (Bratislava: Institute for Public Affairs 1999).
Farrell, B. *Chairman or Chief* (Dublin: Gill/Macmillan 1977).
Goldman, M. F., *Slovakia since independence: a struggle for democracy* (Westport, CT: Praeger 1999).
Malova, D., 'Slovakia', *European Journal of Political Research*, (1994) 413–21; (1995) 463–72; (1996) 453–8; (1997) 481–8; (1998) 513–22. Captions for pix
Mikus, J. A., *Slovakia: a political and constitutional history with documents* (Bratislava: Academic Press 1995).
Waters, T., *Slovak parliamentary elections (Sept. 1998)* (Camberley: Conflict Studies Research Centre 1998).
Wolchik, S., 'Democratization and political partizipation in Slovakia', in K. Dawisha and B. Parrott (eds), *Consolidation of democracy in East-Central Europe* (Cambridge: Cambridge Uuniversity Press 1997) pp. 197–244.

Slovenia

Benderly, J. and E. Kraft (eds), *Independent Slovenia: origins, movements, prospects* (Basingstoke: Macmillan 1997).

Fink-Hafner, D. and J. R. Robbins (eds), *Making a new nation: the formation of Slovenia* (Aldershot: Dartmouth 1997).

Fitzmaurice, J., 'The Slovenian Parliamentary Elections of 10. November 1996', *Electoral Studies*, vol. 16, (1997), 4.

Jansa, J., *The making of the Slovenian state, 1988–1992: the collapse of Yugoslavia* (Ljubljana: Mladinska knjiga 1994).

Mavcic, A. and D. Law, *Slovenian constitutional review: its position in the world and its role in the transition to a new democratic system* (Ljubljana: Nova revija 1995).

Strasek, S., 'The Role of Government in Transition: The Case of Slovenia', *Rivista Internazionale Di Scienze Economiche E Commerciali*, vol. 41, no. 2, (1994), 173 ff.

Zajc, D., 'Slovenia', in S. Berglund, T. Hellén and F. H. Aarebrot (eds), *Handbook of Political Change in Eastern Europe* (Cheltenham: Edward Elgar 1998) pp. 275 ff.

Homepages of governments in Eastern Europe

Links to homepages of governments worldwide

http://www.europa.eu.int/abc/ governments/index en.html
http://www.gksoft.com/govt/en/europa.html
http://www.berlin.iz-soz.de/publications/en/newsletter/socsci-eastern-europe/index.htm (PDF
   version)
RFE/RL newsline, http://*www.rferl*.Newsline.org.
Institute for War and Peace Reporting, http://*www.iwpr.net/*.

Albania

http://mininf.gov.al

Bosnia-Hercegovina

http://www.srpska.org/
Ministry of Foreign Affairs: *http://www.mvp.gov.ba/*

Bulgaria

http://www.government.bg

Croatia

http://www.vlada.hr

Czech Republic

http://www.vlada.cz

Estonia

http://www.riik.ee

Federal Republic of Yugoslavia

http://www.gov.yu/

Hungary

http://www.meh.hu

Lithuania

http://www.lrvk.lt

Latvia

http://www.mfa.gov.lv

Macedonia

http://www.gov.mk/

Moldova

http://www.moldova.md

Poland

http://www.kprm.gov.pl

Romania

http://domino.kappa.ro/guvern/ehome.nsf

Slovakia

http://www.government.gov.sk

Slovenia

http://www.sigov.si

Index